GREECE: A LITERARY COMPANION

GREECE

A Literary Companion

Martin Garrett

JOHN MURRAY

For Helen, Philip, and Edmund

First published in 1994
by John Murray (Publishers) Ltd.,
50 Albemarle Street, London W1X 4BD

The moral right of the author has been asserted

A catalogue record for this book is available from the British Library

ISBN 0-7195-5200-1

Typeset in 12½/12½ Bembo by Colset (Private) Ltd, Singapore
Printed in Great Britain by Biddles Limited, Guildford and King's Lynn

CONTENTS

ILLUSTRATIONS

(between pages 116 and 117)

The author and publishers would like to thank the following for permission to reproduce illustrations: 1, 3, 7: Bodleian Library; 14: Patrick Leigh Fermor; 16: Phil Sayer

PREFACE

We are all Greeks. Our laws, our literature, our religion,
our arts have their root in Greece. But for Greece ... we
might still have been savages and idolators.[1]

Shelley prefaced his dramatic poem *Hellas* with this bold
philhellenic proclamation in 1821. Many before and since have
agreed with him; ancient Greece has continued to appear in
a variety of guises, from Freud's Oedipus to caryatids and
Corinthian columns on museums and banks to the name
of the Diogenes Club for 'the most unsociable and unclub-
bable men in town' to which Mycroft Holmes belongs in
Conan Doyle's story 'The Greek Interpreter'. (Presumably an
Athenaeum is more amiable.)

For centuries, however, the Greece which still existed in
the eastern Mediterranean was little known in Western
Europe except to Levant merchants and a few other adven-
turous individuals. Byron's friend Hobhouse observed:

> At the period when every young man of fortune, in
> France and England, considered it an indispensable part
> of his education to survey the monuments of ancient art
> remaining in Italy, only a few desperate scholars and
> artists ventured to trust themselves among the bar-
> barians, to contemplate the ruins of Greece.[2]

When travellers became sufficiently 'desperate' to come
to Greece (in increasing numbers from the late eighteenth
century onwards), they were usually surprised by what they
saw, although less by the ruins and the landscape than by the
Greeks and their extraordinary failure to correspond with

idealized notions of Pericles and Leonidas. In 1889 Baedeker's *Handbook* still found it necessary to warn its readers against 'the inborn Oriental indolence of the Greek'[3] and there were attempts to argue that this unworthy specimen must be descended not from the noble Hellenes but from invading Slavs. (More affectionate stereotyping occurs in the caricature of theatrically emphatic Greeks with which Edward Lear illustrated his nonsense poem 'There was an old man of Thermopylae . . .')

There were pleasant surprises, too, particularly for those who left their marble-tinted spectacles at home. In 1798 the enthusiastic early philhellene William Eton found not indolence but, the 'Turkish yoke' notwithstanding, 'much energy of character.'[4] Most visitors experienced the passion of the Greeks for hospitality, or admired their bravery and the doggedness of their resistance to the Turkish or, later, German occupiers. Even as travel became easier and more common in the twentieth century, a sense of freshness, of discovery, informed much writing about Greece. Greek drinks, for instance, have exerted a peculiar fascination. To Evelyn Waugh ouzo was 'the drink that tastes like camphorated oil' and retsina 'the one that looks like quinine and tastes like aniseed.' Robert Graves, who had finally come to Greece at the age of sixty-six, was more generous, using ouzo as an image of strength and directness in his poem 'Ouzo Unclouded'. Henry Miller, after a more extended stay, pronounced the ubiquitous glass of cool water the definitive Greek drink.[5]

More broadly, appreciation of Byzantine art, the landscape of rock and olive and oleander, the ancient sites as living places, and the people as inheritors of a long and troubled post-classical history, was disseminated by writers as individual as Peter Levi, Patrick Leigh Fermor, and Lawrence and Gerald Durrell, all visitors who stayed on or frequently returned as most earlier commentators had not. At the same time, responses to Greek places and culture were sharpened by the new confidence of modern Greek literature, made more widely known by the commercial success of translations of the novels of Nikos Kazantzakis and the award of the Nobel Prize for Literature to the poets George Seferis (1963) and Odysseus Elytis (1979).

Responses to Greece have been as various as those of Graves and Waugh to ouzo; but few travellers would challenge Edmund Wilson's diagnosis of its distinctiveness:

When you look down and see the first Greek islands, you are surprised by the difference from Italy, whose dense plantings of parched yellow fields you have so short a time before left behind. Here is a paler, purer, soberer country, which seems both wild and old and quite distinct from anything farther west . . . There is a special apparent lightness of substance and absence of strong colour which characterizes Greece and sets it off from other countries. As you descend into the hot airport, you have a general grateful impression of simplification and gentle austerity.[6]

YUGOSLAVIA B

ALBANIA

MACEDONIA

Edessa
Kastoria
Thessalon

Mt. Olympos
Tempe
Mt. Ossa

CORFU
Ioannina
Meteora
Larissa
Mt. Pelio

EPIROS

PAXOS
Nikopolis
Arta

THESSALY

LEUKAS

Thermopylai
Delphi
Khalkis
Osios Loukas

ITHACA Missolonghi

CEPHALONIA

Patras
Gulf of Corinth
Marath

ZAKYNTHOS
(ZANTE)
IS.

Corinth
PELOPONNESE
Ath

Olympia
Mycenae
AIGIN
PORO

IONIAN SEA

Karitaina
Tripolis

Bassai

Kalamata
Sparta
Mistra
SPETSAI

HYDE

Monemvasi

The Saronic Gulf on an enlarged scale

Marathon
Eleusis
Athens
Piraeus

Corinth
SALAMIS

KYTHERA

Tiryns
Epidauros
Nauplion
AIGINA
POROS

White
Sph

GARIA

HRACE TURKEY

Istanbul

THASOS

Mt.Athos

LESBOS
Mytilene

SKYROS

A E G E A N

CHIOS

S E A

Izmir
(Smyrna)

ANDROS

T
U
R
K
E
Y

TENOS
MYKONOS

YROS
C Y C L A D E S
PAROS
DELOS
PATMOS

NAXOS

TORINI
KOS

DODECANESE RHODES

thymnon
KARPATHOS
Arkadi
Herakleion
R
Knossos
E
istos E T E
Gortys
KASOS
Archaeological sites thus :
∴ Delphi

0

0

50 100

100 200

Miles 150

300 Kms.

Author's Note

Consistent transliteration of Greek place names is all but impossible. Choices are often arbitrary: Mycenae is Latinate but established; Olympus is established, but Olympos is a minor emendation closer to the Greek; Khalkis is a compromise between the traditional Chalkis and the preferred modern Halkis (or Halkida; and the Venetians called it Negroponte).

I should like to thank Hilary Foster, Jane Furnival, Harold Pollins, and Dietrich Warns for their valuable help and advice. Grateful thanks are also due to Gail Pirkis and Kate Chenevix Trench at John Murray.

1

ATHENS

The Acropolis – Coming down from the Acropolis – Syntagma Square, the Grande Bretagne – Schliemann's House – Patisia, the National Archaeological Museum – the New Metropolis, the Old Metropolis – the Tower of the Winds – the 'Lantern of Demosthenes' – Hymettos

Incongruous skyscrapers spring in stooks, wirelesses deafen, sky signs fidget, neon scatters its death ray, trams clash, giant American taxis like winged and elongated boiled sweets screech and squeak along the sweltering asphalt with Gadarene urgency. The fever of demolition and rebuilding has the Athenians by the throat. Streets gape as though bombed, masonry crashes, the dust of a siege floats in the air and the clatter of pneumatic drills has replaced the little owls' note as the city's *leitmotiv*. Rusting whiskers of reinforced concrete prong the sky-line: new hotels soar from the rubble like ogres' mouth-organs.[1]

As he recovered from this encounter with the Athens of the early 1960s, Patrick Leigh Fermor could only conclude that the city was in 'a state of headlong flux.'

A state of mercifully slower flux prevailed in Athens for centuries before this. Ancient monuments gradually collapsed or were adapted for use as churches, mosques, palaces. Stylite hermits lived atop the high columns of the Temple of Olympian Zeus in the fifth century, as did a Muslim *hodja* a few hundred years later. (Until 1860 the remains of his necessarily compact house were to be seen on top of one of the columns.)[2] In the mid-eighteenth century James 'Athenian'

Stuart, sent out to draw or paint the ancient remains for the
benefit of the connoisseurs of the London Society of Dilettanti, found that at the Odeion of Herodes Atticus 'The area
in which were the seats of the spectators, neglected for ages,
has at length acquired a surface of vegetable earth, and is now
annually sown with barley, which . . . the Disdàr-Aga's
horses eat green.'[3] Fairs took place in the open area around
the Theseion or temple of Hephaistos, to which, according
to a drawing of about 1800, one end of a tightrope could con-
veniently be attached.[4] Many Byzantine churches mouldered
away, or were damaged in the sieges and counter-sieges of the
War of Independence (1821–9). For several years after the
fighting had ended, as Demetrios Sicilianos, chronicler of 'Old
and New Athens' records, 'Ruins blocked the streets, and
paths had been made on top of them; walkers had to jump
from hillock to hillock of stones and rubble.'[5] Hundreds of
houses and seventy-two more churches were demolished in the
1830s and 1840s to make way for the new city. Broad boulevards and squares replaced or co-existed with the earlier lanes
and market-places. Museums were opened, and the National
– at first Royal – Gardens grew green amidst the hot and
stony city. Then came faster flux, as the population increased
from 20,000 in 1855 to almost 108,000 in 1889. By 1920
the figure was 293,000 (in 1927 Evelyn Waugh was pleasantly surprised to find Athens 'very much more modern and
smart than I expected – trams, cocktail bars and enormous
blocks of flats'[6]) and since then it has increased steadily
towards the millions and the skyscrapers. Pollution neces-
sitated the removal of the original caryatids from the
Erechtheion to the Acropolis museum in 1977; the *nephos* or
smog arrived, and Athens became, as Arnold Toynbee says,
'Greece's urban octopus' whose tentacles threaten 'to clutch
the whole of Greece in a throttling embrace.'[7]
    The decay and development of the much-mythologized city
has continued to shock visitors since the early seventeenth-
century Scottish traveller William Lithgow lamented, with
baroque inventiveness but real emotion, the terminal decline
of 'the Mother & Well-spring of all liberall Arts and Sciences;
and the great Cisterne of Europe, whence flowed so many
Conduit pipes of learning all where.'[8] But some constants

did remain. The Acropolis and Lycabettos and the surrounding mountains – the garland, as John Addington Symonds put it in the 1890s, 'of air-empurpled hills'[9] – lead the eye upwards and outwards from the streets of the city. Even Leigh Fermor's concrete prongs and – except on the worst days – the *nephos*, cannot make the poet Kostis Palamas' Athens, where 'sky is everywhere', sound entirely ironic to modern ears.[10]

Even the crustiest of sojourners have, on occasion, been surprised by joy. George Gissing spent a rather lonely and melancholy time in Athens in the November and December of 1889. He found the ancient rivers of Kephissos and Ilissos all but dried up, and complained that such was the general aridity of Athens that 'you live in a cloud of dust. It is the duty of a waiter at every hotel to dust the boots and trousers of all who enter. You have not walked ten yards before your boots are white in mid-street.' Rather than face this experience too often, Gissing seems to have spent much of the time reading the classics and writing letters in hotel rooms. Nonetheless, he was forced to admit that everything, even the dust, could be 'transfigured by the sun'.

These vast deserts and dustheaps become unspeakably beautiful when seen from a little distance: they are coloured wonderfully, and their forms keep changing in the strangest way. Impossible to judge of distances here. One hour Mount Hymettus seems twenty miles away, the next you feel disposed to climb it as an after-dinner amusement – every stone is defined from base to summit. The sunsets are of unspeakable splendour. When you stand with your back to the west and look towards the Acropolis, it glows a rich amber; temples, bulwarks and rocks are all of precisely the same hue, as if the whole were but one construction. The marble slopes of Pentelicon become violet and purple and all manner of nameless tints. Impossible for you to imagine what I mean. Impossible for any painter to render such scenes.[11]

Edward Lear – in his lifetime as famous for his watercolours as for his nonsense verse – was one painter who made some creditable attempts to render such scenes. In words as well as paint he celebrated the colour, the light, the space, and the dream come true of his first encounter with Athens. In June 1848 he wrote to his sister Ann:

> The beauty of the temples I well knew from endless drawings – but the immense sweep of plain with exquisitely formed mountains down to the sea – & the manner that huge mass of rock – the Acropolis – stands above the modern town with its glittering white marble ruins against the deep blue sky is quite beyond my expectations . . . poor old scrubby Rome sinks into nothing by the side of such beautiful magnificence.[12]

THE ACROPOLIS

The Theatre of Dionysos

John Addington Symonds, aesthete, poet, and author of the colourful *Renaissance in Italy*, considered modern Athens to be 'an insignificant mushroom.' In the Theatre of Dionysos, on the southern slopes of the Acropolis, there was much more to notice or to imagine. To be told that the present stone semi-circle postdates by several centuries the smaller, partly wooden structure of Sophocles' day, or that the marbled Orchestra was then of hard earth, would have daunted him little.

> The pavement of the orchestra, once trodden by Athenian choruses, presents the tessellated marbles to our feet; and we may choose the seat of priest or archon or herald or thesmothetes [legal officer], when we wish to summon before our mind's eye the pomp of the 'Agamemnon' or the dances of the 'Birds' and 'Clouds' . . . Probably a slave brought cushion and footstool to complete the comfort of those stately armchairs. Nothing else is wanted to render them fit now for their august occupants; and we may imagine the long-stoled greybearded men throned in state, each with his wand and with appropriate fillets on his head. As we rest here in

the light of the full moon, which simplifies all outlines
and heals with tender touch the wounds of ages, it is
easy enough to dream ourselves into the belief that the
ghosts of dead actors may once more glide across the
stage. Fiery-hearted Medea, statuesque Antigone, Prometheus silent beneath the hammer-strokes of Force and
Strength . . . emerge like faint grey films against the
bluish background of Hymettus. The night air seems
vocal with echoes of old Greek, more felt than heard,
like voices wafted to our sense in sleep, the sound
whereof we do not seize, though the burden lingers in
our memory.[13]

In 1904 living people were to be found sitting in the
archons' seats and dancing on the marbles. Isadora Duncan had
come to Greece in search of what she believed to be the ancient
sources of her belief in freedom of movement and expression
(whether balletic, sartorial, or sexual). Accordingly, and to
the amazement or amusement of modern Greeks, the whole
'Clan Duncan' – Isadora with her mother, brothers, and
sister – walked about in 'tunic and chlamys and peplum, and
having put fillets round our hair.'

One moonlit night, when we were sitting in the Theatre
of Dionysus, we heard a shrill boy's voice soaring into
the night, with that pathetic, unearthly quality which
only boys' voices have. Suddenly it was joined by another
voice, and another. They were singing some old Greek
songs of the country. We sat enraptured. Raymond said,
'This must be the tone of the boys' voices of the old
Greek chorus.'

This theory was too exciting to be questioned. On succeeding nights the distribution of drachmas swelled the chorus
until 'gradually all the boys of Athens gave themselves a
rendez-vous to sing to us by moonlight in the Theatre.' Ten
boys, the most effective singers of the oldest songs, were
selected to form a choir. With the help of an Orthodox
seminarian they were trained to sing a chorus of the daughters
of Danaos from Aeschylus' *The Suppliants* to accompany the

energetic Isadora as she attempted to express the emotions of all fifty daughters in dance.

After one such performance, Isadora remembered, 'I could not sleep, and, at dawn, I went all by myself to the Acropolis. I entered the Theatre of Dionysus and danced. I felt it was for the last time.' She went up and stood before the Parthenon, and 'suddenly it seemed to me as if all our dreams burst like a glorious bubble.' She would always be a modern 'Scotch-Irish-American' and could never really become an ancient Greek. This realization was propelled partly by the discovery that the family's money was fast running out. But at least they could take the boys with them to sing at more lucrative engagements in Vienna. They were seen off at the station by a huge crowd which the choir led in a stirring rendition of the Greek national anthem. But in Vienna and Berlin their reception was cooler. Unimpressed by Aeschylus, Byzantine-style singing, and the dancing that went with them, audiences insisted on less demanding entertainment. They told Isadora to forget the Greeks and dance the Blue Danube, the 'schöne Blaue Donau!' To make matters worse, the boys' voices began to break, they threw schnitzels about in fury at not being served proper Greek food, and they climbed out of their windows at night to partake of the night-life of Berlin. They soon had to be sent home to Athens.[14]

Isadora came back to Athens briefly in 1915 and for some months in 1920. She planned to train a thousand children to dance in great Dionysian festivals. But this scheme too was thwarted by money problems, and plans for personal happiness went awry as her latest lover, the pianist Walter Rummel, fell for one of her pupils. She could not recover the rapture she felt in the moonlight in the Theatre of Dionysos, or the calm which, cupped by the hill, it still allows.

The Propylaia

Going through the Propylaia is a rite of passage. Whereas you can survey the wide extent of the Forum in Rome from convenient vantage points, the great Acropolis temples must be progressed to, up steps, through portals, and on up the uneven rocky slope. Every four years the Panathenaic procession, commemorated in the Parthenon frieze, moved along this sacred way, then lined with brightly coloured statues and temples, to bring a new peplos to the wooden figure of Athena in the Erechtheion. The people of the lower town symbolically asserted their awareness of their roots on the holy hill, and they could only do so having passed the great doors of the Propylaia. In one move the rebellious women of Aristophanes' *Lysistrata* bring the city to a standstill by barring and bolting these doors.[15]

From the tenth century the north-west wing was a church, and later an upper floor was added to create a (fairly modest) palace for the Metropolitan of Athens. The most famous resident, from 1182 to 1204, was Metropolitan Michael Akominatos Khoniates. By this time Athens was very much a fading light of Byzantium. Akominatos began his tenure with a grandiloquent sermon about the virtues of the Athenians of old, but was often to feel less than satisfied with his contemporaries in this outpost of empire. (He later discovered that most of his congregation, with their 'barbarous' dialect, understood hardly a word of his preaching.) The solaces of his residence included his library, full of sages and heroes, and the view, both real and imaginary, which it afforded. It was still possible to enjoy

> the temperate, fruit-bearing, all-giving land, honey-sweet Hymettos, serene Piraeus, Eleusis famed for the Mysteries, the plain – so well suited to riding – of the warriors of Marathon, and the Acropolis too, where now I sit and, it seems, tread the highest point of heaven.

But the exaltation was temporary. Akominatos cannot but remember that the 'famous race so fond of learning' has gone and in its place has come 'a boorish people.'[16]

The prelate encountered considerably more boorish people in the Franks who, under Boniface of Montferrat in 1204, captured Athens and expelled him. His cathedral – the Parthenon – was pillaged and his library dispersed. For all his disappointment in the Athenians, Akominatos was fundamentally loyal to them. He wandered for some years, refused offers of attractive sees elsewhere, and finally settled on Keos, where he died in about 1222, and from which he had looked longingly across the Saronic Gulf at the shores of Attica.[17]

Boniface of Montferrat enfeoffed Attica to the Burgundian Othon de la Roche, and the Metropolitan's residence in the Propylaia now became, with sound economy, the residence of the Roman Catholic Archbishop. The Turks, who took Athens in 1456, preferred to house their garrison commander there, with a powder magazine to hand on the ground floor. When this was struck by lightning in October 1656, much injury and damage resulted (as again during the fighting of 1687 and 1826-7; the present building is the result of much restoration) and the unfortunate decision was taken to transfer the magazine to the Parthenon. The other half of the Propylaia, the south-west wing, was used by the Acciajuoli, Florentine dukes of Athens from the end of the fourteenth century, as the base of a huge watch-tower. This conspicuous landmark, known as the Frankish or Venetian Tower, stood until Heinrich Schliemann, full of zeal for the Periclean Acropolis of his dreams and in return for payment of the equivalent of £465, demolished it in 1875.

The Parthenon

In the dark interior of the Temple of Athena Parthenos (the Virgin) glinted the tall statue of the goddess, covered in gold and ivory, and reflected in a pool of water. When the temple was converted into a church in the fifth century the statue was shipped to Constantinople (it probably perished when the Latins seized the city in 1204), an apse was added at the east end, galleries for women were installed, and a campanile (later a minaret) was erected. But the most dramatic change was the piercing of arched windows which flooded the once dark temple with light. Metropolitan Michael Akominatos' cathedral church in the late twelfth century was an 'exceedingly beautiful, brightly shining, and graceful royal palace, the holy dwelling-place of the true light which shines from the Mother of God.'[18]

Traces of the splendour of the cathedral, quite at odds with the impression the building makes now, were seen by Jacques

Spon and Sir George Wheler in 1676 when it housed a mosque and a powder-store. The apse was marked off by pillars of jasper; although the altar had been removed, its canopy remained, 'sustained by four Porphyry Pillars, with beautiful white Marble Chapters, of the *Corinthian* Order'; an archiepiscopal throne of marble also remained, an ancient seat, we now know, carried up from the Theatre of Dionysos.[19] Eleven years after this description, in 1687, Doge Morosini's bombardiers began the process responsible for the modern appearance of the Parthenon. Further damage during the War of Independence, and the classical purism of German and Greek archaeologists soon afterwards, completed the process. Amongst much else was removed the smaller mosque built within the shattered Parthenon, the 'petites ruines turques parmi la grande ruine grecque' seen by Gustave Flaubert in 1851.[20]

A few traces of the church lingered on. In the mid-nineteenth century children were still collecting little gold cubes from the apse, demolished in 1835.[21] In December 1889 George Gissing saw, on the interior walls, 'fading pictures of saints, with aureoles about their heads, relics of the time when the Parthenon was a church. Strange thoughts these excite!'[22] They were strange thoughts, presumably, because Gissing came, like the great majority of nineteenth- and twentieth-century visitors, with clear classical expectations. Alphonse de Lamartine came with such expectations in August 1834, and had them triumphantly fulfilled. Having meditated long on the wide vistas from the Acropolis, peopling them in imagination with ancient ships, forests, Athenians passing in their waves to and from Piraeus, he found it easy to 'rebuild' the 'majestic simplicity' of the Parthenon.

> It was a single thought in stone, as one, as intelligible as ancient thought itself. Only from near at hand were the richness of the materials and the inimitable perfection of the decoration and the details apparent. Pericles wanted to make of it as much a bringing-together of all the masterpieces of man's genius and man's hand as an act of homage to the gods, – or rather, the whole Greek genius was offering *itself*, through this emblem, as a

homage to the Divinity! The names of all those who dressed a stone or moulded a statue for the Parthenon became immortal.

Even the ruins of the Parthenon retained vitality for Lamartine: the fallen blocks and columns were like great oaks resting on each other in the Forêt de Fontainebleau, they were white like the foam on huge waves, they demanded of the beholder the same emotion he would feel for 'creatures who once had, or who might still have, life and feeling.'[23]

Classical preparation was not always so useful. Thackeray, alias Michael Angelo Titmarsh of *Notes of a Journey from Cornhill to Grand Cairo*, found it difficult to take much interest in Athens because he had 'the same recollection of Greek in youth that I have of castor-oil.'[24] Textbook reproductions of the Parthenon, besides (not to mention the lifesize concrete replica erected on a low mound in Nashville, Tennessee in 1922–32), had a habit of doing the original an injustice. There were, as Robert Byron remembered when he first came to Athens, watercolours of the Parthenon as 'a row of grooved cinnamon ninepins against a sky the colour of a faded butcher's apron.' Byron (a distant relation of Lord Byron, usefully if sometimes embarrassingly for a traveller in Greece) was twenty-one, fresh from Eton and Oxford, and remembered all too clearly 'those yellowed photographs that invariably adorn the dining-rooms of British pedagogy – photographs enlarged to accentuate every scratch and chip into a deep and crumbling abrasion.' Because of such pictures, artistically educated people are beginning to loathe 'anything of the nature of a "Greek Ruin".'[25] Pleasantly surprised by the real Parthenon, on this occasion he praises its texture and colour and setting, but, probably with the ninepin pillars and yellowing monochromes in mind, preferred to write about Byzantine art.

Even the original was too much for William Golding, who in his younger days had belonged to 'British pedagogy.' His friend Peter Green describes walking with him on the Acropolis under grey skies one March:

A curious expression came over Bill's face. He stopped, blew his nose with a loud trumpeting sound, and stared, briefly, at the Western world's biggest cultural cliché, clearly resenting its long and all-too-influential shadow. '*Aargh*,' he said. Into that curious noise he injected all the censorious impatience produced by years of peddling Greek culture to lymphatic schoolchildren. Then he found a comfortable block, and settled himself down in it – with his back squarely turned to the ostensible object of our visit. Little by little he relaxed, taking in the hazed industrial gloom of Piraeus, the squalid proliferation of sugar-cube houses creeping out to embrace the lower slopes of Mt Parnes, the big jets whining down past us on their approach to Ellenikón airport . . . 'Ah,' he said at last, 'now *this* is what I call the right way to look at the Parthenon.'[26]

No two encounters with the Parthenon are the same. It can be viewed from many different angles and, after more than two millennia, from many different mental positions. Exposed on its hill in the bowl of the mountains, it is played upon by changing light. Its colour and texture can look as different at morning and evening, in winter or summer, as Monet's series paintings of Rouen Cathedral or the grainstacks. As a result, observers have reached some very different conclusions about the colour: for Flaubert (in February) it was predominantly reddish brown, for Robert Byron 'sun-kissed satin,' for H.V. Morton, in a more homely analogy, 'a curious milky gold, the colour of crust on Devonshire cream.'[27] Kostis Palamas, living and working near the Parthenon for many years, could only conclude that it 'takes its colour from all our thoughts and all our dreams.'[28]

One way of coping with the temple's apparent refusal to settle into a single easily described appearance is to invoke the balancing of opposites, particularly movement and stillness. Morton suggests that the Parthenon 'has a quality of life which suggests a bird alighting from the air, in that brief moment as it closes its wings and is still poised and balanced.'[29] Lamartine also spoke in terms of movement miraculously stabilized, of 'lumière pétrifiée' and 'le plus parfait poème en pierre écrit sur la face de la terre.'[30]

One of the most stimulating accounts of a first encounter

with the Parthenon occurs in Peter Levi's *The Hill of Kronos*.
His involvement with Greece began in 1963, when he
was thirty-two, as a form of escape from the restraints of
his Jesuit vocation and the cold of Oxfordshire. Later he
became more involved in archaeology, wrote more poetry, left
the priesthood, and married. Greece was important at each
stage of this personal journey. It acted as a release from
English self-control, as linguistic stimulus (Levi writes poems
in Greek as well as English) and poetic inspiration, as a source
of friendships (especially with George Seferis, one of Greece's
foremost modern poets), and spur to political involvement (he
did much to help Greeks courageous enough to speak out
against the Colonels' tyranny of 1967–74). So it is with
Greece in his blood that Levi looks back at one of his early
inspirations, the Parthenon, and tries, like so many before
him, if not to fix, at least to express, its indeterminacies.
Here are

> the restrained geometry, the impressive and deliberate
> size, the harmony and proportion and the splendid
> physical impact that we call classical. It has the animal,
> not only the spiritual, qualities of man. It has the peace
> and the subtlety that oriental buildings have. At the same
> time there is something naive and stark naked about that
> wonderful white marble. Is it white? Is it cream? Not
> a dead white or a salt white, but fresher than milk or
> cream, fresher than a white cloud, crisper than white
> silk. The marble exists because of the light, because of
> the blazing purity and strength of Greek sunlight. That
> light does still exist, more brilliant than the sun or the
> sea or any stone or mineral. The akropolis belongs more
> to the sky than to the earth; it is made of light and of
> white marbles, dark marbles, pillars, shadows.[31]

The Parthenon Frieze

'De Greeks were godes! de Greeks were godes!' cried the
Swiss painter Fuseli when he first saw the sculptures of the
Parthenon frieze, while John Keats, in more English manner,
would gaze at them for an hour at a time 'rapt in revery.'[32]

The 'heifer lowing at the skies' in 'Ode on a Grecian Urn' probably derives from the frieze. But of course Fuseli was striding about, and Keats sitting, not on the Acropolis but in London. (In the Park Lane gallery in the first case; by 1817, when Keats saw the sculptures, they had been transferred to the British Museum.)

Lord Byron responded differently to the work of Phidias when Lord Elgin first removed the marbles: wasting thousands of pounds on 'Phidian freaks,/Misshapen monuments and maim'd antiques' qualified Elgin for a place in the angry young man's general blacklist, *English Bards and Scotch Reviewers*.[33] Once he had actually seen the denuded Parthenon in 1810 Byron was even more enflamed against Elgin, now as a plunderer and enemy to Greeks rather than just an admirer of 'freaks'. In 'The Curse of Minerva' he wishes on Elgin, on Minerva or Athena's behalf, vengeance beyond the tomb in the form of 'many a branding page and burning line.'[34] Unluckily for Elgin, Byron's lines were quite enough lastingly to tarnish his reputation. There are few records of immediate reactions to the spoliation in Greece itself, but as early as January 1803 the Athenian teacher Ioannis Benizelos was lamenting that the Parthenon without the frieze was like a noblewoman deprived of all her jewels.[35]

The arguments for and against Elgin's actions have often been rehearsed, together with the lengthy tale of his difficulties in transporting his trophies, persuading others of their artistic merit, and selling them. In the end the British Museum paid him far less for the marbles than he had spent on them. Less well known are the depredations of other sculpture hunters. Not content with blowing up the temple, the victorious Francesco Morosini attempted to remove Zeus in his chariot from the west pediment of the temple, but as his workers detached the cornice it fell to the ground and was completely smashed.[36] C.R. Cockerell, in 1814, was more fortunate with his loot. Cockerell, who spent seven years in southern Europe and Turkey, studying, drawing, and taking part in the discovery of the Aigina and Bassai marbles, was still three years from his return to take up an architectural career in England. The Turkish 'disdar or commandant of the castle on the Acropolis' had taken a great liking to him. Indeed

Cockerell charmed wherever he went. His physical apearance seems to have helped: the British Ambassador in Constantinople, Stratford Canning, noted on his passport, with evident delight and in Italian, the *lingua franca* of the day, 'occhi, negri e splendente; naso fino . . . fronte, di marmo . . . in somma Apollo lui stesso.' ('Eyes: black and lustrous. Nose: noble. Brow: of marble. Altogether, the very likeness of Apollo.') When this noticeable young man came to take his leave, the Disdar told him that he would make him a present.

> He said he knew that Cockerell was very fond of old sculptured stones, so if he liked to bring a cart to the base of the Acropolis at a certain hour at night (it could not be done in the daytime for fear of giving offence to the Greeks) he would give him something. Cockerell kept the appointment with the cart. As they drew near there was a shout from above to look out, and without further warning the block which forms the right-hand portion of Slab I. of the South Frieze now in the British Museum was bowled down the cliff. Such a treatment of it had not been anticipated, but it was too late for regrets. The block was put on to the cart, taken down to the Piraeus, and shipped at once. Cockerell presented it to the British Museum, and its mutilated appearance bears eloquent testimony to its rough passage down the precipices of the Acropolis.[38]

The Erechtheion

Visitors to the Acropolis have mostly taken at least a polite interest in the Erechtheion as a whole, perhaps sparing a word for the elegance of its Ionic pillars or the way in which its irregularity – it incorporates several earlier shrines – complements the clarity and harmony of the Parthenon. But the caryatid porch has excited stronger feelings. Lord Elgin liked it enough to remove one of the six caryatids. (Another disappeared in Turkish times; the remaining originals are kept in the Acropolis Museum to protect them from corrosive air more dangerous than any Scot or Turk.) Virginia Woolf approved of the statues, although she was a little uneasy about their size (one and a half times larger than life): 'The fat Maidens who bear the weight of the Erechtheum on their heads, stand smiling [with] tranquil ease, for their burden is just meet for their strength. They glory in it; one foot just advanced, their hands, one conceives, loosely curled at their sides.'[39] (In fact, as later copies in Rome and at Hadrian's Villa near Tivoli suggest, they held in their right hands *phialai* – flat, rather saucer-like drinking vessels.[40]) The problem of size was not to be brushed aside so easily for Brian de Jongh, author of the *Companion Guide to Greece*.

> The heavy drapery of the Caryatids may have been meant to harmonize with the fluting of the columns of the Parthenon, but these six hefty maidens, in spite of their brave yet self-conscious simper, seem to be crushed by the weight of the ornamental roof they support on their cushioned heads.[41]

The most surprising chapter in the history of the Erechtheion began in 1463 and continued until at least the 1670s. Wheler notes that the Turkish commander 'made it his *Seraglio* for his Women.'[42] Perhaps, if he noticed them, the commander enjoyed the contrast between the rather prim-looking stone maidens outside and the expected welcome within.

COMING DOWN FROM THE ACROPOLIS

Coming down from the Acropolis in a group has its own appeal. Virginia Stephen (Woolf) was travelling with her brothers Thoby (who contracted typhoid and died soon after returning to England) and Adrian, her sister Vanessa, and Violet Dickinson. In her journal she describes the scene in the narrow streets descending the hill on an autumn evening in 1906:

> The lights are flaring, & you walk in a curious soft air, blue with daylight still, though the lamps are pouring yellow into it. It is still quite warm, & the atmosphere

has a curiously tangible quality to it; the streets are crowded & people come swarming down them, happy & garrulous, in crowds.[43]

For the lone stroller the appeal is different. On the afternoon of 20 January 1945 Harold Macmillan, taking advantage of a precarious truce between the factions struggling for control of Athens during the first stage of the Greek Civil War,

went to the Acropolis and on the way there and back pottered about old streets and found old bits of temples and market-places. This is really a most attractive city. It somehow gains by there being so comparatively little to see, and all of it so lovely.

In different circumstances Macmillan might have lingered longer over those temples and market-places, and we shall return to them presently. But some relaxation was needed after the stress of the recent battle for Athens, during which he had maintained a suitably British stiff upper lip, making such notes in his diary as 'The street just outside the Embassy is rather dangerous and bursts of machine-gun fire pour down it from time to time.'[44] Inside the embassy, a stray bullet missed the future Prime Minister's head by a couple of inches, but existence under siege was made more tolerable by the genial presence of Osbert Lancaster as Press Attaché, and by the decision to break into the well-stocked wine cellar of the former Ambassador. To silence the remonstrations of the new Ambassador, Rex Leeper, Macmillan is said to have penned the following impeccably English note: 'I have decided that in sieges it is permissible to drink the former ambassador's champagne. Harold Macmillan, Minister of State.'[45]

Evelyn Waugh was freer to relax in the Athens of 1929. He had come first a few years earlier, as an undergraduate, when, he claimed, he spent most of his time in an alcoholic stupor thanks to an encounter with 'a one-legged Maltese, who gave us cocktails made out of odd drugs and a spirit of his own distilling.' On his return, as part of a Mediterranean cruise, he felt somewhat more sober, although the memory of a more respectable brand of alcohol seeps into his idea of the colour of the Acropolis, not snow-white 'but a singularly beautiful tone in very pale pinkish brown; the nearest parallel to it of Nature that I can think of is that of the milder parts of a Stilton cheese into which port has been poured.'

Apart from this brief sally, Waugh eschewed classical Athens during this second visit, written up in *Labels*. He preferred to write about the atmosphere of 'Dickensian conviviality' in a taverna in 'the poorer part of the town.' Here he watched men dancing 'with very severe expressions on their faces but a complete lack of self-consciousness' and watched a heated political argument with baffled amusement.

There was an elderly man with a curly grey beard who was much moved. He roared and pounded on the table with his fist; he pounded on his glass, broke it, and cut himself. He stopped arguing and began to cry. Immediately everyone else stopped arguing too and came over to comfort him. They wrapped a grubby handkerchief round his hand, which was not, I think, at all seriously injured. They gave him beer and bits of bad ham on matches; they patted him on the back and put their arms round his neck and kissed him. Soon he was smiling again and the discussion was resumed, but as soon as he showed signs of excitement, they warned him with smiles, by moving his mug farther across the table.[46]

SYNTAGMA (CONSTITUTION) SQUARE, THE GRANDE BRETAGNE

Syntagma Square and the boulevards which radiate from it were designed as the imposing centre of a new, unequivocally European city in the early years of Greek independence. The royal palace (completed in 1840) was built to dominate its north side, and King Otho and Queen Amalia took an enthusiastic part in a social life far removed from that of the crumbling Athens of a few years earlier. Amalia's maid of honour, Julie von Nordenflycht, remembered the square for its band which played on Sundays (a reminder, perhaps, of the royal homeland, Bavaria), its six cafés, and its picturesque mixture of Hydriot ladies in their island costume, 'the latest Paris fashions, and foreign naval uniforms.'[47]

In these years, however, with much of Athens still being planned, built, or reconstructed, Syntagma's pretensions to cosmopolitan elegance were bound to strike some observers as premature. Thackeray seized on the absurdity of the situation in his *Notes of a Journey from Cornhill to Grand Cairo*, remembering the King riding out 'in a gilt barouche and an absurd fancy dress' from his 'huge plaster of Paris palace' into a square containing not Nordenflycht's six cafés, carriages and a band, but 'six houses, three donkeys, no roads, no fountains.'[48]

When Thackeray mocked the square in the autumn of 1844 it had recently acquired its modern name, in circumstances which gave more than comic meaning to the idea of a fancy-dress king who 'goes out to drive (revolutions permitting) at five.' For Nordenflycht's description does not mention the divisions between the 'picturesque' and essentially powerless strollers and the German-dominated ruling group. Otho was eventually deposed in 1862; in 1843, mass protests had forced him to curtail some of his own powers and dismiss some of his more hated ministers. In March 1844 he read the new constitution to the crowds from the palace balcony, and the square became Syntagma.

Ever since the 1840s, Syntagma has attracted the crowds. David Hogarth, Director of the British School of Archaeology, described the scene in the 1890s:

Democracy makes the charm of the square. On a spring evening, ere the sea side has come into vogue, you may see any and every Athenian type sitting cheek by jowl with any other, or strolling up and down among a motley gathering of diplomatists, tourists, and figures from the Levant lands. Family parties or groups of friends sit happily round little tables, justifying their occupation with perhaps only one *consommation* among the lot, perhaps with none at all. But no-one cares . . . Outwardly, it is a sombre crowd, for aspiring Greece wears black coat and black hat, and only rarely may you see the starched *fustanella* kilt, blue gaiters, bordered zouave and vest, and soft red-tasselled cap, which the exploits of the Suliotes and the vanity of King Otho imposed as a national dress.[49]

Julie von Nordenflycht would have found much here to delight her, democracy notwithstanding; Thackeray might have had a different sort of fun placing the aspiring classes in Vanity Fair.

In 1915 Isadora Duncan, on her brief second visit to Athens, danced here to a massive non-paying audience. She danced, and the audience sang, the Marseillaise in a characteristically spirited attempt to swing the Greek political balance in favour of joining the French and British allies in the First World War and against the neutrality espoused by King Constantine I. He was forced into exile in 1917. (Constantine was restored in 1920 but expelled again in 1922; Greek monarchs, ever since the removal of King Otho in 1862, have been prone to misfortune: George I, admittedly after fifty years on the throne, was assassinated in 1913; Alexander died from a monkey-bite in 1920; George II was forced to spend most of his reign in exile; Constantine II fled abroad in 1967 and officially lost his throne when the monarchy was abolished by plebiscite in 1974.) Charismatic though Isadora undoubtedly was, the unpopularity of Constantine I was presumably not the result of her intervention. By the time of his exile she had long returned to France, by steamer and the fast Mercedes of a 'homosexual sultan' whom she had allegedly kidnapped.[50]

Whether such goings-on disturbed the smooth running of the Hotel Grande Bretagne, to the north-east of the square, is not recorded. This is the most mentioned establishment in the brief history of the Greek hotel industry. It was built as an elegant private house in 1843, and became a hotel in the 1870s. Waugh dined and took cocktails here in more sophisticated surroundings than the taverna celebrated above; his friend Robert Byron dined daily on the 'inevitable mutton' in the summer of 1925, and maintained that 'the whole of business and political Athens' from the Prime Minister down 'was usually focused on' the prolonged midday meal; Gerald, Lord Berners, composer, painter, writer and practical joker, enlivened his stay at the hotel with Osbert Sitwell by baying fearsomely one night at the 'vulpine, rather toothy' manager who, he insisted, 'was in fact a werewolf'; Edmund Wilson, reporting for the *New Yorker* on the aftermath of war in 1945, succeeded in spite of the lethargy of the staff in obtaining a one-third share of a bullet-riddled bedroom.[51] The hotel had been deemed suitably comfortable and central for successive Greek, German and British rulers in the 1940s; Harold Macmillan and his staff were 'a little shaken' by the discovery of large quantities of dynamite under the hotel on the eve of Winston Churchill's visit to help arrange a truce between the warring factions at the end of 1944.[52] A serious assault on its elegance occurred as a result of the urge to modernize which swept post-war Athens. The Grande Bretagne was entirely re-built in 1958. Patrick Leigh Fermor was there soon afterwards to mourn its demise.

> The old hall had acquired the vast and aseptic impersonality of an airport lounge. (Greek architects have forgotten the saying of their ancestor Isocrates about man being the measure of all things.) Beyond it, the bar, the noisy and delightful meeting place of many years, had become a silent waste dotted with lost and furtively murmuring customers dwarfed by their habitat into air-conditioned skaters on a rink of marble.[53]

SCHLIEMANN'S HOUSE

Continuing up Panepistimiou or University Street (officially called Leoforos Eleutherios Venizelou after the charismatic and controversial between-the-wars statesman) from the Grande Bretagne one passes the grandiose home built for Heinrich Schliemann by Ernst Ziller in 1877–80, Iliou Melathron, the Palace of Ilion. Many years later Schliemann's daughter remembered the palace as a magnificent but uncomfortable place where her father would work, standing at a high desk.[54] The more reverential Carl Schuhhardt left this account of the successful archaeologist and businessman at home:

Dr Schliemann generally spent the intervals of rest at Athens. His palatial house in the *Rue de l'Université* reminds us at every point of the world in which its owner lived and moved. In the mosaic floors the chief specimens of the Trojan vases and urns are represented. Along the wall run friezes with classical landscapes and pictures from the Greek epic, with appropriate Homeric quotations. The visitor was admitted by the porter Bellerophon and conducted by the footman Telamon to the master, who was generally found reading one of the Greek classics, and stopping at intervals to complain of the number of Stock Exchange lists brought by the morning post from Paris, London, and Berlin.[55]

PATISIA, THE NATIONAL ARCHAEOLOGICAL MUSEUM

Among the spacious streets off Omonia Square is Leoforos 28 Oktovriou, formerly called Patisiou. The whole area was Patisia, descended from the rural Paradisia where, in the mid-sixteenth century, the wealthy aristocratic nun St Philothei (born Rhigoula Benizelou) owned a farm. She angered the Turks by buying large numbers of Greek women out of slavery, until in 1589 some Turks came to the farm, found her at prayer, and 'beat her so severely that she succumbed to her wounds.' Philothei did many good works, and died for her charity; but she did not always endear herself to her fellow Athenians. Engaged in various property disputes, she fulminated against them in a letter to 'the great Logothete, Ierax' as 'a people without religion, decision or shame, wicked and reckless, with mouths open for insults and reproaches, grumbling, barbarous-tongued, loving strife and trouble and gossip, petty, loquacious, arrogant, lawless, crafty, inquisitive, and wide-awake to profit by the misfortune of others.'[56]

At number 61 Patisiou lived the family of Maria Kalogeropoulos, better known as Maria Callas. She was already singing sufficiently notably for her colleagues in the Royal Opera company to protest against her taking leading roles before her elders and betters, when the British arrived in Athens and she started administrative work at British

headquarters. As a result, her life was in danger as soon as
civil war broke out on 4 December 1944 (her twenty-first
birthday). Callas could never forget the contrast between the
habitual calm of Patisiou and its appearance in 1944. It was

> literally covered with broken glass and all sorts of
> wreckage that had fallen out of windows as a result of
> the constant machine gun fire: gray and silent. A tremen-
> dous, unnerving silence that would last sixty seconds, to
> be broken, once a minute, by the communists' terrible
> 'blind volley,' shots at regular intervals that could hit
> anyone and had the specific aim of wearing down the
> populace's nerves. Even now I can't explain to myself
> how I could have run desperately through the midst of
> that devastation, under fire, and arrived safe and sound
> at British headquarters.[57]

Callas attributed her survival only to the assistance of 'the
good Lord.'

Also in 28 Oktovriou is the National Archaeological
Museum, filled, as Peter Levi fondly noted in his diary, with
'Archaic painted snakes . . . tartan or striped black and red'
and 'hair of statues as dense as foliage, like flowerless,
unscented jasmine.'[58] Lady Diana Cooper rather breathlessly
summed up her impressions of the very full collection in 1936:

> Duff and I, a bit irritable, plodded off at 9 to another
> temple and a museum where the Mycenae dug-ups are
> kept. Most finely-chased cups that maybe Agamemnon
> drank from, and gilded masks for the faces of the dead,
> and much gold, jewellery and many swords. Actually the
> things that Homer wrote about.[59]

No doubt the Coopers also paused briefly to admire the
bronze figure of Poseidon in the act of hurling, with almost
nonchalant majesty, his missing trident (or possibly his
thunderbolt, in which case he is Zeus). The trident arm was
brought to the surface off Cape Artimision by fishermen in
1926, and the rest of the statue two years later. They also

found the later, distinctly less Olympian figures, also in bronze, of a charging, straining horse and its diminutive, also straining rider. These figures have a special resonance for the child narrator in Eugenia Fakinou's novel of 1982, *Astradeni*. The eponymous heroine and her family have been forced by economic necessity to leave the simple communal life of the island of Symi (near Rhodes) for a cramped flat in a depressed neighbourhood of Athens. The town seems crowded, superficial, corrupt. On Symi there were no cars. At school the girl is mocked and even punished for the way she dresses, for her innocent religious devotion, her island pronunciations, and her habit of responding emotionally to her studies. On a school trip to the museum, while the teacher's pet gathers material for a precise factual essay on the best known exhibits, Astradeni responds to the statues which best sum up her trapped, exiled position:

> The boy on horseback you thought would spur his horse and jump over all fences and ride free beyond all museums all over Greece. He would ride up mountains and down to the plains; he would jump over streams and gallop on without stopping ever.
> I think the boy and the horse are the most fenced-in creatures I've ever seen in my life.

But this 'childish gibberish' has no place in a 'proper essay', says the teacher, and all Astradeni's attempts to gallop away (except in memory to Symi) will, sadly, come to nothing.[60]

THE NEW METROPOLIS, THE OLD METROPOLIS

The new cathedral or metropolis in Mitropoleos Square, completed in 1855, incorporates materials from as many as seventy demolished or collapsed Byzantine or Byzantine-style churches and chapels. By general agreement the resulting structure lacks any distinctive graces; few have argued with Baedeker's judgement that 'the interior is sumptuous, but destitute of taste.'[61] The lost churches are irreplaceable, but a strong impression of their world – the candelabra, golden vestments, earnest golden saints and brooding Christs of more than a thousand years of Byzantine culture – can be gleaned at the Byzantine Museum. (The museum was originally converted, rather improbably, from the 1840s palazzo of the Duchesse de Plaisance, an eccentric French-American hostess formerly married to one of Napoleon's generals.)

One of the churches which did survive, very near the new cathedral, and long all but swamped by the Bazaar, is the squat twelfth-century old or small metropolis, or church of the Virgin 'Gorgoepiköos', swift to grant requests. The exterior decoration is exuberantly eclectic, featuring an ancient relief with the signs of the Zodiac and the Attic seasons, medieval beasts and crosses, and, added in the thirteenth century, the arms of the de la Roche and Villehardouin rulers of Athens. Baedeker found all this quite interesting, but was rather put off by 'the flat, uncouth representations of animals . . . of Byzantine workmanship.'[62] The structure of the church as a whole, however, was already widely recognized as what David Hogarth, in the mid-1890s, called 'a marvel of miniature proportions and mellow tones.'[63] Appreciation and conservation of the city's medieval remains, so often swept aside by the town planners and the archaeologists, was at last beginning.

THE TOWER OF THE WINDS

The Tower of the Winds began, in the Roman agora or forum in the first century AD, as an ingenious hydraulic timepiece. Water, supplied by aqueduct from a spring on the Acropolis, steadily filled a cylinder within the tower from which passers-by could tell the time. Long after this practical function had ceased, and most of the forum had disappeared from sight, visitors continued to take notice of the tower's curious octagonal structure and fanciful external decoration. According to the seventeenth-century Turkish traveller Evliya Chelebi, the old Greek philosophers had done their magic work here, blessing Athens from plagues and serpents, and although at the birth of the Prophet such spells became null and void, entering the building was still a tried and tested protection from malaria.[64] The tower was known then as the Tent of Plato or the School or Tomb of Socrates. Later, painters felt moved to paint it, and architects to imitate it: James 'Athenian' Stuart drew and painted it and designed a version of it at Shugborough in Staffordshire, and it is imitated more closely in the Radcliffe Observatory in Oxford. The figures of the winds themselves have had a mixed reception. Flaubert, who treasured all things absurd and incongruous, gave this brief judgement: 'Swollen legs, their weight alone would prevent the body from flying.'[65]

Had Flaubert visited the tower in Turkish times, he might have seen something nearer to flight in the dances of the dervishes whose *tekke* or religious house it then was. The devotional frenzy of the dancing frightened and fascinated a succession of early-nineteenth-century spectators. The noted watercolourist Hugh William Williams (whose productive Continental tour in 1816–18 earned him the epithet 'Grecian') was of Welsh birth but resident since childhood in Edinburgh, and felt that only Burns could furnish a fit comparison for the whirling of the dervishes: 'The witches' dance in Alloway Kirk, as seen by Tam o' Shanter, could not have exceeded the rapidity of their motions.'[66] Thomas Smart Hughes, about to become a clergyman, was moved more to outrage than wonder by the spectacle, but found himself mesmerized nevertheless.

The frantic gestures, horrible outcries, and inconceivable exertions of these fanatics, urged on by superstitious enthusiasm and stimulated by emulation, made us absolutely shudder at such a degradation of human nature. A sheik or priest presided over the orgies who stood upon a raised step and appeared to limit the time of operation by counting the beads of a rosary; but the movements were regulated by the deafening noise of three small kettle-drums which were beat violently with short elastic sticks. A single person first gets up and goes hopping or jumping round the room, throwing his head backwards and forwards or twirling it like a harlequin, uttering every now and then a hideous noise like the loud grunting of a pig. After a little time another starts up and catching him around the waist accompanies him in his revolutions which soon become most vehemently accelerated; then another and another succeeds until the first is quite surrounded and almost suffocated by the throng; in this manner holding each other with a tight grasp they go round and round leaping and crying out, as if engaged in a trial of lungs, hoo hoo, ullah ullah, hoo ullah.[67]

THE 'LANTERN OF DEMOSTHENES'

In 1676 Jacques Spon and Sir George Wheler were paying guests at Athens' recently opened 'Convent of Capuchin Missionaries.' The convent incorporated, they were interested to find, a 'little round Edifice of white Marble, very like a Lanthorn; whose Roof is sustained by six *Corinthian* Pillars.' Here, they were told, Demosthenes 'would shut himself up, to follow the Studies of Eloquence with greater privacy; having, the more to engage himself not to appear in Publick, cut off one half of his Beard.' The travellers might simply have shrugged and noted down the explanation, as most of their predecessors would have. But Spon and Wheler, observant pioneers of the Enlightenment, examined the structure in minute detail, read the inscription on the upper part of the frieze, and came much of the way to the modern conclusion that this is no lantern but the duller sounding Choregic Monument of Lysicrates, set up in celebration of the victory of 'the Lads of the Tribe of Achamas' – a chorus of boys competing in the festival of Dionysos – and their sponsor or *choregos*, Lysicrates.[68]

Foreigners continued to stay at the Capuchin house – little other accommodation was to be had – until it burnt down in 1821. (The 'lantern' was unscathed.) On 20 January 1811 Byron wrote from there to his Cambridge friend Francis Hodgson.

I am living in the Capuchin Convent, Hymettus before me, the Acropolis behind, the temple of Jove [the

Olympeion] to my right, the Stadium in front, the town to the left, eh, Sir, there's a situation, there's your picturesque! nothing like that, Sir, in Lunnun, no not even the Mansion House. And I feed upon Woodcocks & red Mullet every day, & I have three horses (one a present from the Pacha of the Morea) and I ride to Piraeus, & Phalerum.

Amongst those also living in the convent, Byron had told Hodgson the previous autumn in one of his less sophisticated shafts of wit, were 'one Fri*ar* (a Capuchin of course) and one Fri*er* (a bandy legged Turkish Cook).' As well as putting up guests like Byron, the abbot ran a small boys' school on the premises. The abbot apparently enjoyed the arguments between the three Catholic and three Orthodox pupils, while his visitor engaged with some of the boys in horseplay and a degree of sexual dalliance. (Byron notes that the abbot's favourite, Giuseppe, obviously one of the Catholics, slept in the 'Lantern'. More idealistic later tradition has it that this was Byron's cramped study or library.)[69]

Although he complained of the lack of books, Byron evidently felt more settled in the convent than he had in his first Athenian lodgings with the Makri family, in a now demolished house in Odos Theklas in whose courtyard, remembered Byron's companion John Cam Hobhouse, grew 'five or six lemon trees, from which during our residence in the place, was plucked the fruit that seasoned the pilaf.'[70] Here the poet improved his Greek, flirted – probably no more – with the three Makri sisters, and was inspired by twelve-year-old Teresa to implore in verse, 'Maid of Athens, ere we part,/Give, oh give me back my heart!'[71] Byron clearly took the relationship less seriously than Teresa's optimistic mother, who, he wrote to Hobhouse, 'was mad enough to imagine I was going to marry the girl.'[72] But the poem made Teresa a tourist attraction for some years.

HYMETTOS

Wheler and Spon visited Mount Hymettos and the small monastery on its lower slopes, Kaisariani, in a mood to relax after their diligent annotations of antiquity. The honey of Hymettos had been proverbial for its sweetness since classical times, and the monks at Kaisariani, from the eleventh century onwards, became equally famous for their skill in superintending the bees. Wheler had little to say about the monastery – lacking in architectural merit but remaining rustically restful among its pines and poplars – and much about the honey.

> The Convent is well enough built for that Country, where they do not strive to excel in stately Buildings; but rather to hide themselves as much as they can in obscurity from the World. This Mountain is celebrated for the best Honey in all *Greece*, of which it makes a great quantity to send to *Constantinople*, where it is much esteemed for making *Sorbets*.

He willingly tested the honey's reputation: 'we eat of it very freely, finding it to be very good; and were not at all incommodated with any Gripings after it ... It is of a good consistence, of a fair gold-colour, and the same quantity sweetens more water than the like quantity of any other doth.'[73]

Beyond Kaisariani Hymettos slopes up towards its traditionally violet crown. Let us leave Athens, however, by returning to its smaller hills and the distinctive atmosphere recorded in Peter Levi's diary.

> Lemon and black butterflies on the hill of Philopappos. The last light on the west end of the akropolis. Apricot cream distant marble. The bright white broken thing and the bright blue unbroken sky. Heat. Smell of pines and sage and thyme. Creaking cicadas. Bright, warm moon and stars like woodworm.[74]

2

ATTICA AND CENTRAL GREECE

Piraeus – Sounion – Daphni – Eleusis – Marathon – Khalkis – Aigina – Poros – Hydra – Spetsai – Osios Loukas – Delphi

This area includes many of the places most famous in Greek history and legend and most visited by later travellers: the mound for the fallen at Marathon; the knoll of Leonidas' last stand at Thermopylai (the pass itself has disappeared, river silt replacing it with a plain, but the knoll remains and on it a memorial stone repeating the much-quoted epitaph 'Go tell the Spartans, thou who passest by, / That here obedient to their laws we lie'); the religious centres of Eleusis and Delphi; Aigina the ancient rival of Athens; Hydra and Spetsai, the homes of the ship owners and seamen who gave early impetus to the struggle for independence in the 1820s.

Also in central Greece are towns and whole areas which have been more subject to fortune and fashions. Euboia and its splendid Venetian capital Negroponte (now Khalkis) attracted few visitors in later centuries. Thebes was renowned from Mycenaean times onwards. Its name was perpetuated in the myths of Oedipus (Oidipous, 'swollen foot') who killed his father and married his mother to become the ill-fated, self-blinding King of Thebes, and of his daughter Antigone who suffered burial alive rather than leave her brother's corpse to rot: stories beloved of Sigmund Freud, dramatized by Sophocles, Aeschylus and Jean Anouilh (*Antigone*), providing a title for Shelley's satirical burlesque *Swellfoot the Tyrant*. Yet – except under the medieval Dukes, especially the lavish, castle-building Nicolas de St Omer in the late thirteenth

century – Thebes itself attracted little post-classical com-
ment. The remains were fairly scanty, the stone a dull grey,
Sophocles sufficient on the page. Thebes was at least, however, spared the fate of the region of Boeotia more generally.
The *Dictionary of Greek and Roman Geography* of 1856, a mine
of information about ancient topography, politics, customs,
and place-associations, reminds us that

> The Boeotians are represented as a dull and heavy race,
> with little susceptibility and appreciation of intellectual
> pleasures. It was especially their lively neighbours the
> Athenians, who reproached them with this failing,
> which they designated by the name of *anaesthesia*. Their
> natural dullness was generally ascribed to the dampness
> and thickness of their atmosphere, but was probably as
> much owing to the large quantities of food which they
> were accustomed to take, and which the fertility of their
> country furnished in abundance.[1]

PIRAEUS

'Alas! alas! The Piraeus is a great busy manufacturing town,
and has mill-chimneys which vomit fumes,' wrote George
Gissing to his friend Eduard Bertz in December 1889.[2]
Worse was to come after the opening of the Corinth Canal
in 1893, when the new link between Adriatic and Aegean
made Piraeus the most important Greek port. Concrete spread
until the scanty remains of the ancient port were linked con-
tinuously to Athens in one vast conurbation. Already in 1687
the Venetian general and doge Francesco Morosini, having
defeated the Turks, had removed the regal sitting lion which
guarded the main harbour and explains the mediaeval name
'Porto Leone'. It bore an inscription from earlier times pro-
claiming in runes how the rebellious Greeks had been punished
by none other than the future King of Norway, Harald
Hardrada, then in Byzantine service. With a similar beast
from Athens, it now guards the Arsenal in Venice.
   But Piraeus is not all concrete. Variety is provided by the
contrast between the main industrial harbour and the smaller

Zea and Mikrolimani. It was probably in one of these two harbours that Patrick White experienced one of his happiest moments in Greece:

> But the fish . . . ! That is really something . . . Last night we went to a place near the water in Piraeus and feasted with many cousins [of his close friend Manoly Lascaris] on clams in the shell, fried baby kalamaria, prawns about six inches long, little red rock cod, of tender, melting flesh (these are perhaps the best of all), and an enormous fish, I don't know what, grilled in the piece, with crisp, salty black and golden skin. All this with plenty of retsina, of course, and raw salads.[3]

SOUNION

Location, colour, and Lord Byron between them explain why the columns of the Temple of Poseidon at Sounion have become so famous. They command a wide sea-view from the southernmost headland of Attica, the locally quarried stone is unusually white, and Sounion figures in the final invocation of the song 'The Isles of Greece'.

> Place me on Sunium's marbled steep,
> Where nothing, save the waves and I,
> May hear our mutual murmurs sweep.[4]

Roads now efficiently link Sounion and Athens. But when Byron and Hobhouse first ascended the 'marble steep' in January 1810 it was by way of many a winding track. Such a remote place had its dangers for the traveller, as Byron discovered during a second expedition to Sounion at the end of the year. He supplied the details in a letter to Hobhouse, who by this time was safely back in England.

> At that time five and twenty Mainotes (pirates) were in the caves at the foot of the cliff with some Greek boatmen their prisoners. – They demanded of these who were the Franks above? One of the Greeks knew *me*,

and they were preparing to attack us, when seeing my Albanians and conjecturing there were others in the vicinity, they were seized with a panic and marched off. – We were all armed (about 12 with our attendants) some with fusils & all with pistols and ataghans, but though we were prepared for resistance, I am inclined to think we are rather better without a battle. – Some of the Greeks whom they had taken, told me afterwards they saw me with my double barrell mounted on a chestnut horse, and described the rest of our party very accurately. – Two of them arrived yesterday, released, but stripped of every thing by the Mainotes. – These last deliberated some time, but as we were in a very advantageous postion among the columns, ignorant of our numbers, and alarmed by some balls which whizzed over their heads by accident, they kept to the shore, and permitted us to depart in peace. – The Albanians, my Turkish bandy legged Cook, a servant of Lusieri's & myself had guns and pistols, the rest side arms and pistols, but how we should have carried on the war is very doubtful.[5]

It seems Byron could not quite make up his mind whether to be more relieved at his escape or sorry to have missed the chance of a gun-battle in a romantic setting.

Several of the 'Isles of Greece' are visible to the south-east, even Melos on a clear day. Much nearer at hand to the east, and with less pleasant associations, is the rocky, windswept island of Makronissos. During the Greek Civil War thousands of Communists were detained here by the government. Among the prisoners were the poet Yiannis Ritsos and the composer Mikis Theodorakis, later best known for the film-scores of *Zorba the Greek* and *Z* (based on Vassilios Vassilakis' novel about the murder of the left-wing deputy Grigorios Lambrakis in Thessaloniki in 1963). Theodorakis' belief in the artist's duty to protest, and his known Communist allegiances, resulted in his arrest by the Germans, assault by political opponents, and detention in concentration camps on the islands of Psitalea, Ikaria and, from December 1948, Makronissos. The aim of the camps was to force the prisoners to renounce their politics. The rightist authorities had very different ideas to Theodorakis on how best to employ human creativity and on the proper focus of Greek culture.

[The prisoners] were assigned to open roads, break up rock piles, build walls, and use whatever skills or vocational training they had in re-creating the 'Golden Age' of Athens. This revival of ancient culture devised by the camp authorities included miniature replicas of the Parthenon, the Acropolis, and ancient theatres. They were also forced to erect buildings to house their keepers, and chambers designed for their own torture.[6]

They were forced to carry rocks until they dropped, and deprived of sleep by harassment and bright lights. Thousands were either shot or died – as Theodorakis nearly did – under torture. After this he was sent to hospital on the mainland, then back to Makronissos; final release only came after a further breakdown in his health. When a new right-wing regime seized power in 1967, Theodorakis was again arrested and imprisoned, this time in Averoff gaol in Athens. He was released thanks mainly to international pressure, but the Colonels continued to ban his songs. It was illegal either to sing or to possess them. But Theodorakis was not so easily silenced: during his later imprisonment, he continued discussing and composing music, and this time he also succeeded in smuggling songs out.

DAPHNI

Othon de la Roche, the first Frankish Lord of Athens, made the monastery of Daphni over to his fellow-Burgundians, the Cistercian monks of Bellevaux, in 1205. Othon went home to France twenty years later, but his successors, styled Dukes from 1260, chose Daphni as their place of burial. The only visible trace of this custom today is a sarcophagus in the cloister, marked with fleurs-de-lis and snakes, which probably contained the remains of the last de la Roche Duke, Guy II. In his time (he died in 1308) he was one of the most powerful men in Greece, Lord of Argos and Nauplion, Lord of Lamia, regent of the Peloponnese, with his capital and rich castle in Thebes.[7]

Later rulers treated Daphni with less reverence than the de la Roches. The last Duke of Athens before its capture by the Turks, the unsavoury Franco Acciajuoli, is even alleged to have personally beheaded his aunt Chiara, a possible dynastic rival, as she knelt at prayer in the monastery church one day in 1455.[8] The Turks left Daphni unmolested, but also unprotected from the raids of corsairs. Western travellers had, at first, little to say about the crumbling buildings which drew their attention mainly because there had once been a temple of Apollo on the same site. Dr Richard Chandler of Magdalen College, Oxford, who had been commissioned by the Society of Dilettanti to report on classical inscriptions and remains, did however express some interest, mixed with disapproval, in 1776.

> The monastery of Daphne is a mean and barbarous edifice, enclosed within a high wall. Before the gate is a well of excellent water. The church is large and lofty, and reputed the most antient in Attica. The inside of the dome is adorned with a figure of Christ in Mosaic, much injured.[9]

It was this eleventh century Christ Pantocrator of the dome which seized the attention of later observers. Less evidently 'injured' following restoration between 1889 and 1897, it was hailed now by Murray's *Handbook for Travellers in Greece* as a 'very noble mosaic of our Saviour, in the attitude of blessing.'[10] Others have found the mosaic more unsettling. The viewer is confronted, suggested Brian de Jongh in his *Companion Guide to Mainland Greece*, by a 'terrifying Messianic vision'.

> Depicted in bust, Christ raises one hand in blessing, the long bony fingers of the other clasping a jewel-studded Book of Gospels. The face, with the superbly arched eyebrows and the mouth of a man who is, beyond all things, decisive if not forgiving, is austere, Eastern, implacable. It is a Christ of Nemesis.[11]

ELEUSIS

Early Eleusis did not welcome visitors. Non-initiates who wanted to know more about the Mysteries of Demeter were deterred by stout walls around the sanctuary, fear of divine retribution, and the earthly threat of the death penalty. In fact the details of the ceremonies practised in the dark Telesterion hall are still unknown, although they were evidently connected with death, rebirth, and the cult of Demeter, goddess of fertility, and her daughter, Kore or Persephone, who returned each six months, in spring, from the Underworld.

For many centuries after the rites and the processions had stopped, the site seemed numinous to local people. Even today, amid the flame and smoke of industrial Eleusis, it may be possible to hear, with Richard Stoneman, 'a few echoes of august sanctity', a memory of *The Magic Flute*.[12] But Edward Daniel Clarke, Cambridge mineralogist and collector of trophies for the galleries of his university, took a more practical attitude to the site in 1801. Arriving at the edge of the village, he came upon the upper parts of a statue representing, he was convinced, Demeter herself 'in colossal majesty among the mouldering vestiges of her once splendid sanctuary.' The majesty was not enhanced by the fact that the statue was buried to the neck 'in the midst of a heap of dung,' but even this was less inappropriate than at first appeared.

> The inhabitants of the small village which is now situated among the ruins of *Eleusis* still regarded this *Statue* with a very high degree of superstitious veneration. They attributed to its presence the fertility of their land; and it was for this reason that they heaped around it the manure intended for their fields.

Not surprisingly, the peasants who had such a direct need of the statue were reluctant to let Clarke take it away. But, undeterred, he obtained permission from the Voivode or Governor in Athens, 'aiding my request by letting an English telescope glide between his fingers.' He then constructed an ingenious wooden frame on which to transport the statue, hired one hundred men and fifty boys to work the ropes, levers, and rollers, and prepared to set to. But at this point the goddess seemed to intervene. As the workforce considered how best to undertake their task,

> an ox, loosed from its yoke, came and placed itself before the Statue; and, after butting with its horns for some time against the marble, ran off with considerable speed, bellowing, into the Plain of *Eleusis*. Instantly a general murmur prevailed; and several women joining in the clamour, it was with difficulty any proposal could be made. '*They had been always*,' they said, '*famous for their corn; and the fertility of the land would cease when the Statue was removed.*'

Eventually they were persuaded, and made a beginning by removing the dung. But no steps could be taken towards moving the statue until the village priest, entreated by Clarke and given some menacing hints by the local Turkish governor, donned full vestments, gathered the people together, and struck the first pickaxe into the soil. (Whether the priest or the statue represented a more powerful divine authority was a little uncertain.)

The villagers' prediction that the ship carrying their statue would be wrecked was later confirmed off Beachy Head, but a successful salvage operation was conducted, and Clarke's 'Demeter' (in fact a Roman-period caryatid from her sacred precinct) still stands, faceless but possessed of a certain heavy grace, in the Greek galleries of the Fitzwilliam Museum in Cambridge.[13]

George Bernard Shaw, writing to a friend following a brief visit in 1899, was as cavalier to Eleusis in word as Clarke had been in deed. Athens fared no better.

> If you pine to see glorious Athens, buy a few second hand classical columns & explode a pound or two of dynamite among them, and there you are . . . Of course it is all a Godsend to English tourists, since they have heard about Socrates & Co, and can recognize a Corinthian capital as 'artistic' at the first glance; but to the unsophisticated eye of the natural man the whole thing is simply

exasperating. Take the prettiest seaside hill you know and dump down the tombstone makers' yards in the Euston Road upon it in a heap, smashing the stones as much as possible in the process, and you have Eleusis.[14]

MARATHON

'That man is little to be envied whose patriotism would not gain force upon the plain of Marathon, or whose piety would not grow warmer among the ruins of Iona!' declared Dr Samuel Johnson in 1773. 'I really believe I should walk over the plain of Marathon without taking more interest in it than any other plain of similar features,' riposted Samuel Taylor Coleridge sixty years later.[15] Neither writer went to Greece (Coleridge was on the point of setting out from Malta when he accepted the post of Public Secretary there instead), but Marathon, where the Athenians routed the Persians in 490 BC and whence the first 'Marathon' was supposedly run by the messenger who carried news of the victory to Athens, had become proverbial.

In the spring of 1925 the composer Dame Ethel Smyth visited Marathon. At sixty-seven, she had forged a career against much opposition from the male establishment. Her best-known work is probably her opera of 1906, *The Wreckers*. A suffragette, she wrote the 'March of the Women' and in 1912 supervised its most famous performance, 'conducting its strains with a toothbrush from the window of a cell in Holloway prison.'[16] As this last detail may suggest, she cultivated a reputation for eccentricity, conducting in happier circumstances clad in tweeds, a tie, and a three-cornered hat, and wearing them unabashed in a photograph printed at the end of her *Three-Legged Tour in Greece*. The tour was like a three-legged race, she explained, since she was travelling with her great-niece Elizabeth, one trying to speed up while the other tried to slow down to the other's pace.

At Marathon, as the two ascended the mound, crowds of children pursued them and, 'regardless of the fact that the plain is one mass of wild flowers,' pressed on them bouquets in the hope of cash returns. Exasperated, Dame Ethel turned eccentricity to account:

As they approached, each one trying to outrun the others, I myself hastily plucked a bouquet and presented it with many smiles and floods of English to an elect tormentor, with the result that, baffled, and I think terrified, the whole band retired and left us in peace. People with a perhaps dangerous lunatic in their train had better be avoided. I make a present of this tactic, which was successfully employed on many a future occasion, to any traveller heartless enough to use it.[17]

On 11 April 1870 a group of wealthy foreign visitors to Marathon faced graver difficulties. The day had started well. 'We arrived at the Tumulus,' recorded Lord Muncaster, 'about 11 a.m., and there we stopped and had our luncheon, and made ourselves jolly; the gentlemen walking to the shore, and looking for Persian remains, gaily chaffing one another the while about the brigands.' But the threat from brigands remained, to the subsequent embarrassment of the Greek authorities, a very real one. Soon after leaving Marathon the party was ambushed by a gang mostly composed of 'ill-favoured and villainous-looking murderers.' The women and child in the party were soon released, but large ransoms or an amnesty (or, later, both) were demanded in exchange for the men. After some cold, wet, and miserable experiences being moved from hill to hill around Athens, Muncaster was sent off to the city to arrange terms for himself and his companions. Negotiations were protracted, and eventually came to nothing. Intervention was unsuccessfully attempted, and during the confused events of the night of 21–22 April the four remaining captives were murdered near Dilessi.[18] The King and Queen, ministers and diplomats attended the funerals, but relations between Greece and the Western powers were temporarily soured by the incident. The British press branded all Greeks as brigands, and the Greek press angrily protested that the killers could not be Greeks – they must have been Albanians, Vlachs, infiltrators from Turkey. The victims are commemorated in stained glass in the east window of the Anglican church in Athens, St Paul's.

KHALKIS

Industrial Khalkis, on the long large island of Euboia but linked to the mainland by successive bridges across the narrow Euripos channel since 411 BC, is an unromantic place. It must have looked very different in its earlier, Venetian guise as the cosmopolitan Negroponte or Black Bridge, centre of colonial administration, high finance, and the Catholic church. Jan Morris imagines it in *The Venetian Empire: a Sea Voyage*:

> Khalkis was the show-place of the Venetian Aegean, and in old prints it is drawn bristling with towers and turrets, surrounded entirely by moat and sea-wall, and tight-stacked upon the water's edge. Its site remains extraordinary. The Euripos is one of the world's enigmas, for through it there rush, as through a mighty funnel, as many as fourteen powerful tides a day, in alternate directions. . . . The Venetians built actually on top of the channel, in the middle of a double drawbridge, a fortified tower that marked their imperial frontier. It was a romantic, Rhenish-looking construction, if we are to believe the old pictures, and so remarkable was the place, so suggestive the movement of the waters beneath it, that local rumour held it to be an enchanted castle, guarded by fairies or demons.

An early phase in the long decline of Venice was signalled by the loss of this 'show-place' to the Turks in 1470. By land and sea the huge army of the formidable Sultan Mehmet II, conqueror of Constantinople, advanced to claim the prize. Pontoon bridges were thrown across the Euripos, and heavy cannon pounded the walls relentlessly. But the defenders' fate was sealed by the aberration of the Venetian Admiral, Niccolò da Canale, who seems to have lost his nerve and turned back at the very point when his fleet appeared to be about to smash through the pontoons and raise the siege. Canale, whose skills had been diplomatic rather than military, was relieved of his command and banished from Venice for life. But by that time the citizens and garrison of Negroponte had suffered a sadder fate. Most of them were butchered in the streets when, the day after the Canale fiasco, the Turks had burst through the walls. Some women and small children lived to be enslaved. Worse was in store for the Bailie or colonial governor, Paolo Erizzo. He fell victim to Mehmet's lethal sense of humour, as John Julius Norwich explains: 'Erizzo, who had taken refuge in one of the towers, gave himself up only on the condition that he might keep his head; Mehmet, true to his promise, had his body severed at the waist instead.'[20]

In April 1941 the threat to Khalkis came from the air. Roald Dahl was a fighter-pilot based at Eleusis. A small group of Hurricanes was doing what it could to delay the relentless progress of the invading Germans. One of Dahl's missions was to prevent German planes from bombing an ammunition ship which the Greeks were trying to offload at Khalkis. At 6.15 one morning he had the unforgettable view of Euboia from the air which he describes in his second volume of autobiography, *Going Solo*.

> The little town with its sparkling white houses and red-tiled roofs stood on the edge of the waterway, and behind the town I could see the jagged grey-black mountains where I had chased the Ju 88s the day before. Inland, I could see a wide valley and there were green fields in the valley and among the fields there were splashes of the most brilliant yellow I had ever seen. The whole landscape looked as though it had been painted on to the surface of the earth by Vincent Van Gogh. On all sides and wherever I looked there was this dazzling panorama of beauty.[21]

It was so dazzling that for a near-fatal instant Dahl failed to see the enemy plane close beneath him. Fortunately he was able to make a rapid vertical escape, and lived to tell this and many another tale.

AIGINA

The flesh even of classically aware nineteenth-century travellers was weak. In 1832 the Romantic poet Alphonse de

Lamartine, 'tired of museums', sensibly avoided the one on the island of Aigina. He would have seen, besides, only a 'graveyard of the arts', for 'fragments detached from place, purpose, context are dead; marble-dust which lives no longer.' Instead, he spent two 'delicious hours' sitting or strolling in a garden of cypresses and orange-trees.[22]

Lamartine's lack of enthusiasm for the museum was perhaps sharpened by the knowledge that the 'Aigina Marbles' had, twenty years earlier, been discovered by two Englishmen and two Germans and were now safely in Munich. Prominent among the unearthers of the Munich marbles was Charles Robert Cockerell. He came to the Temple of Aphaia, then a jumbled ruin known as the Temple of Jupiter, in the spring of 1811. With his friends and followers he camped nearby and enjoyed an on-site rustic idyll.

We got our provisions and labourers from the town, our fuel was the wild thyme, there were abundance of partridges to eat, and we bought kids of the shepherds; and when work was over for the day, there was a grand roasting of them over a blazing fire with an accompaniment of native music, singing and dancing. On the platform [the floor of the temple] was growing a crop of barley, but on the actual ruins and fallen fragments of the temple itself no great amount of vegetable earth had collected, so that without very much labour we were able to find and examine all the stones necessary for a complete architectural analysis and restoration.

More exciting than architectural analysis, however, was the expedition's archaeological scoop.

On the second day one of the excavators, working in the interior portico, struck on a piece of Parian marble which, as the building itself is of stone, arrested his attention. It turned out to be the head of a helmeted warrior, perfect in every feature. It lay with the face turned upwards, and as the features came out by degrees you can imagine nothing like the state of rapture and excitement to which we were wrought. Here was an altogether new interest, which set us to work with a will. Soon another head was turned up, then a leg and a foot, and finally, to make a long story short, we found under the fallen portions of the tympanum and the cornice of the eastern and western pediments no less than sixteen statues and thirteen heads, legs, arms &c., all in the highest preservation, not 3 feet below the surface of the ground.[23]

Local representatives wanted the statues to stay on Aigina, but the Westerners paid them off with forty pounds. The French, British, and Prussian governments hoped to obtain them for their burgeoning rival museums, and Cockerell's *Journal* refers periodically over the following three years to the continuing difficulty of deciding the fate of the statues. After being stored first on Zakynthos and then on Malta, they found a home in Munich as a result of a mismanaged (or possibly 'arranged') auction in which they were sold to the Prince of Bavaria for a sum considerably smaller than his rivals were prepared to offer.

Modern archaeologists wince at the way untrained excavators enthusiastically dug up the marbles ('Soon another head was turned up'!), packed them into crates, and moved them around the Mediterranean. Some might also lament Samuel Gridley Howe's treatment of the ruins of the temple of Apollo, on a promontory near Aigina town, in the winter of 1828–9. His motives were, however, philanthropic. He first came to Greece after qualifying in medicine and surgery at Harvard in 1824. Where many Europeans had come out full of uplifting words about solidarity with the descendants of Pericles (soon followed, as often as not, by disillusion and departure), or had naïvely handed over funds and supplies to the rival faction leaders, Howe and a number of other American sympathizers were determined to bring practical aid to the poor and dispossessed. For a time he succeeded in establishing a free hospital on Poros. Then, in December 1828, he conceived his scheme for the provision of employment on Aigina for thousands of refugees from Turkish controlled areas.

After revolving in my mind various plans of relief to these suffering beings, I have resolved to commence a work upon which I can employ four or five hundred persons, give them their bread, and at the same time benefit the public; viz., the repairing of the port here, which, from the destruction of the piers and the accumulation of mud and filth, is reduced to a state nearly resembling a marsh upon its border, preventing the boats from approaching near the shore and giving out an unpleasant and unwholesome odour. To remedy this and render the port at once commodious, salubrious, and beautiful, requires only that a solid wall should be built around the border of the port a little way within the water, and then filled up behind with stones and earth; after that is done the mud should be dredged from the port within the wall and the whole filling be covered with stones. In this way a fine wharf will be formed along the whole border of the port; boats can approach and unload at it; all the dirt will be removed, and the port rendered excellent.[24]

The task was made easier by the use of stone blocks from the ruins of the temple of Apollo, whose one column was left intact and remained a landmark for those approaching Aigina town from the sea. Unusually, as William St Clair points out, the ancient Greeks had lent their successors some practical assistance.[25]

POROS

Poros is rarely mentioned by early travellers. The temple of the Sanctuary of Poseidon, where the Athenian orator Demosthenes took poison rather than give himself up to the Macedonians, was largely dismantled by Hydriotes for their own building purposes. Not surprisingly on such a small island, almost joined to the mainland, it was the point of arrival, the colourful harbour, which appealed to those who did write about it once the twentieth century began to notice it. For Henry Miller, 'To sail slowly through the streets of Poros is to recapture the joy of passing through the neck of the womb'; it was a moment to store up and exempt from the general hopelessness of Europe in 1940.[26] Lawrence Durrell, recommending his old friend's rhapsody more than thirty-five years later, adds his own tribute:

> Poros is a most · enchanting arrangement, obviously designed by demented Japanese children with the aid of Paul Klee and Raoul Dufy. A child's box of bricks that has been rapidly and fluently set up against a small shoulder of headland which holds the winds in thrall, it extends against the magical blue skyline its herbaceous border of brilliant colours, hardly quite dry as yet; the moisture trembles with the cloud-light on the wet paint of the houses, and the changing light dapples it with butterflies' wings. As the harbour curves round, everything seems to move on a turntable hardly bigger than the hurdy-gurdy of a funfair, and you have the illusion that without getting off the ship you can lean over the rail and order an *ouzo*. And this sense of proximity is increased so that you seem to be sailing down the main street with the inhabitants walking in leisurely fashion alongside the ship. You feel that finally they will lay friendly hands upon the ropes and bring it slowly to a halt.[27]

Henry Miller had visited Poros with, amongst others, George Seferis. Seferis returned six years later, exhausted and frustrated after years of war, exile, and administrative duties in Athens. In a seaside house in Poros he had at last the opportunity to write, firstly in the brilliant light, later shutting the blinds against its overwhelming, brain-emptying beauty. When not working on poetry or his essay on Cavafy and Eliot, he spent hours cutting or carving wood, enjoying simple pleasures and absorbing images.

> Poros, enclosed as it is, nonetheless reminds me how few things I need, that I should dispense with things that prevent me from seeing. What I have here before me is enough: a piece of driftwood on the beach, the brassy sound from the [naval] Training Camp, the lithographs

in the grocery stores of the town, the blank faces suffice
for me to write what I wish. I no longer believe very
much in wide horizons.

He experienced, as Miller and Durrell had in their different
ways, an 'unconquerable intoxication with every living
thing.'[28]

HYDRA

Alexander Kinglake became one of the most popular Victorian
travel-writers when *Eothen* – 'from the east' – was published in
1844. Although his journey bypassed Greece, he did encounter
Greeks, including seamen.

Our mate was a Hydriot, a native of that island rock
which grows nothing but mariners and mariners' wives.
His character seemed to be exactly that which is generally
attributed to the Hydriot race; he was fierce, and
gloomy, and lonely in his ways.[29]

Hydra, whose inhabitants were among the main proponents
of revolution in the 1820s, perhaps sounds an unlikely home
for heroes. But lack of soil capable of cultivation had always
forced the Hydriots to look outward from their rock in order
to earn a living. George Finlay, the historian who came to
Greece as a young volunteer in 1823 and stayed until his death
in 1878, described the Hydriots' eminently practical way of
life in the years before the war. (There had been a sharp decline
since the later years of the conflict, he felt.)

Seen from the sea, it presents a noble aspect, forming
an amphitheatre of white houses, rising one above the
other round a small creek which can hardly be used as
a port. The houses cling like swallows' nests to the sides
of a barren mountain, which towers far above them, and
whose summit is crowned by a monastery of St. Elias.
The streets are narrow, crooked, unpaved lanes, but the
smallest dwellings are built of stone, and near the sea
some large and solidly-constructed houses give the place

an imposing aspect. In these houses the wealthy primates
of Hydra resided at the breaking out of the Revolution.
They lived, like most Albanians, a frugal, and it may
even be said, a penurious life. In their dress, their education, and their character, indeed, there was very little
difference between the primate, the captain, and the
common sailor of Hydra. The rich Hydriot usually
displayed his wealth in erecting a large building near the
sea, which served as a dwelling for his family and a
warehouse for his goods. In some of the rooms the sails
and cordage of his ships were kept; in others he lived.[30]

SPETSAI

With Hydra (and with Psara, near Chios, until the massacre
there in 1824), Spetsai or Spetses was one of the three 'Naval
Islands' which dominated Greek sea-trade in the eighteenth
century and scored important successes against the Turks in
the early stages of the War of Independence. One of the early
naval commanders was Lascarina Boubelina, the widow of a
wealthy victim of Turkish aggression. An anonymous *History
of Modern Greece from 1820*, published in 1823, explains how

she equipped and armed at her own expence [*sic*] three
frigates, and, like a modern Amazon, she took the command of one, ranged herself in the ranks among the
captains of the fleet. Neither the dangers of war, the
perils of navigation, nor the fatigues of so rude a
campaign, could alter her resolution. She embarked,
taking with her her young sons, and said to them as they
went on board, 'my dear children, the barbarians we are
going to fight against have murdered your unfortunate
father, you must, like me, avenge his death.'

Boubelina, the author notes admiringly, 'forgot the natural
weakness and timidity belonging to her sex; she only bore in
mind, to revenge the murder of her husband, and this desire
was so great, that she would not entrust that care to any one
else; and all Greece applauded this generous feeling.'[31]
The anonymous patriot has embroidered Boubelina's story.

It was pirates rather than the Turkish authorities who had killed her husband, but her father had died as a victim of Turkish oppression. Besides, Greece needed heroes, and needed them to be known abroad. The front matter of the anonymous *History* carries this advertisement: 'Just published, Price 3s. 6d. A Whole Length Portrait of the celebrated Heroine of Greece, BOBELINA, in the Greek Costume, at the Battle of Argos.' Statues and portraits of Boubelina with her cutlass and pistol were soon to proliferate on Spetses, particularly after her death in action – although this took the form of a family feud rather than the Greek struggle – in 1825. She became a kind of secular patron saint of the island. Official tributes, naturally, fail to mention the alleged vigour of her sexual appetite. This aspect of her fame may, of course, reflect the nervousness of a male-dominated society before such a commanding and formidable female. Kazantzakis' Zorba, not a man to be nervous of women, cheers the fading Mme Hortense, who claims once to have consorted and cavorted with the admirals of several nations, by calling her his 'Boubelina'.

The novel especially associated with Spetses is John Fowles' *The Magus*. The Villa Yasemia, near Agia Paraskevi, is the original of Bourani in the novel. Guidebooks feel conscience-bound to admit, however, that Fowles' island of Phraxos is a more tranquil and remote place than Spetses can have been for several generations. Silence is the distinguishing characteristic of Phraxos.

> Out on the hills one might pass a goatherd and his winter flock (in summer there was no grazing) of bronze-belled goats, or a bowed peasant-woman carrying a huge faggot, or a resin-gatherer; but one very rarely did. It was the world before the machine, almost before man, and what small events happened – the passage of a shrike, the discovery of a new path, a glimpse of a distant caïque far below – took on an unaccountable significance, as if they were isolated, framed, magnified by solitude. It was the least eerie, the most un-Nordic solitude in the world. Fear had never touched the island. If it was haunted, it was by nymphs, not monsters.[32]

OSIOS LOUKAS

Robert Byron described the view as he descended towards the monastery of Osios Loukas, after a gruelling mountain mule-ride, in June 1926:

> Sheer below to one side stretched great sort of flying buttresses of bluey grey earth, about 200 feet down, where they were met by smaller and more luminous ones, a purply pink – and on them very *bright pink* clumps of oleanders. Beyond a vast panorama of infinitesimal cultivated patches, olive trees and huge mountains rising again. Around one, yellow clumps of broom and hundreds of strange thistles, whose leaves looked as if they had been dipped in Reckitts blue – while huge iridescent beetles buzzed from bloom to bloom – and swallowtails, marbled whites, white admirals and all the blues flying everywhere.[33]

As champion of all things Byzantine, Byron was in his element in the large eleventh-century pilgrims' church, glowing, thanks to imperial patronage, with gold and marble, porphyry and jasper. It was, he wrote to his mother ('Darling Mibble'), 'all marble panelled, just as we use wood – with even the veins of the marble transposed so as to make a pattern like our dining-room table.' Less was to be said for his flea-infested monastic guest-room.[34]

The Austrian poet and dramatist Hugo von Hofmannsthal was, so far as we know, untroubled by fleas when he stayed at Osios Loukas in 1908. In *Moments in Greece* he absorbs the timeless atmosphere of daily life in the monastery:

> Everything breathed peace and a scent-sweetened serenity. From below, a fountain murmured. On a bench sat two older monks with ebony-black beards. Opposite them, on a second-floor balcony, leaned another of uncertain age, his head on his hand. Small clouds sailed across the sky. The two monks rose and went into the church. Two others came down a staircase. They also wore the long black gowns, but the black caps on their heads were

not so high, and their faces were beardless. Their gait had the same indefinable rhythm: as far removed from haste as from slowness. They disappeared simultaneously through the church door, not so much like men entering a house as sails vanishing beyond a rock, or as great unobserved animals stalking through the forest and disappearing behind trees. Inside the church faint voices began chanting psalms, following an age-old melody. The voices rose and fell; there was in them something endless, as remote from lamentation as from desire, something solemn which might have been sounding from eternity and continue to sound far into eternity.[35]

DELPHI

Lucy Honeychurch, in *A Room With a View*, was about to travel to 'silly Greece' and round the world with the Miss Alans when she was persuaded instead to admit her love for George Emerson and return to Florence with him. But the elderly Alans went on to 'either shrine of intellectual song – that upon the Acropolis, circled by blue seas; that under Parnassus, where the eagle builds and the bronze charioteer drives undismayed towards infinity.'[36] (E.M. Forster himself found Greece less exhilarating than Italy when he was there on an organized tour in the spring of 1903, but the expedition did result in an unfinished historical story set in Mistra, 'The Tomb of Pletone', and the more characteristic and readable 'The Road from Colonus', in which 'a hollow tree not far from Olympia' vouchsafes the staid Mr Lucas an all-too-short glimpse of eternal happiness.)

Delphi became a 'shrine of intellectual song' because of its location between the great rocks where the eagles nest. Here, it was believed, was the omphalos, the earth's navel, a fit meeting-place for the divine – channelled through the oracular trance of the priestess – and the human. Rose Macaulay found the god lingering in *Pleasure of Ruins*:

Imagine . . . the Pythian priestess at her job, bathed and purified by the cold Castalian springs, frenzied by the sacred laurel between her teeth, seated on the tripod over

the intoxicating air that welled up from the deep till she
spoke what she received from the oracle, sending men
to death or conquest, loss or victory, or (often) merely
confusing or deceiving them, for Apollo, though usually
succeeding in saving his face, was full of wiles. Long
since expelled from his dubious, rewarding job, he still,
we may assume, haunts his sanctuary, brooding among
his broken treasuries, hiding his face among the goats and
crags, or breaking out with radiance that lights all the
great jumbled mass of mountain peaks and the Gulf of
Salona below.[37]

Earlier visitors, arriving when the treasuries, the Temple of
Apollo, the theatre, and the stadium, were all buried under
the village of Kastri, were sometimes disappointed in their
search for the numinous. The early nineteenth-century watercolourist Hugh William Williams describes how

The Castalian spring being quite close at hand, we were
led to it first . . . in which we immediately saw the
Pythia in imagination lave her streaming hair. Our classic
dreams, however, were soon dismissed by the appearance
of a dirty washerwoman trailing a piece of cloth in the
sacred stream – the stream of Castaly.[38]

Kastri survived until the early 1890s, rivalry between
French and German archaeologists having procured a stay of
execution for it. But once the French had won the contest,
the inhabitants of the village were forcibly removed to the
present 'Delphi', at a discreet distance from the sanctuary. One
area of the newly uncovered site, the theatre, with its
sweeping view, was particularly useful to the poet Angelos
Sikelianos. Here in 1927, with his American wife Eva Palmer
Sikelianou, he staged the first of his multiple festivals of
drama, dancing, and athletics in an ambitious attempt to
realign the corrupt modern world with the ancient harmonies
of Delphi. The festivals combined, as Oliver Taplin says in
the book accompanying his television series *Greek Fire*, 'weird
ideas about the origin of tragedy and the Eleusinian mysteries
with oriental mysticism and a feminism connected with
Isadora Duncan's dancing.'[39] Many found all this simply

absurd and Sikelianos, whom a younger poet, George Pavlopoulos, once overheard eloquently addressing a tree in the National Gardens in Athens, something of a figure of fun.[40] But, as Taplin goes on to argue, Sikelianos helped inject a new confidence into Greek theatre; practical results included the establishment of regular modern performances in the theatre at Epidauros. And at Delphi in 1927 there was one famous moment when contact with the gods seemed to have been established. At the end of a production of Aeschylus' *Prometheus Bound*, eagles flew down from the Phaidriades, the 'Shining Rocks', and appeared to menace the god-defying Prometheus: 'Some say they heard thunder!'[41]

Indoors, in the museum, dwells Forster's bronze charioteer. Charles Ricketts, designer, aesthete, collector, described him in 1911.

> The doors let in a flood of morning light upon the sudden appearance of the Charioteer. At a few paces from us on a low pedestal he stands like a column of bronze; the sun catches the inlay of his eyes which flash for an instant, and puts a gleam about the corners of his arrogant lips. The apparition is startling: this effigy of a beautiful and sullen young tyrant, long dead, seems to have come to life. Or was he living behind the locked door and become immobile this instant only? His arms and feet still show the sleek grain of the living flesh from which they seem actually to have been cast; the ringlets and wire eyelashes glimmer and glitter in the light.[42]

Most descriptions of Delphi, including Ricketts' of the charioteer, are bathed in sunlight; Stephen Spender, teaching in Cincinatti, remembered a hauntingly different scene:

> When I had come back from India once, I went to Delphi on a shining starlit night and I noticed how with star and moonlight brilliant on tree-like columns, there seems a geometric relationship between stars and temples, as though there were lines drawn between the stars illustrating the heavenly signs, as depicted in old globes of the heavens.[43]

3

THE PELOPONNESE

Corinth – Mycenae – Tiryns – Nauplion – Epidauros – Sparta –
Mistra – Monemvasia – Kythera – Mani – Olympia –
Bassai – Karitaina

The Peloponnese, suggests the ancient geographer Strabo, 'is the acropolis of Greece as a whole.'[1] Access from the northern mainland is limited by the narrowness of the isthmus, and easy sea approaches are rare; indeed 'Peloponnesos' means 'the island of Pelops'. (The medieval name, Morea, may refer to its shape – 'mulberry-leaf'; Strabo and others had compared it to a plane-tree leaf.) The integrity of the near-island was essential to the Greek victory over the Persians and the Spartan victory over the Athenians in the Peloponnesian War; the mountains which seem to radiate from the central peaks of Arcadia also made the peninsula the securest power-base for rebellion against the Turks.

The War of Independence dates officially from the moment when, on 25 March 1821, Metropolitan Germanos of Patras raised the standard at the monastery of Agia Lavra, near Kalavrita in the northern Peloponnese. (It seems that the famously fierce Maniots, in the south, were actually first in the field.) The mountainous central and western Peloponnese was the territory of a very different rebel leader, resilient amid all reverses and popular in local song, picture, and story, Theodore Kolokotronis. He and his followers the 'Kolokotronaioi' were so bold, declares a popular *tavlas* or table-song perhaps not calculated to appeal to the likes of Metropolitan Germanos, that they not only came to church on their horses but stayed on them while taking part in the service.[2]

This has long been a land of myths and myth-makers, from the bloody story of the Atreids, the descendants of Pelops, onwards. Atreus brought down the gods' curse on his family by serving his brother his own children for dinner; the better known effects of the curse include the murder by Klytaimnestra of Agamemnon, King of Mycenae and leader of the Greeks at Troy, followed by the revenge of their children Orestes and Elektra, Orestes' pursuit by the Furies for the crime of matricide, and the intervention of the gods and the court of Areopagus to protect and pardon him. Early dynastic rivalries probably shaped the myth, but its deeper psychological roots are attested to by the fascination it has held not only for Homer, Aeschylus, Euripides, and Seneca, but for more consciously psychological modern artists like Hugo von Hofmannsthal and Richard Strauss (*Elektra*), and Eugene O'Neill (*Mourning Becomes Electra*). For Heinrich Schliemann the story was substantially true; it gave him the faith to dig for Agamemnon at Mycenae and discover the remains of an actual civilization of the 'Heroic Age'.

All but the most scientific accounts of the ruins at Mycenae and Tiryns tend in some way to be coloured by grim associations with the curse of Atreus. So too Sparta, which dominated the Peloponnese in the classical period, is coloured by an image which, although founded on fact, is certainly one-sided: 'Spartan' austerity, unthinking obedience, ritual character-building floggings, and a diet of occasional black broth. Few classically aware readers can have been entirely surprised to hear from Captain William Humphreys, a disenchanted Philhellene volunteer, that the Moreots or Peloponnesians in 1824 were 'inhospitable, intractable, stubborn and cowardly . . . insensible to kindness . . . penurious and dirty . . . dishonest in their dealings, their natural acuteness and intelligence of disposition are exercised only to deceive.'[3]

But the Peloponnese is much more various than the tale of Atreus, the Spartan myth, or Humphreys' dreadful natives suggest. Ancient Corinth was as known for wine and pleasure as Sparta for gruel and virtue. ('Spartan' came to mean austere, while Corinth catered to the body by providing the word 'currant'.) The Byzantine lords of Mistra and Monemvasia and the Frankish castellans of Karitaina or Khlemoutsi held court, feasted, jousted and fought battles in distinctive medieval manner and built in styles far removed from Cyclopean walls or lion gates. Sizeable modern ports have grown up near or around the ancient Corinth and Patras. Arcadia has led a dual existence as pastoral myth and more rugged actuality: myth again struggles valiantly with the facts in William Lithgow's description of how

> amongst these rocks my belly was pinched, and wearied was my body, with the climbing of fastidious mountains, which bred no small grief to my breast. Yet notwith-standing of my distress, the remembrance of these sweet seasoned Songs of Arcadian Shepherds which pregnant Poets have so well penned, did recreate my fatigated corpse with many sugared suppositions.[4]

Both imaginatively and literally true, old and new, have continued to be combined as when Benjamin Disraeli, touring the Argolid just after the War of Independence, wrote home to his father: 'Napoli [Nauplion] is a busy place for Greece; Argos is rising from its ruins; Mycenae has a very ancient tomb or temple of the time of their old kings, massive as Egyptian.'[5]

CORINTH

Homer's 'wealthy Corinth' – wealthy because it controlled trade routes across the narrow isthmus between the Corin-thian and Saronic gulfs – had an early reputation for wild living, luxury and prostitution.[6] In 146 BC Roman legion-aries sacked the city of sin, and it remained in ruins for a century; but the new city founded by Julius Caesar soon became as prosperous and as notorious as its predecessor. Its remains, mixed with some earlier survivals, notably seven of the columns of the Temple of Apollo, are more evidently urban than most Greek sites. There are traces of shops, and a street-plan is easily discernible. But the atmosphere is far from civic, especially in March and April, when the site is covered in yellow chrysanthemums. For Odysseus Elytis (awarded the Nobel Prize for Literature in 1979) this is part of 'The living land that passion joys in opening,' a joyous place for 'drinking the sun of Corinth/Reading the marble ruins.'[7]

The memory of deep-drinking, light-hearted Corinthians lasted long enough for the tapsters at the Boar's Head tavern in Eastcheap to hail Prince Hal as 'a Corinthian, a lad of mettle, a good boy.'[8] But in the town itself the houses and churches of later, poorer times grew up among the columns and along the ancient processional way. (These accretions were removed with the combined aid of an earthquake in 1858 and American archaeologists after 1896.) When Sir George Wheler and Dr Jacques Spon came here in 1676 they found people more concerned with protecting themselves from attack by corsairs than with the pleasures of the body; those who could afford to had two houses, one in the town and one, for emergencies, high above in the citadel on the Acro-Corinth.[9]

But even Acro-Corinth, the 'hoary rock' of Byron's *The Siege of Corinth*, was not impregnable. Together with the lower town it was recaptured from the Venetians by the Turks after a fierce siege in 1715. This ended amid spectacular carnage when – quite possibly by accident in real life, but as a final gesture of defiance by the Venetian governor in Byron's romantic tale of a century later – the powder store was set alight and buildings, Turks and Christians all 'In one wild roar expired!'[10] What was left was, apparently, a pitiful sight by the time Hon. Frederick Douglas, a young traveller with a particular sympathy for the sufferings of modern Greeks as well as the loss of their ancient glories, came upon it in 1811.

Corinth, the seat of all that was splendid, beautiful, and happy, [has been] degraded to a wretched straggling village of two thousand Greeks, whose pale countenances and emaciated figures proved the deadly influence of the atmosphere which surrounded them.[11]

To escape this battered and disease-ridden site, New Corinth was founded in 1858 by the sea, several miles away. A new commercial centre rapidly grew up. But the proverbial ancient luxury was not so rapidly regained, at least not for travellers. According to Heinrich Schliemann there were no hotels: the only accommodation he could find was a wooden bench in a 'wretched cook-shop.' Persecuted by mosquitoes, he decided to leave, only to find that the proprietor had locked him in and disappeared. Putting to good effect the strength he usually reserved for prising ancient artefacts out of the ground, Schliemann eventually managed to pull out two of the iron bars covering the window-opening, jumped out into the street, and got some uninterrupted sleep on the beach.[12]

Soon the needs of moneyed travellers were better catered for, especially once the unprecedented engineering feat of the Corinth Canal was completed in 1893. Tourists came to marvel; in 1903 *Cook's Continental Time Tables, Tourist's Handbook, and Steamship Tables* was still devoting a third of its 'General Information' item on Greece to facts and figures about the canal. Statistic-hungry Edwardian travellers were informed that it was '20,000 ft. long, 26 ft. 3 in. deep, 68 ft. 11 in. broad,' 'crossed by one railway bridge, 141 ft. above sea level' and, 'being fitted with Electric Light' was 'navigable both by day and night.' Hotels were built, and acquired a more cosmopolitan patina than that provided by Schliemann's inn. Electricity began to be fitted in some buildings as well as along the canal, and in the advertising pages of *Cook's*, the Pelopides brothers were able to offer specialized care at the Palmyra Hotel: 'Near the mineral Spring Baths especially frequented by the great reputation for sufferings of Gravel, Rheumatism, Urinary Gravel, the Stomach, etc., etc.'[13]

Few visitors, whether suffering from those misfortunes or not, have been charmed by modern Corinth. After a major earthquake in 1928 it was rebuilt, this time in what Osbert Lancaster calls unequivocally 'as nasty an example of twentieth century urban architecture as can be found in Europe.'[14] But even architectural carbuncles can inspire modern poets. Stephen Spender, whose tastes had always been more catholic than Lancaster's, found himself brooding on the image of the modern town many years after he had visited it in the 1930s. This was the scene which, in memory's curious way, lingered longest:

There is comfort and reassurance in being able to remember things vividly – to count them over again and again in one's mind. For instance the glaring white streets of Corinth, the flyblown cafés opposite the sea, the shops full of oranges and other fruits. The very first time I went into Corinth, the streets were crowded and from a balcony of one of these low, almost Moroccan houses, there was a mad orator speaking in a voice that seemed to direct the crowd listening to him below.[15]

MYCENAE

In 468 BC the Mycenaeans pitched huge blocks of stone at the men of Argos as the latter charged at the ancient Lion Gate. Eventually the Argives captured the city of Agamemnon and forcibly expelled the inhabitants. But Mycenae lived on in two forms: firstly in the minds of those who read Homer and the Greek dramatists, and secondly where it had always stood, now silent in its stone cocoon. (The blocks hurled at the Argives continued to obstruct the gate until 1876.) The two were brought together when Heinrich Schliemann became passionately convinced, as he told Gladstone, that 'Homer does not describe myths, but historical events and tangible realities.'[16] Thanks to a highly successful career as a self-made businessman, he had the means to pursue his conviction.

Schliemann came to the windy hill of Mycenae determined to repeat his first success at Troy. 'For the first time during 2,344 years, the Acropolis of Mycenae has a garrison,' its watchfires blazing out across the plain of Argos at night 'like the signal which warned Clytemnestra and her paramour' of Agamemnon's return from Troy.[17] Schliemann's triumph followed as inevitably as Agamemnon's murder: with extra-ordinary speed he unearthed an unlooted royal or noble grave circle and its spectacular golden artefacts, revealing a culture then almost unknown and pre-dating Pericles' Athens by a millennium and more, and pronounced it all Homeric. On the surface, this was important to him as a point scored against the sceptics. Deeper down, it mattered as the near-miraculous fulfilment of the dreams of a lifetime. At times his on-site conduct resembled more that of 'The lunatic, the lover, and the poet' who are 'of imagination all compact' than that of the serious investigator. As Leo Deuel points out in his selection from Schliemann's writings:

After beholding the relatively well-preserved face in the first grave – the last that he emptied – he declared, in a telegram to the Greek minister of education, that it resembled the features of Agamemnon as they had previously *appeared* to him. In all seriousness, he considered his own imagination conclusive proof. In ecstasy he lifted the golden face mask of the buried prince and kissed it.[18]

Schliemann was at once a romantic dreamer – the owner of the mask must have lived centuries before Agamemnon, if indeed such a person ever existed – and someone who saw himself as a discoverer, an explainer. When his second wife, Sophia Engastromonou, bore a son, he was named Agamemnon and the proud father solemnly laid a copy of *The Iliad* on the baby's head.[19] But at the Orthodox christening, Agamemnon's sister Andromache remembered, Schliemann publicly displayed a more scientific attitude to the child's well-being when, outraged by the priest, he suddenly 'whisked out a thermometer and took the temperature of the holy water. There was a great commotion; the priest was outraged. It took my mother's gentle intervention to reinvest the water with holiness.'[20] This temperature-checking, measuring, digging, practical side of Schliemann would have appealed very little to Henry Miller, Mycenae's best-known American chronicler. Miller was fascinated by feelings, impressions and the sort of urges polite Victorians did not talk about in public. To him Mycenae is anything but explicable. The bloody story of the Atreids (cannibalism, human sacrifice, husband-killing, matricide) and the brooding presence of the rocky acropolis are out of harmony with the beautiful golden artefacts and the gleaming light on the surrounding hills and plain. 'There are two distinct worlds impinging on one another – the heroic world of daylight and the claustral world of dagger and poison.' On balance the mysterious and sometimes frightening darkness prevails, with the practical consequence that Miller cannot bear to descend the slippery staircase leading to the dark, heavy-roofed 'secret cistern'. The contrast with the open, straightforward classical theatre of Epidauros could not be greater.

Mycenae, like Epidaurus, swims in light. But Epidaurus is all open, exposed, irrevocably devoted to the spirit. Mycenae folds in upon itself, like a fresh-cut navel, dragging its glory down into the bowels of the earth where the bats and the lizards feed upon it gloatingly. Epidaurus is a bowl from which to drink the pure spirit: the blue of the sky is in it and the stars and the winged creatures who fly between, scattering song and melody. Mycenae, after one turns the last bend, suddenly folds up into a menacing crouch, grim, defiant, impenetrable. Mycenae is closed in, huddled up, writhing with muscular contortions like a wrestler. Even the light, which falls on it with merciless clarity, gets sucked in, shunted off, grayed, beribboned. There were never two worlds so closely juxtaposed and yet so antagonistic. It is Greenwich here with respect to everything that concerns the soul of man. Move a hair's breadth either way and you are in a totally different world. This is the great shining bulge of horror, the high slope whence man, having attained his zenith, slipped back and fell into the bottomless pit.[21]

A writer of very different background and opinions, C.S. Lewis, visited Mycenae in 1960. His friend Roger Lancelyn Green remembered his cry of awe and surprise on seeing the Lion Gate: 'My God! The curse is still here.'[22] No doubt fifty years of familiarity with the tale of the Atreids, and the imagination which had recently shaped the *Chronicles of Narnia*, go some way to explain this response. But Mycenae on its bleak hill, guarded by lithe but headless stone lions, its grave circle within the larger circuit of the mighty walls, certainly ought to symbolize something.

TIRYNS

Tiryns lacks Mycenae's spectacular setting. The citadel rises only eighteen metres from the plain of Argos. Adjoining citrus groves, and a view where green is a dominant colour even in summer, are unlikely to inspire the terror Henry

Miller experienced at the roughly contemporary fortress of Agamemnon. But here too the 'Cyclopean' walls remain impressively solid, a satisfyingly weighty, rocky contrast with the more delicate grace of the Parthenon and other classical remains. In essence we can see what the second century traveller Pausanias described: 'The wall, which is the only part of the ruins still remaining, is a work of the Cyclopes made of unwrought stones, each stone being so big that a pair of mules could not move the smallest from its place to the slightest degree.'[23]

Schliemann, not content with such vagueness, at once measured the stones, finding most 7 feet long and 3 feet thick (some even larger) and calculating that the walls themselves had originally been about 60 feet high.[24] Eight years after his initial probings, and with the triumphs of Mycenae and the second Trojan 'campaign' behind him, Schliemann returned to complete the job in March 1884. He employed between sixty and seventy workers to attack the site, armed with 'necessary apparatus', 'viz 40 English wheelbarrows with iron wheels; 20 large iron crowbars; one large and two small windlasses; 50 large iron shovels; 50 pickaxes; 25 large hoes, known all through the East by the name of *tschapa*, and used in vineyards; these were the greatest use in filling the baskets with *débris*.'[25]

Pickaxes typify the methods of most archaeologists in this period, with Schliemann especially keen on their application to anything which overlay the Homeric 'truth' and the possible Homeric treasures. Soon the horseshoe-shaped fortress and its corbelled galleries were beginning to take on their present appearance, and Schliemann was able to report to the Greek minister of education, in a letter not remarkable for its modesty, that he had brought to light 'the great palace of the legendary kings of Tiryns so that now and for evermore (until the Last Judgment) no book on ancient art can ever be published that does not include my plan of the Palace of Tiryns.'[26] Needless to say, the plan has continued to be modified by a century of more careful work on the site.

But Tiryns did not belong, for Schliemann any more than to more casual observers, only to the world of books on ancient art. He too lingered over the view across the green

plain to the mountains and, in the distant haze, the bay.
Having travelled widely as a phenomenally successful businessman, he had a huge range of comparisons on which to draw,
even if in the end it is the 'mighty deeds' of the mythic Argives
which give the following view the palm:

> The panorama which stretches on all sides from the top
> of the citadel of Tiryns is peculiarly splendid. As I gaze
> northward, southward, eastward, or westward, I ask
> myself involuntarily whether I have elsewhere seen aught
> so beautiful, and mentally recall the ascending peaks of
> the Himalayas, the luxuriance of the tropical world on
> the Islands of Sunda, and the Antilles; or, again, I turn
> to the view from the great Chinese wall, to the glorious
> valleys of Japan, to the far-famed Yo-Semite Valley in
> California, or the high peaks of the great Cordilleras, and
> I confess that the prospect from the citadel of Tiryns far
> exceeds all of natural beauty which I have elsewhere
> seen. Indeed the magic of the scene becomes quite over-
> powering, when in spirit one recalls the mighty deeds
> of which the theatre was this plain of Argos with its
> encircling hills.[27]

NAUPLION

On 11 July 1827 Admiral Sir Edward Codrington, British
commander-in-chief in the Mediterranean, walked doggedly
to the headquarters of the newly established Provisional
Government of Greece in Nauplion. The morning sun was
'roasting', especially if you were wearing nineteenth-century
naval uniform. The admiral was shown up some rickety
wooden stairs to a room with no ceiling, where swallows
darted among the rafters. He proceeded to read the government a lecture, the first of many, on the folly of Greek
fighting Greek while the Turkish menace continued. They
listened politely, but even as Codrington spoke the feuding
went on. The previous evening fire had been exchanged
between snipers in the fortress on the steep rock of Palamidi
and those in the town beneath. The crackle of musketry could
still be heard at noon, when Codrington was writing home

to his wife from the safety of his flagship, the *Asia*, about 'the filthiest town, with the worst streets and most wretched houses, I ever saw.'[28]

Codrington found the whole situation exasperating, not least because he was the representative of a neutral power and could not impose his views by force. On the basis of his experiences at Nauplion he wrote to his son, with an appropriately nautical turn of phrase, that 'a good man does not know how to steer by' the Greeks. It is as if 'their mountains being barren of vegetation were the cause of their minds being barren of virtue.'[29] But Codrington was not permanently disenchanted: in October 1829 it was he who, by his interpretation of uncertain orders, intervened decisively to defeat the Turks in the Battle of Navarino, thus doing more than almost anyone else to ensure Greek independence.

By this time the first President of the fledgling Greek state, Count John Kapodistria, had arrived in Nauplion. His successful career abroad, culminating in a period as adviser to Tsar Alexander I, had done little to prepare him for the sheer complexity of the problems which awaited him in Greece. He arrived in the midst of financial crisis, a rebellion on Hydra, and faction fighting which only increased in ferocity after the victory of Navarino. To make matters worse, Kapodistria was convinced that he knew, and must at all costs carry out, the will of God for Greece. He found it well-nigh impossible to compromise. He was popular with peasants, but managed to offend those with real power. Attempts at centralization went down badly with the warlords and regional chiefs; vested interest thwarted his plan to redistribute to the peasantry all land confiscated from the Turks.[30] He succeeded, with Russian aid, in defeating a rebellion in the Mani, but reckoned without the Maniots' pride and their predilection for vendetta when, in 1831, he dared to imprison one of the most powerful members of the Mavromikhalis family, Petrobey (Petros, recognized as Bey of the Mani by the Turks in 1815 but already virtually independent from them; an early hero of the War of Independence). Kapodistria's worst mistake, however, was to place Petrobey's brother Constantine and son George under surveillance only. The historian George Finlay narrates the consequences:

At early dawn on the 9th October 1831, Capodistrias walked as usual to hear mass in the church of St Spyridion [patron saint of his native Corfu]. As he approached the low door of the small church, he saw Constantine Mavromichales standing on one side and George on the other. He hesitated for a moment, as if he suspected that they wished to address him, and would willingly have avoided the meeting. But after a momentary pause, he moved on to enter the church. Before he reached the door he fell on the pavement mortally wounded by a pistol-ball in the back of the head. In the act of falling he received the stab of a yataghan through the lungs, and he expired without uttering a word.[31]

Constantine was seized and killed forthwith; the unrepentant George was tried and executed on 22 October. The President's death solved nothing. A period of near anarchy was followed by the short-lived euphoria of the opening years of the reign of King Otho, the Bavarian prince who entered Nauplion in triumph, aged seventeen, to take up his post on 30 January 1833. Faction soon flared again.

But in 1834 the capital moved to Athens, and Nauplion was left in comparative peace. In happier circumstances, visitors no longer found it a filthy or a wretched place. Osbert Lancaster was here just after the Second World War, and recorded his impressions of a town 'decidedly western European' thanks to its earlier Venetian heritage, with even the 'austere functionalism' of the citadels of Palamidi and the Acronauplion 'heraldically relieved by escutcheons and winged lions over the various gateways.' This no longer seemed a likely setting for political assassination as Lancaster settled down to observe and sketch the houses whose wrought-iron balconies,

together with the extraordinary richness and beauty of the innumerable tiny gardens, often no more than three whitewashed petrol-cans alongside a doorstep, attached to the cottages clustered around the foot of Itsh-Kaleh . . . lend a charming air of light opera to the whole town.[32]

EPIDAUROS

Going to the theatre was among the cures which the priests of Asklepios prescribed for the sick at Epidauros. Some members of modern audiences find the remedy painful: after a long session on the ancient stone seats, as the Australian novelist Patrick White remarked, you leave 'understanding at last about the purge of ancient Greek tragedy.'[33]

Sir Peter Hall, who came to Epidauros in 1975 to make a television film, was more positive. He came with Sir Denys Lasdun, whose design for the National Theatre's main auditorium, the Olivier, was partly inspired by Epidauros. Hall recognized, above all, the close relationship between the theatre and the wooded hills behind.

It's exactly as if someone had said to me, 'The Globe has after all been preserved on the South Bank, come over and have a look at it, then you might understand something about staging Shakespeare. For here is a Greek theatre, and a masterpiece of architecture as well. Yesterday the Roman theatre by the Acropolis [the Odeion of Herodes Atticus] had left me cold: a brutal confrontation, the audience looking at the performers as their victims. But here, in a Greek theatre, everything grows out of the landscape. The first impression is one of intimacy, yet it holds 15,000 people. The second is one of perfect, simple geometry, yet every geometric calculation is slightly altered in the interest of grace and of humanity. Most extraordinary of all is the way the auditorium grows out of the hillside and, as you sit in it, seems to continue into the landscape, making a whole world of which the spectator feels a part. Why did they site it here? Because for the Greeks the landscape was alive, and full of gods who had a positive relationship with man. It is interesting to make a comparison with the Romans. They were engineers; like us they could move mountains. A Roman road cuts straight through the landscape, indifferent to its form. A Greek road is sensitive to the landscape, sensitive to its gods. So are their theatres.[34]

SPARTA

At the height of Sparta's power, the Athenian historian Thucydides prophesied that, if one day the town was abandoned, future generations would refuse to believe that it had ever been a city of any reckoning in the world.[35] Defended not by mere walls but by the spectacular bulk of Mounts Taygetos and Parnon, Sparta was more a group of villages than a city. It never had huge gorgeously adorned temples, and much of what little stone there had been was later removed to help with the building of nearby medieval Mistra. What remains now is mostly Hellenistic or Roman.

The stones of Sparta were outlasted by its reputation for tough single-mindedness, adherence to unchanging laws handed down through the generations from the semi-legendary Lycurgus, firm oligarchic government, and military discipline and success. In the eighteenth and nineteenth centuries Sparta had almost as many admirers as its great rival, the more mercurial and artistic Athens. Exactly how the Spartans made themselves so strong was a familiar conundrum. Did their famous black broth offer an explanation? Henry Blount, travelling in 1634, thought that only the newly fashionable coffee could have provided the necessary stimulus: this 'is thought to be the old blacke broth used so much by the *Lacedemonians*, and dryeth ill humors in the stomacke, comforteth the brain, never causeth drunkennesse, or any other surfeit, and is a harmelesse entertainment of good fellowship.'[36] In reality, the ancient broth seems to have consisted of pieces of pork in pig's blood.

Travellers had great expectations of the capital of the Spartans. Whether they had read their Thucydides or not, they found the sparseness of the ruins disorientating. François-René de Chateaubriand finally came upon the site in the early hours of 18 August 1806 after delays and false starts and a temptation to acquiesce in the common belief that Sparta had been incorporated in Mistra. As the sun rose he looked down from the top of the acropolis.

What a magnificent spectacle! But how melancholy! The solitary stream of the Eurotas running beneath the remains of the bridge Babyx; ruins on every side, and not a creature to be seen among them. I stood motionless, in a kind of stupor, at the contemplation of this scene. A mixture of admiration and grief, checked the current of my thoughts and fixed me to the spot: profound silence reigned around me. Determined, at least, to make echo speak in a spot where the human voice is no longer heard, I shouted with all my might: 'Leonidas! Leonidas!' No ruin repeated this great name, and Sparta herself seemed to have forgotten her hero.[37]

As the day went on Chateaubriand tried to identify the ruins. He watched silent lizards on scorching walls, the 'dozen half wild horses feeding here and there upon the withered grass,' a shepherd 'cultivating a few water-melons in a corner of the theatre.' He read fragments of inscriptions. (Many had been smashed in 1729 by a less reverent French visitor, the Abbé Fourmont, in order to conceal how far his 'copies' were inventions.) He strolled among 'reeds and rose-laurels' by the winding Eurotas, and departed reluctantly at dusk, 'with a mind absorbed by the objects which I had just seen, and indulging in endless reflexions. Such days enable a man to endure many misfortunes with patience, and above all, render him indifferent to many spectacles.'[38]

Not everyone enjoyed Chateaubriand's Spartan mood piece. The Breton's very presence in Greece in 1806 was, said the passionately patriotic Maurice Barrès nearly a century later, a dereliction of duty: at a time when Napoleon's France was gearing itself for the 'sublime' campaign which would culminate in the great victory of Jena, 'Leonidas!' was 'a naïve outburst of Celtic enthusiasm' from a man seeking to mask his own inaction by dwelling on departed glories.[39] (Chateaubriand, who had mixed feelings about Napoleon, had resigned from government service in 1804.) Throughout the First World War Barrès, as a daily columnist in *L'Echo de Paris*, demanded renewed acts of Spartan or Napoleonic heroism from the French people. Apparently, however, national affairs were secure enough in 1900 for him to visit Greece with a clear conscience. He admired the ancient Spartans' unswerving dedication to their state, their attempt to produce a 'master-race'. (Some Nazis also took an interest in Sparta.) But he could not forget France for more than a few moments. On arrival in the new town of Sparta – founded next to the ancient remains in 1834 and, as Baedeker notes, 'laid out on a remarkably regular plan, with broad, quiet streets, lined with low houses surrounded by gardens' – Barrès met the town magistrate and the pharmacist.[40] He says – it is difficult to determine how much of this really occurred – that they were keen to talk with him because they were due to visit the Paris Exhibition. On their way to show him the vestiges of the ancient town, they expressed their joy as Greeks that they would soon be able to see the *Venus de Milo* in the Louvre. Barrès reflected that the French also had *their* national Venuses, not lacking in arms, and to be found at the Folies Bergères. Perhaps wisely, he seems to have kept this witticism to himself. Half proudly, half apologetically, his guides announced 'There it is, the famous Sparta.' The Greeks went on chattering about the coming joys of the restaurants of Paris while Barrès, with mixed feelings, contemplated the Eurotas and 'the meadow where once the maidens of Sparta, rubbed with oil, wrestled naked with the boys,' and now 'a wretched little girl was bothering a restive pig.'[41]

On the luxuriant plain, where flowers and vegetables, barley and maize grew amongst olive groves, sycamores, plane trees and mulberry bushes, Barrès could not find the Sparta he was looking for. Its spirit survived rather, he concluded, in the awe-inspiring, dominating presence of Taygetos. At one point he solemnly assures the reader that the mountain moved him no less than when, in younger days, he recognized a little man talking to the poet Leconte de Lisle as none other than Victor Hugo. Otherwise, even Paris is forgotten for a time as Barrès hymns the mountain:

What strength and what grandeur there is in the movements of Taygetos, leaning expansive on the plain with its invitation to softer delights, thrusting its five snowy peaks into the sky. No amount of boldness on the part of a writer could do justice to this shining forceful mass, these solid colours, indivisible, une- quivocal, these violent variations, which ascend with ease tier upon tier from the zone of the oranges to that of the sparkling ice.[42]

MISTRA

Mistra, unlike most earlier Greek sites, does not have one or two clear defining elements – a marble temple crowning the hill, a broad theatre cut into it. Here is a whole hill of ruins and partial ruins, a lower, middle, and upper town of domed monasteries and churches with their frescoes in varying states of preservation, courtyards, houses, the shell of a palace where grass now grows, a fortress, mosques. Mistra started as a Frankish castle in 1249 (traditionally when Guillaume de Villehardouin, Prince of Achaia, noticed the strategic advantages of 'a wonderful hill' near Sparta[43]), but in Byzantine hands from 1261 expanded to become a walled city and an important provincial centre. Its cultural high-point was in the late fourteenth and early fifteenth centuries. It was at this time that the neo-Platonist and virtually neo-pagan philosopher George Gemistos Plethon was writing, teaching, and debating here, at a safe distance from Constantinopolitan disapproval. This was also the period when many of the surviving frescoes were produced, and when Despots of the imperial family governed from Mistra, a period colourfully imagined by Patrick Leigh Fermor in *Mani*:

> [A] succession of purple-born princes reigned: strange and stately figures in their fur-trimmed robes and melon-crowned caps-of-maintenance. The libraries filled with books, poets measured out their stanzas, and on the scaffolding of one newly-risen church after another painters mixed their gypsum and cinnabar and egg-yolk and powdered crocus and zinc and plotted the fall of drapery and described the circumference of haloes.[44]

On 6 January 1449 the church of the Metropolis (or possibly the smaller Palace Church of St Sophia) was crowded out for the first and last coronation of a Byzantine emperor in Mistra. In order to end uncertainty over which of the family of

John VIII was to succeed him, the Empress Mother had
taken the bold step of despatching the imperial crown direct
to her son, Despot Constantine. As Constantine XI he was
killed fighting heroically when the Turks took Constantinople, after centuries of gradually eating up its territories, in
1453. The probable site of the coronation, marked by a
Byzantine two-headed eagle in the Metropolis, has a sacred
status for Greeks. And as the last flowering of Byzantium
(Mistra itself did not fall to the Turks until 1460) it is at once
inspiriting and deeply sad for a people which sees itself as the
heir of that civilization. The painter Photis Kontoglou had
particular reason to be aware of the melancholy of the place,
as one of the thousands of Greeks forced out of their homes
in Turkey in the 1920s. Amid the 'water-eaten walls' of
Mistra, she reflected on the sufferings of emperors and
ordinary people alike. The grassy shell of the palace of the
Despots impressed on Kontoglou a sense of gradual, inevitable
decay. The Despot perished, then his clothes, then the
wooden parts of his palace, the roofs, the floors. At last the
walls too began to crumble, until finally

> there remained standing a single column of wall, beaten
> by wind and becoming more slender, more decayed, until
> it reached the point at which even nature was ashamed
> to order one of her valiant envoys, the air, the earth-
> quake, the thunder-bolt, to finish off such an adversary.
> Then a crow flew over and settled lightly on the top
> of this column, and there as it began to preen its wings
> for lice, suddenly the stones fell apart and rumbled
> down with a hollow noise, as if dissolved back into the
> earth.[45]

Maurice Barrès was in a happier frame of mind when, fresh
from his visit to Sparta, he climbed the hill, entranced by the
sparkling light. As the orange trees became less frequent he
went on past the palace and up the steep way to the fortress.

> Eventually I reached the summit of the citadel. Barley
> is grown amid the debris and the cisterns. What space,
> what light! On my left rose a deserted peak where only

clumps of pines grew; behind us extended the steep slopes of Taygetos, strewn with sparkling villages and crowned with glaciers.

Ahead and to the right was the consolation of many who have made the steep ascent to the citadel, the vast, light-filled plain.

> Sheer, beneath my feet, the silvered ruins flashed on the lead-coloured hill. From my champenois battlements [the Villehardouin family originated from Champagne], over Byzantine churches, I saw the voluptuous garden which conceals the ruins of Sparta. The Eurotas flows towards the sea, amid the hills which mark out its valley, beneath a cloud of dust blazing red, ochre and green in the sun. From Taygetos to the Menelaion, from the isle of Cythera to the mountains of Arcadia, I behold, I breathe, the valley of Lacedaemon.[46]

MONEMVASIA

The steep rock of Monemvasia, separated from the Malea peninsula by a causeway – the eponymous *moni emvasis*, 'single entrance' – was for much of its history a proud, independent place. The early inhabitants, often refugees from the invading hordes of Huns and Avars further north, made their stand here. They crammed the inhospitable-looking slopes with houses and at least fifty churches, producing the lower town whose appearance today is described by Jan Morris:

> Crisscross and confusing run its alleys through the wreckage, like the runs of weasels or city-foxes, and its houses are jumbled cheek-by-jowl on the escarpment above the sea, sometimes almost on top of each other, so that the lanes have to burrow and probe beneath them, here and there opening out into a little plaza with a church, or a neglected esplanade along the sea-wall.[47]

Piracy helped to achieve virtual independence for Monemvasia under Byzantine rule, and inaccessibility long kept it

Greek. But it at last seemed to have met its match when, in 1246, Guillaume de Villehardouin succeeded his father and brother as Prince of Achaia, lord of much of the Peloponnese and perhaps the most powerful man in Greece. His chivalrous martial exploits were retold in the fourteenth century in the Greek verse *Chronicle of Morea* (also extant in French, Aragonese, and Italian). One of Guillaume's first actions on becoming Prince, the *Chronicle* recounts, was to muster a great army for the siege of Monemvasia. The army hemmed-in the town by land, while four Venetian galleys blockaded it by sea. The Prince was thoroughly determined; seeing the arrogance of the Monemvasiots he 'swore by God's blessed name that he would not leave until he had taken the fortress.' But the Monemvasiots held out for three years, until, having 'nothing to eat, they ate the rats and cats. Nothing more remained but to eat each other.' When at last, in 1248, their leaders did agree to surrender, it was on their own conditions: they must not be robbed or dispossessed but treated as 'free Franks, owing no service but the use of their boats, and that with fixed stipend.' (In other words their feudal service would be due only by sea, and they would be paid for it.) Once the treaty had been sealed, the three archons, members of the noblest families, brought the keys of the castle across the causeway to Prince Guillaume and did homage to him. He rewarded them with fiefs and magnificent chivalric gestures: 'gracious and benevolent man that he was, he treated them generously and honourably, making them gifts of chargers and palfreys, and of robes of scarlet and gold.'[48]

The romantic pageantry did not, however, usher in a new golden age of French Monemvasia. Defeated at the Battle of Pelagonia in 1259, Guillaume was forced in 1261, as the price of his freedom, to surrender Monemvasia, together with his newly built fortresses of Mistra and Le Grand Magne (Mani) to Michael Palaiologos, whose other great success of that year was to regain the Byzantine imperial throne from the Latins. The thirteen years of Frankish overlordship left little or no mark on the surviving buildings of Monemvasia. Under Byzantine and then Venetian protection the rock went on to survive the Turkish onslaught until at last it surrendered to the superior forces of Suleiman the Magnificent in 1540.

In Monemvasia the elements are never far away. This, of course, is especially true for visitors who make the effort to climb up to the citadel. In the autumn of 1948 the ascent was obligatory for Kevin Andrews, working on a study of the Frankish castles of the Peloponnese while attached to the American Academy in Athens, and an amateur mountaineer to boot.

> From the summit I looked down on to a ledge once sealed against possible assault by a wall with a ruined bastion at one end; through its fallen floor the water tearing like white fangs along the shoreline. Clouds were blowing up from Cape Malea over the grey water of the Cretan sea. Birds called and cackled in the cliffs, and wild pigeons dived down the open face of the red rock like darts hurled into the abyss. It began to rain. Over the long summit of the rock thin grasses blew and stalks of asphodel rattled on withered roots and flew up into the air. Four ruined towers rose pale in the swirling mist, and an old woman with bare, bloodstained feet leaped from one rock to another, flinging stones to right and left of a small herd of goats and screaming shrilly above the wind.[49]

KYTHERA

The tradition that Aphrodite was born on Kythera – either wafted ashore or emerging from a shell here – filled classical and Renaissance love poetry with the adjective 'Cytherean'. Later, the image of a shaded, fertile paradise for lovers was enhanced by Watteau's painting *L'Embarquement pour Cythère* and Debussy's piano piece, *L'Île joyeuse*. In the twentieth century, unable to live on a diet of love alone, many of the inhabitants of the real, more arid island emigrated to Australia. Visitors had always been rare. One of them was the successful merchant Lewes Roberts, whose account was published in 1638. At the Venetian castle he was told a tale about two prominent followers of Aphrodite, but remained unimpressed.

Out of the Castle of the chief town of this Isle, was
Helena the wife of Menelaus stolen by Paris, where
during my abode here, the Castelan did show me, and
lodged me in the chamber whence, as he would have me
believe, she was ravished; but, if it were so, her lodging
I am confident was better than mine, for a soft board
was my best bed, & God knows with what sorry cover-
ings and appurtenances.[50]

In 1814 Kythera, like the distant Ionian islands with which
it formed the 'Septinsular Republic' or 'Heptanese', passed
from French to British rule. The poet Gérard de Nerval was
in no doubt about the deleterious consequences of this:
Kythera is lost as Aphrodite's isle, there are no shells like the
one the Nereids chose for Aphrodite, there are no shepherds
and shepherdesses like those in Watteau's painting landing on
flowery shores in their garlanded galleys. Instead, there is a
'gentleman' (the English word stands out with contemptuous
emphasis from the French text) shooting woodcocks and
pigeons, and some dreamy Scottish soldiers missing the fogs
of home. Worse, what from the sea appears to be a statue,
standing yet, of the patron goddess of the island, proves on
closer view to be a three-armed gibbet with one victim in
position.[51]
Nerval had not, in fact, been close enough to Kythera to
see any gibbets, although he had sailed some miles to the south
of it on his way to his only Aegean landfall at Syros. His vision
resulted from a blend of Anglophobia, an imagination increasingly verging on the hallucinatory, and some wide reading.
Nevertheless, his account was influential at home. Most
famously, it was the 'point de départ' for Charles Baudelaire's
bitter contrast, in 'Un Voyage à Cythère', between the over-
invoked fantasy island, the 'Eldorado banal' of those 'old
boys' the respectable poets, and the rotting corpse on the
gallows.[52] Myths seem to fasten on Kythera with a peculiar
tenacity.

MANI

For centuries the Maniots had the reputation of being as fierce and inhospitable as their craggy, arid peninsula. They were, declared Sir George Wheler, both 'famous Pirates by Sea, and Pestilent Robbers by Land.'[53] Murder in Mani in the early nineteenth century, reported George Finlay, 'answered the same purpose as duelling in other countries where the state of society was less barbarous, and assassination was a privilege of the Maniat gentility.'[54] From their mountains – the Taygetos range divides Mani – they defied attempts by the Byzantines and Turks to dominate or tame them. They provided some of the most vigorous fighters in the War of Independence, then went on to become a thorn in the side of the independent Greece for which they had fought. Attempts by government troops to bring them to heel in the 1830s failed embarrassingly.

Most of the Maniots' energy, however, seems to have gone into fighting each other. (The few outsiders who penetrated far into the peninsula usually report a warm welcome, but the myth remained.) The better to conduct their vendettas, the Nyklians – the landowning class whose curious name conceivably derives from the Maniot connections of the Frankish lords of Thebes, Nicholas II and III de St Omer – erected tall towers from which to shoot at one another.[55] There were and are so many towers that villages like Kitta and Vatheia are reminiscent either of San Gimignano or, as Patrick Leigh Fermor puts it, 'bundles of petrified asparagus.'[56]

It was presumably from a tower that Father George of Lagia, in south-eastern Mani, had a rock dropped on his head in the mid-eighteenth century. He survived thanks to the ministrations of Dr Papadakis, also of Lagia, whose manuscript casebook records a wealth of similar misadventures, many of them to priests who were, as Peter Greenhalgh and Edward Eliopoulos say in their guide to the area, 'evidently in the thick of the fighting among their wolf-like flocks.' Father George also suffered a stiletto through the foot; a musket wound to the shoulder brought low Father Dikeolias of Boularii; and Father Zervyolatis of Tserova sustained multiple injuries: 'bullets (2) in thigh, straight through; severe sword wounds.' Apparently 'only the good doctor himself was sacrosanct, for he was always neutral and far too useful to all sides to be offended.'[57]

Feuds became much rarer by the end of the nineteenth century, but memories were long. In the 1950s Leigh Fermor encountered 'indestructible elders' who discoursed on the fights they had seen and, further back, 'those old battles between rough-hewn grandees in their grandparents' and great-grandparents' days.' Reminders were not far to seek: all around the old men as they reminisced, 'battered with cannon-balls and pocked with bullets, assaulted by time and decay, disapproved of, legislated against and condemned by regime after regime and as bold as brass – stand the wicked and indelible towers.'[58]

Some of the 'wicked' edifices do, however, have a kindlier side, as Leigh Fermor discovered in Vatheia. A tower-owning family entertained him on their parapeted roof, high above the accumulated heat of the summer's day. Table, chairs, and basket-loads of food and wine were hauled up sixty feet by rope. Maniot hospitality was reasserted and Leigh Fermor provided with one of those romantic and slightly surreal scenes he delights in describing. (A more surreal escape from the heat elsewhere in *Mani* was arrived at by dint of dining at a restaurant table, fully dressed and waist-deep in water, off the quay at Kalamata.)

> The night was still. As our tower-top was the highest in Vatheia, the others were invisible and we might have been dining in mid-air on a magic carpet floating across dim folds in the mountains. [When we were] standing up, the other tower-tops came into sight, all of them empty and clear under the enormous moon. Not a light showed, and the only sounds were the shrill drilling note of two crickets, a nightingale and a faint chorus of frogs, hinting of water somewhere in the dry sierra.[59]

OLYMPIA

Every four summers in antiquity, as every summer now, Olympia was a crowded place. Warring tribes and cities lay down their arms and, their passage made easier by the then navigable River Alpheios, the Olympic athletes and spectators and pilgrims converged on the stadium and the sacred grove of Zeus from places as far distant as Spain. Kings of Macedon competed in the chariot races, the Emperor Nero invented singing and poetry contests so that he could win them, the rich painter Zeuxis strutted about with his name embroidered in letters of gold on his robes.[60] 'There is no modern parallel for Olympia,' writes Judith Swaddling in her book about the ancient games; 'it would have to be a site combining a sports complex and a centre for religious devotion, something like a combination of Wembley Stadium and Westminster Abbey.'[61]

The setting of Olympia is unusual among Greek sites: a wooded, grassy plain between low hills and the river – 'romantic and park-like rather than classical,' says Osbert Lancaster.[62] Visitors received a less tranquil impression, however, when full-scale excavation was under way from 1875 onwards. One of the first visitors to watch the German archaeologists and Greek peasants digging was the young Oscar Wilde. He left no record of his impressions, but did later maintain to Charles Ricketts that 'I was sent down from Oxford for being the first undergraduate to visit Olympia.'[63] He had announced the jaunt in question to the Dean of Magdalen in a letter of 2 April 1877, explaining that his former tutor, J.P. Mahaffy, had persuaded him to come to Greece.

> The chance of seeing such great places – and in such good company – was too great for me and I find myself now in Corfu. I am afraid I will not be able to be back at the beginning of term. I hope you will not mind if I miss ten days at the beginning: seeing Greece is really a great education for anyone and will I think benefit me greatly, and Mr Mahaffy is such a clever man that it is quite as good as going to lectures to be in his society.[64]

The Dean, though he can rarely have received such a superbly plausible note of absence, was evidently not amused. On his return Wilde was rusticated – sent down for what remained of the term – and fined £47.10s. (The money was, however, returned the following summer in consideration of Wilde's good performance in Finals.)

John Pentland Mahaffy, Professor of Ancient History at Trinity College, Dublin, and soon to be knighted, was a respectable choice of guide. The purpose of his visit was to write up Olympia for the second, extended edition of his *Rambles and Studies in Greece*, published the previous year. But his impressions of Olympia were not primarily those of a classicist: his aesthetic responses were much those Wilde – who had written joyously to his mother about the silvery olive trees of Corfu – might be expected to share. Mahaffy relished the spring approach to the site, contrasting it with the baked July vistas which those coming to the games must have had, but found the digging distasteful.

> We found the meadows green with sprouting corn and bright with flowers, and all along the slopes the trees were bursting into bud and blossom, and filling the air with the rich scent of spring. Huge shrubs of arbutus and of mastich closed around the paths, while over them the Judas tree and the wild pear covered themselves with purple and with white, and on every bank great scarlet anemones opened their wistful eyes in the morning sun.
>
> When we came to the real Olympia the prospect was truly disenchanting. However interesting excavations may be, they are always exceedingly ugly. Instead of grass and flowers, and pure water, we found the classic spot defaced with great mounds of earth, and trodden bare of grass. . . . We found hundreds of workmen, and wheelbarrows, and planks, and trenches, instead of solitude and the song of birds.[65]

Fifty years later Evelyn Waugh was not particularly impressed by 'the ruins which extend for acres and acres of waste land at the bottom of the hill.' But he did have more to say for the museum. It was the Christmas holidays, 1926–7, and Waugh was trying to forget that he was an unhappy teacher at a school for 'backward boys' at Aston Clinton in Buckinghamshire. Mercifully he was sacked in

February 1927 and began to fictionalize his woes in *Decline
and Fall* later that year, but in January at Olympia he
still needed the consolations of ancient art. He found
'quite marvellous' the Parian marble Hermes, attributed to
Praxiteles, which was at the time 'kept in a separate shed in
charge of the village idiot, embedded in concrete before a grey
plush curtain.'[66]

Hermes had moved to the main museum, which had been
rebuilt, by the time the American 'Beat' poet Allen Ginsberg
noted in his journal his more personal and explicit response
to the naked god:

> The smile on Hermes' face is very soft & familiar. The
> part I would like to lay my head, if it were soft, [is]
> against his mid breast. All the human muscle curves &
> ripples over the belly & side to the armpits – the pubic
> hair shaved except for right above the ball & the cock
> is missing, which must have been a fine piece of polished
> creamy marble, long tipped . . . His bellybutton not
> very deep but just a touch & small valley. The lyre shape
> curve of the lower belly from the waist.[67]

Sexual activity features directly in some of the other
sculpture in the museum. Nikos Kazantzakis was particularly
struck by the west pediment of the Temple of Zeus, where
the drunken centaurs attempt to carry off the women and
youths of the Lapiths on either side of a ten-foot tall Apollo.
He saw the struggling figures as both timeless and the product
of a particular historical moment, the period just after the
Persian Wars. The great artist sees beyond the 'spasmodic,
often incoherent actions of mortal men' to 'the great currents
that sweep souls along.' History is transposed upwards into
mythology, Greeks and Persians into lapiths and centaurs,
spiritual and bestial. Not just the body but 'the forces that
shape the body' are depicted.

> These creative forces seethe visibly beneath the translu-
> cent skin. The symposium has come to an end, the cen-
> taurs have got drunk and rushed to grab the Lapithaean
> women. A centaur flings out his leg and embraces a

woman, and at the same time squeezes her breast with his gross hand. The woman appears to have fainted from the pain, and from some mysterious, ineffable pleasure. Elsewhere the strugglers bite and stab at one another, the beast is let loose, wild orgasm explodes, primeval scenes of human against ape men are revived before us. A strange calm, however, pervades all this incredible, primordial passion: because, serene in the midst of the frenzied mortals, unseen by the combatants, extending simply his right arm, stands Apollo.[68]

BASSAI

Mahaffy, Wilde, and, later, Kazantzakis, made their way from Olympia southwards until they came to what an earlier traveller, William Mure, describes as 'a wilderness of rugged rocks, studded with knotty old oaks, thickening here and there into masses of forest.' There, in Mure's 'recess or hollow of the summit of a long table-topped mountain,' they came upon the Temple of Apollo at Bassai.[69]

It was more to the taste of the Irish travellers than Olympia. Excavations had ceased long before; they had been at their most vigorous in 1811, when Charles Cockerell, following the movements of a fox in the ruins, lighted upon the lapiths and centaurs of the temple frieze. This was subsequently acquired by the British Museum. It was some consolation for the loss of the Aigina marbles to Munich. (By the time Olympia was excavated, it was illegal to export such notable finds from Greece.) The temple had, as Mahaffy saw it, all the aesthetic appeal which muddy Olympia lacked.

It is built of the limestone which crops up all over the mountain plateau on which it stands; and, as the sun shone upon it after recent rain, was of a delicate bluish-gray colour, so like the surface of the ground in tone, that it almost seemed to have grown out of the rock, as its natural product. The pillars are indeed by no means monoliths, but set together of short drums, of which the inner row are but the rounded ends of long blocks which reach back to the cella wall. But as the grain of the stone runs across the pillars, they have become curiously wrinkled with age, so that the artificial joinings are lost among the wavy transverse lines, which make us imagine the pillars sunk with years of fatigue, and weary of standing in this wild and gloomy solitude. . . . Their ground being a pale grayish-blue, the lichens which invade the stone have varied the fluted surface with silver, with bright orange, and still more with a delicate rose madder. Even under a mid-day sun, these rich colours were very wonderful, but what must be the effect at sunset?[70]

Nikos Kazantzakis came to Bassai ready to ponder rather more deeply than this, although this time without the aid of the on-site sculpture which had directed his thoughts at Olympia. He was sunk in thought when the caretaker, an old woman, emerged from her hut to welcome him with figs and grapes. Their conversation took a rather un-archaeological turn:

'And what's all this here?' I ask her.
'Eh, can't you see, my child? Rocks!'
'Then why do people come to see them?'
The old woman hesitated for an instant. Then, lowering her voice, she asked me: 'Are you a foreigner?'
'No, Greek.'
She became more confident, shrugged her shoulders.
'Simple-minded Franks!' she said, bursting into laughter.[71]

KARITAINA

At Karytaena begins the true Arcadia – the land of crag and wood and torrent, home of Pan and the Dryads . . . It lies over the face and summit of a beetling crag; one side is separated by a deep gorge from another rock whereon stands a grand old Frankish tower, and the other overhangs the bed of the roaring Alpheus.[72]

The dramatically located 'Frankish tower' noticed by Richard Ridley Farrar in 1880 was built in 1254 by Geoffroy de Bruyères, one of the barons of Prince Guillaume de Villehardouin. Over the centuries the castle gradually decayed, but its commanding position again made it useful in the 1820s, when it was refortified by Gennaios Kolokotronis, son of the Peloponnesian warlord Theodore Kolokotronis. The father had used Karitaina as a base for a while soon after the outbreak of the struggle for independence in 1821, staying probably in a now-ruined house high up on the steep castle path. On that occasion his forces had been rapidly dispersed by a well-organized Turkish attack. It was partly to avoid a repetition of this ignominy that the fortress was repaired and much strengthened in 1825. A more immediate spur to action was the relentless progress of Ibrahim Pasha and his Egyptian troops through the Peloponnese in a campaign which very nearly succeeded in returning all the Greeks to Turkish rule.

In his last years Kolokotronis, who was virtually illiterate, was persuaded to recount his memories to George Tertzetis, librarian of the Greek parliament. Brave heroes before Agamemnon and Achilles, Tertzetis had warned him, were forgotten because they had no Homer to record their deeds.[73] Kolokotronis obliged, supplying practical details – how, for instance, Gennaios had biscuits baked and exchanged them for gunpowder, bought up large supplies of lead from Zakynthos, and settled in with two hundred men to await developments – but also relating more appropriately Homeric incidents and speech. Ibrahim was determined to remove the defenders of Karitaina who had dared to obstruct his progress; in the meantime, he decided systematically to destroy all fruit-bearing trees in the region of Messenia. Theodore Kolokotronis replied, with majestic wrath, on behalf of the Messenians, that to fight with 'the senseless trees' is not legitimate warfare; besides, 'We will not submit – no, not if you cut down every branch, not if you burn all our trees and houses, nor leave one stone upon another!' The earth will remain Greek, and will bear again. 'If only one Greek shall be left, we will still go on fighting, and never hope that you will make our earth your own – dismiss that from your mind.'[74]

Perhaps one look from old Kolokotronis should have been enough to deter his enemies. 'He had a stentorian voice,' recorded Ioannis Gennadios, dweller in a very different world as Greek envoy to St James's in the 1890s, 'and an irresistibly piercing glance, to which his hooked nose leant the aspect of an eagle; and with the long hair, traditional to the Palikar [bold warrior], floating about him, he looked . . . like one of those splendid rocks which project from the Aegean.' He wore, as he would continue to do in many a popular patriotic print, a high-crested helmet 'declaring that his mind was with the Greeks of old.' Because of his unrivalled experience he was known as '*O Geron tou Moreos*', the Old Man of the Morea (the usual name of the Peloponnese at the time).[75] A less partial account might have added that he had a reputation for ordering massacres. But his complete dedication to the cause cannot be doubted.

It was, however, through a mixture of subterfuge and luck that Karitaina was not taken by Ibrahim. Gennaios exploded gunpowder in 'four or five hollow places' (dungeons or treasure-houses from the days of Geoffroy de Bruyères?) and allowed the growth of a rumour that cannon had been found in the castle. Access to the inner fort was carefully restricted to prevent the truth from being winkled out. As a result, or so Kolokotronis would have us believe, Ibrahim was deterred from attacking Karitaina. In fact, the defenders did have cannon, but only two of them.[76] Up on the windy ramparts, as they surveyed the hills of Arcadia, they must have been, bold palikars though they were, a little uneasy that their bluff would be called.

4

THE IONIAN ISLANDS, MISSOLONGHI, EPIROS

Zakynthos – Cephalonia – Ithaca – Leukas – Paxos – Corfu – Missolonghi – Epiros – Arta – Nikopolis – Ioannina

In June 1386 Corfu tendered its formal submission to the Doge of Venice, Antonio Venier. The envoy insisted politely that

> The Lion [of St. Mark] does not tyrannize over other beasts. He requires, indeed, submission, but leaves to each the freedom and power granted by nature. You, generous Lion, will not forget your habits. Therefore we hope that you will . . . not destroy our liberties.[1]

Corfu was to remain under Venetian rule until the extinction of the Republic in 1797; Venice also ruled the other Ionian islands apart from Leukas by the end of the fifteenth century, and Leukas from 1684. After Venice, there were brief periods of French and (nominally at least) Russo-Turkish rule, before the establishment of a British Protectorate in 1815. The 'liberties' hoped for in 1386 were made available chiefly to the (usually Italian or Italianate) ruling classes, but the cultural climate was at least freer under European than Ottoman rule. The most notable demotic Greek verse for centuries was written by Dionysios Solomos and Andreas Kalvos, Italian-trained poets, in the Ionians.

Solomos and his colleagues were also, however, inspired by the movement for independence on the mainland in the years before 1821. When the Turkish threat was removed, Ionian energies began to be channelled into the campaign for union with the Greek state. Not even Gladstone's oratory – he was shouted down by an angry mob at Argostoli in Cephalonia – could persuade the islanders to settle for reform under continuing British jurisdiction; such voluble expressions of feeling combined with financial considerations to persuade Britain, with some reluctance, finally to cede the islands to Greece in 1864.

Recently, there have been more drastic changes in the Ionian Islands. A major earthquake destroyed most of the Venetian and British period buildings on Cephalonia and Zakynthos in 1953, although many have since been rebuilt. And in the late twentieth century Corfu in particular has become a crowded, much-built-over place, largely unrecognizable as the paradise painted by Edward Lear and described by Lawrence and Gerald Durrell. It seems, however, that things to come were being signposted as long ago as the visit of the geologist Professor D.T. Ansted to 'the beautiful ridge near Pelleka' [Pelekas] in 1863. He described it as

> among the places resorted to for celebrating that singularly British institution the picnic. Large deposits of oyster shells and broken champagne bottles will clearly indicate to future generations the important uses and sacred character of the place, and long after Great Britain has ceased to act as the Protecting Power of the Ionian Islands, long after even our roads – the most durable mark of England's Empire – have become obliterated, future travellers will discover in their search after the remains of a former people, these unmistakable proofs of the taste and habits of the western rulers of the world.[2]

ZAKYNTHOS (ZANTE)

Zakynthos is renowned for fertility; in spring its air, Andreas Kalvos proclaimed in his poem about his native island, 'enriches the sea by the scent of its golden lemons.'[3] For centuries its economy relied on the export of citrus fruits, white wine, and especially currants, which were in such demand in England, said the traveller William Biddulph in 1599, that

'the Greeks wonder what we use to do with so many . . .
and ask sometimes whether we use to dye with them, or feed
Hogs with them.'⁴ Inherited privilege allowed the Venetian-
descended ruling class to keep most of the proceeds of this
trade and to live in some state in the palazzi (mostly rebuilt
after the earthquake of 1953) in the town of Zakynthos. In
the eighteenth and early nineteenth centuries the palazzi
blazed with the light of grand receptions and masked balls,
and rang with Italian declamations and extempore sonnets for
the more elegant *cognoscenti*.

Into this unlikely milieu was born in 1798 Dionysios
Solomos, the founding father of demotic Greek poetry.
Solomos was the legitimized offspring of the immensely
wealthy landowner and tobacco importer Count Nicolas
Salomon or Solomos. Educated for a decade in Italy, he began
to write Italian verse there, and continued to do so on his
return to Zakynthos in 1818. He did, however, have a Greek
mother, a tendency to serious thought, and liberal sympathies
not shared by his ultra-conservative relatives. He was an ideal
target for the eloquence of the persuasive Greek patriot and
historian Spyridon Trikoupis, soon to win renown for his
stirring address over the body of Lord Byron. Unlike Byron,
Solomos seems to have had no intention of physically joining
the fight for independence across the narrow seas, but
Trikoupis was able tactfully to nudge him in a no-less-useful
direction.

> 'Your poetical talent assures you a distinguished place on
> the Italian Parnassus. But the highest positions there are
> occupied already. The Greek Parnassus has not yet found
> its Dante.' At his request I then gave him a sketch of
> the position of our language and literature. 'I don't know
> Greek,' he said, 'how could I write well in Greek?' And
> in fact he knew the spoken tongue very imperfectly. I
> said, 'The language which you imbibed with your
> mother's milk is Greek. So you can easily bring it back
> to your memory.'⁵

Solomos indeed had no training in formal literary Greek as
used by academics and administrators in the lands ruled from

Istanbul; his decision to refresh his memory of the demotic and to adapt it to the writing of serious poetry was of immense significance in the one-hundred-and-fifty year struggle between adherents of the archaic official *katharevousa* or 'pure' Greek, and the more modern and informal demotic. (Uglier incidents in the struggle included the death of eight people in riots provoked by the publication of the first few instalments of a demotic version of the Gospels in 1901, and the belated imposition of compulsory *katharevousa* in education and public life by the Colonels of 1967–74.)

In May 1823, only a few months after Trikoupis' rallying call, Solomos was at work on his best known poem, the long and impassioned 'Hymn to Liberty'. Against the will of the purists, part of the poem was eventually adopted as the Greek national anthem in 1863. Rudyard Kipling's version appeared in 1918.

> We knew thee of old,
> Oh, divinely restored,
> By the light of thine eyes
> And the light of thy Sword.
>
> From the graves of our slain
> Shall thy valour prevail
> As we greet thee again –
> Hail, Liberty! Hail![6]

Solomos, like one of his heroes, Byron, woke up to find himself famous. (Trikoupis took a copy of the hymn to Missolonghi, but arrived too late.) Solomos found it more difficult than Byron, however, to build upon this early success. For the rest of his life, first on Zakynthos and from 1828 on Corfu, periods of creativity alternated with bouts of hard drinking and depression. But this sort of pattern corresponded well with the popular nineteenth-century image of the poet, and Solomos died in 1857 a national hero. Ten years later, his brother Demetrios brought his bones back to Zakynthos to rest in the marble tomb on the ground floor of what is now the Solomos museum in Agiou Markou Square.

CEPHALONIA

Cephalonia is more rugged than the other Ionian islands.
In 1936 Duff Cooper, Secretary of State for War, suffered
'acute vertigo' during a four-hour excursion by 'crazy vehicle'
along roads like 'goat-paths, no wider than a car's axle, with
crumbling precipitous edges and a surface of shifting shingle.'
Lady Diana Cooper was, in a way, luckier.

> I get only abject terror. He can shut his eyes at least,
> while I have to drive the car with my hands and feet and
> eyes, but I can carry away a picture of the heights and
> cliffs and wine-dark sea. Poor Duff has only his lids to
> remember.[7]

The Coopers' ride would have been even rougher but for
the work, in the early nineteenth century, of the British
Resident in Cephalonia, Colonel Charles Napier. During his
six years in office Napier built 134 miles of road – of which,
says his biographer, '96 miles were blasted through the living
rock' – bridges, market-places, and a prison, and established
a convent school.[8] (The earthquake of 1953 unfortunately
removed most traces of his work.) He also succeeded in doing
much to break the feudal privileges of the Cephalonian
aristocracy. Napier was hampered in carrying through some
of his plans, however, by the attitude – from indifference to
personal enmity – of his superiors on Corfu, the Lord High
Commissioners Sir Thomas Maitland and Sir Frederick Adam.
He was eventually relieved of his post on trumped-up charges
of negligence. Back in England, he was exonerated and offered
the Residency of Zakynthos, but refused on the grounds that
only a return to Cephalonia would satisfy the demands of
injured honour. Subsequently he found glory in a different
sphere of imperial endeavour, the conquest of India.
   Napier admired, and was admired by, his most famous
visitor to Cephalonia, Lord Byron. Napier was a man of action
and Byron at least aspired, amid contradictory impulses, to
be one. Anxious not to be identified too readily with one
Greek faction or another, he bided his time on Cephalonia
between August and December 1823 before finally setting off

for Missolonghi. He stayed in a small villa (another casualty of the earthquake of 1953) at Metaxata, and there found, as he took up his interrupted journal on 17 October 1823, a rare degree of reflective tranquillity.

> . . . standing at the window of my apartment in this beautiful village – the calm though cool serenity of a beautiful and transparent Moonlight – showing the Islands – the Mountains – the Sea – with a distant outline of the Morea traced between the double Azure of the waves and skies – have quieted me enough to be able to write . . . which (however difficult it may seem for one who has written so much publicly – to refrain) is and always has been – a task and a painful one.[9]

ITHACA

Byron left Cephalonia to spend a few days on Ithaca in August 1823. Like his companion, Edward John Trelawny, he evidently enjoyed the contrast between 'the arid wastes and barren red hills of Cephalonia' and Ithaca's 'verdant valleys, sparkling streams, and high land, clothed in evergreen shrubs.'[10] And of course there were the Homeric associations to be appreciated. Byron duly wrote to Teresa Guiccioli that he had 'visited the places to which the remembrances of Ulysses and his family are attached.'[11] The notoriously unreliable Trelawny, who tends to touch up memories and mix times and places for the sake of a good story, gives a more colourful account of the visit:

> After landing, it was proposed to Byron to visit some of the localities that antiquaries have dubbed with the titles of Homer's school, – Ulysses' stronghold, & c.: he turned peevishly away, saying to me, 'Do I look like one of those emasculated fogies? Let's have a swim. I detest antiquarian twaddle. Do people think I have no lucid intervals, that I came to Greece to scribble more nonsense? I will show them I can do something better: I wish I had never written a line, to have it cast in my teeth at every turn.[12]

Heinrich Schliemann went to Ithaca solely because of Homer. Although no great discoveries awaited him here, he evinced the same energy and conviction which would soon strike gold, and 'prove' Homer a historian as much as a poet, at Troy and Mycenae. Having established to his own satisfaction that 'Dexia is the site of the harbour of Phorcys, where the Phaeacians first put the deeply sleeping Odysseus ashore,' he launched his assault proper. He searched determinedly for Odysseus' palace on Mount Aëtos, so steep and boulder-strewn that 'one often has to crawl on all fours.' Enthusiastically he ripped out of the soil vases, two of which, he thought it 'very possible', contained the ashes of Odysseus and Penelope. In his haste – working with a pickaxe – he accidentally broke most of the vases. Tired of such vandalism, he read the relevant passages from *The Odyssey* to the Ithacans he met. They were, we have Schliemann's word for it, enraptured.[13]

In 1963 the modern world arrived dramatically on the small island of Skorpios, just to the north of Ithaca, in the shape of the millionaire shipping magnate Aristotle Onassis. He bought it for $110,000, spurred on by his rival Stavros Niarkhos' recent purchase of Spetsopoula, off Spetsai. Onassis had, as his biographers say, 'found his island kingdom.'[14] Here in 1968, with journalists and photographers attempting to invade by small boat (some of those who swam ashore were allowed to stay), he married Jackie Kennedy, and here in 1975 he was buried.

LEUKAS (SANTA MAURA)

In AD 968 Liudprand, Bishop of Cremona, spent a few miserable days on Leukas. He was returning from an embassy to Constantinople, where he was snubbed as the representative of his master, the Emperor Otto the Great, who had the gall to claim succession to the Roman emperors. Liudprand vented his spleen by becoming an early luminary of the anti-retsina movement – 'To add to our troubles, the Greek wine we found undrinkable because of the mixture in it of pitch, resin and plaster' – and by scrawling on the walls and table of his wretched accommodation a poem beginning 'Trust not the Greeks'.

Liudprand reached Leukas in December, where he was 'most unkindly received' by the bishop, a eunuch. All Greek bishops

> are both poor and rich; rich in gold coins wherewith they gamble recklessly; poor in servants and utensils. . . . They do their own buying and selling; they close and open their doors themselves; they are their own stewards, their own ass-drivers, their own 'capones' [eunuchs] – aha, I meant to write 'caupones' [inn-keepers], but the thing is so true that it made me write the truth against my will.

For bishops to be either eunuchs or inn-keepers, Liudprand pointed out triumphantly, violated canon law. As for the acquisitiveness, he was prepared to stretch a point and admit that the bishop of Leukas had heavy taxes to pay to Constantinople.[15] But by this time nothing could please Liudprand about the Greek lands except for the prospect of leaving them.

John Addington Symonds felt quite differently as he sailed past the cliffs of Leukas on his way back from Athens to Italy.

> Here Sappho leapt into the waves to cure love-longing, according to the ancient story; and he who sees the white cliffs chafed with breakers and burning with fierce light, as it was once my luck to see them, may well with Childe Harold 'feel or dream he feels no common glow.' [Following a spectacular storm] a rainbow rose and grew above Leucadia . . . spanning with a horseshoe arch that touched the zenith, the long line of roseate cliffs. The clouds upon which the bow was woven, were steel-blue beneath and crimson above; and the bow itself was bathed in fire – its violets and greens and yellows visibly ignited by the liquid flame on which it rested. The sea beneath, stormily dancing, flashed back from all its crests the same red glow, shining like a ridged lava-torrent in its first combustion. Then as the sun sank, the crags burned deeper with scarlet blushes as of blood, and with passionate bloom as of pomegranate or oleander flowers. Could Turner rise from the grave to paint a picture that

should bear the name of 'Sappho's Leap', he would paint it thus: and the world would complain that he had dreamed the poetry of his picture.[16]

PAXOS

Viscountess Strangford, traveller, writer, and future nursing reformer, was bored on Paxos in 1863.

> We spent the next wind-bound day in laborious idleness, as there is no earthly thing to see or do at Paxo, and it was too hot, till late in the evening, even to walk along the unaccountably numerous stone paths of the island. Paxo, in fact, may be briefly described as a construction of stone walls, stone paths, and olive trees; no other green thing is visible, and scarcely one single clod of earth.[17]

There was more to see a few years earlier, during Gladstone's official visit. He had come to the Ionians to consider constitutional reforms, but was also eager to pursue his interest in the possibility of union between the Anglican and Orthodox churches. Consequently he had the following encounter, recorded by Major-General Ferdinand Whittingham:

> At Paxo, as everywhere else he showed the most unbounded veneration for the dignitaries of the Greek Church. In Corfu, he had excited the, perhaps illiberal, disgust of the English, by publicly kissing the hand of the Archbishop and dutifully receiving his blessing . . . The simple Bishop of Paxo appears, also, to have been ignorant of the etiquette which the High Commissioner Extraordinary practised with ecclesiastical dignitaries. Mr Gladstone, having taken and respectfully kissed the Bishop's hand, leaned forward to receive the Orthodox blessing. The Bishop hesitated, not knowing what was expected of him; and not imagining, perhaps, that a member of the Anglican Church could require his benediction. At last, however, he perceived the truth, and, bending forward, he hastened to comply with the

flattering desire of the Representative of the British Crown. But at this moment, unfortunately, Mr Gladstone, imagining that the deferred blessing was not forthcoming, suddenly raised his head, and struck the episcopal chin. The Resident and other spectators of the scene had considerable difficulty in maintaining the gravity befitting so solemn an occasion.[18]

CORFU

The shipwrecked Odysseus is welcomed by Nausikaa, princess of the Phaeacians, to 'wave-washed' Skheria (Corfu, traditionally), a place so remote that its inhabitants 'have no dealings with other mortals.'[19] In later times other mortals arrived as colonists from ancient Corinth, as rulers from the west, and finally as tourists from every direction and in such numbers that Nausikaa's peaceful land has now all but disappeared beneath 'ferro-concrete hideosity.'[20]

British affection for Corfu has, ironically, been one cause of this state of affairs. Earlier British influence had pleasanter results, including the imperial grandeur of the older public buildings in Kerkyra (Corfu town) and the traditions of playing cricket and drinking ginger-beer or *tstinti birra*. Most of the palaces, villas and theatres date from the times of the first two holders of the office of Lord High Commissioner of the Ionian Protectorate, the often despotic Sir Thomas Maitland and the usually vainglorious Sir Frederick Adam. Adam lavished money on building himself the palace of Mon Repos ('a very desirable Regent's Parkish (only better) house', Lady Diana Cooper later observed[21]), and equipping himself and his entourage with fine uniforms. ('Corfu is filled with paid idlers!' railed Colonel Charles Napier from Cephalonia.[22]) Maitland was shrewder but more eccentric and, if one credits Napier's rather biased testimony, 'constantly drunk'.[23] The best known anecdote about him, set in the imposing and then brand-new neo-classical palace of St Michael and St George, goes as follows:

> On one occasion, the Senate having been assembled in the saloon of the palace, waiting in all form for his

Excellency's appearance, the door slowly opened and Sir
Thomas walked in, attired in a shirt, a red nightcap, and
a pair of slippers. In this state he walked into the middle
of the room with his hands before him, looked round
at the assembled senators, and then said, addressing the
secretary of the Senate, 'Damn them . . . tell them all
to go to hell!' and walked back to his room with a
grunt.[24]

By this and more sophisticated methods Maitland and his
successors prevented the Greeks of the Ionian Islands from
obtaining more than a token role in decision-making.

In spite of or because of this exclusion, Greek culture
flourished on Corfu during the nineteenth century. Dionysios
Solomos, the 'National Poet', lived in Kerkyra from 1828 until
his death in 1857. (The house in Arseniou Street, destroyed
by Second World War bombing, has been restored as a
museum.) Other residents included Solomos' fellow-poet and
fellow-Zantiot Andreas Kalvos, and the historian Spyridon
Trikoupis. English and Greek culture were not, however,
wholly separate, thanks especially to the efforts of another
eccentric Englishman, Frederick North, Earl of Guilford. In
1824, thirteen years before a university was established in
Athens, he founded the Ionian Academy, at which both
Kalvos and Trikoupis taught. Guilford compensated for the
indifference of much of the colonial ruling class by being as
Greek, or at least as ancient Greek, as possible. Napier
reported that 'He goes about dressed up like Plato with a gold
band round his mad pate, and flowing drapery of a purple hue.
His students' dress is very pretty and said to be taken from
ancient statues.'[25] More practically, he bequeathed his library
of 25,000 books to the Academy at his death in 1828.

A later aristocrat who felt drawn to Corfu was the Empress
Elisabeth of Austria. In the 1890s she had built, and occasionally lived in, the Achilleion palace. Nine years after her
assassination in 1898 it was bought by Kaiser Wilhelm II,
who underlined the intended association with Achilles by
erecting in the garden a massive statue of the hero, inscribed
'To the greatest of the Greeks from the greatest of the
Germans.' (The inscription was removed after the First World

War.) After 1918 the building was left mostly unoccupied and began to decay. In the summer of 1936 a party including King Edward VIII (shortly to abdicate), Wallis Simpson, and Duff and Diana Cooper, had to break chains and cut through barbed wire in order to reach the former palace. Lady Diana describes the visit:

> Then came a forty-minute climb of beauty – one endless flight of steps bordered by symmetrical cypresses culminating in a charming 1890 statue of the Empress Elizabeth in marble skirt and collar of modish cut. The top when reached (dead with fatigue) showed a tremendous view and a colossal figure of Achilles erected by the Kaiser, and a house the size of Chatsworth of such hideosity that it takes seeing to believe. Pompeian in style. The electric light is installed with great fancy – baskets full of electric-light flowers, groups of plaster cherubs blowing electric-light bubbles.[26]

The Achilleion opened as a casino in 1962.

Also on Corfu in the 1930s were the Durrell family. The island nourished Lawrence's exoticism and the ten-year-old Gerald's passion for fauna. The whole family were supported by surely the most Anglophile Corfiot this century, their ubiquitous, noisy, great-hearted friend, driver and factotum, Spiro Hakiaopoulos.

> It was Spiro who, on discovering that our money had not yet arrived from England, subsidized us, and took it upon himself to go and speak severely to the bank manager about his lack of organization. That it was not the poor manager's fault did not deter him in the least. It was Spiro who paid our hotel bill, who organized a cart to carry our luggage to the villa, and who drove us out there himself, his car piled high with groceries that he had purchased for us . . .
>
> That he knew everyone on the island, and that they all knew him, we soon discovered was no idle boast. Wherever his car stopped, half a dozen voices would shout out his name, and hands would beckon him to sit

at the little tables under the trees and drink coffee. Policemen, peasants, and priests waved and smiled as he passed; fishermen, grocers, and café-owners greeted him like a brother. 'Ah, Spiro!' they would say, and smile at him affectionately as though he was a naughty but lovable child. They respected his honesty, his bellige-rence, and above all they adored his typically Greek scorn and fearlessness when dealing with any form of Govern-mental red tape.[27]

Gerald Durrell spent most of his time on Corfu wandering the countryside in search of scorpions, mantids, and turtles. To the young naturalist's eye even the garden of the 'Strawberry-Pink Villa' was

a magic land, a forest of flowers through which roamed creatures I had never seen before. Among the thick, silky petals of each rose-bloom lived tiny, crab-like spiders that scuttled sideways when disturbed. Their small, translucent bodies were coloured to match the flowers they inhabited: pink, ivory, wine-red, or buttery-yellow. On the rose-stems, encrusted with greenflies, lady-birds moved like newly painted toys; lady-birds pale red with large black spots; lady-birds apple-red with brown spots; lady-birds orange with grey-and-black freckles. Rotund and amiable, they prowled and fed among the anaemic flocks of greenfly. Carpenter bees, like furry, electric-blue bears, zigzagged among the flowers, growling fatly and busily. Humming-bird hawk-moths, sleek and neat, whipped up and down the paths with a fussy efficiency, pausing occasionally on speed-misty wings to lower a long, slender proboscis into a bloom . . . As an accom-paniment to all this activity there came from the olive-groves outside the fuchsia hedge the incessant shimmering cries of the cicadas.[28]

Adults have found Corfu equally alluring. Edward Lear based himself here for varying lengths of time between 1848 and 1866 partly for commercial reasons – paintings were easier to sell and commissions to acquire in colonial society than on

the mainland – and partly through sheer love of the giant
olive-trees, orange groves, and limestone hills of the island.
These could make him forget even his persistent irritation
with the superficiality of 'fiddle faddle poodly-pumpkin' colonial high society. In December 1857 Lear wrote to his friend
Chichester Fortescue:

> There is one thing here which cannot be grumbled at
> – at present, at least. The weather, it has been simply
> cloudless glory, for 7 long days & nights. Anything like
> the splendour of olive-grove & orange-garden, the blue
> of sky & ivory of church & chapel, the violet of moun-
> tain, rising from peacockwing-hued sea, & tipped with
> lines of silver snow, can hardly be imagined. I wish to
> goodness gracious grasshoppers you were here.[29]

Even as professedly unromantic an observer as Evelyn
Waugh succumbed, if with irony intact, to the spell.

> Frankly I had never heard of the place when, after my
> first visit to Greece, I stopped there for a few hours in
> a vile ship called the *Yperoke*, where I was travelling
> second class in barely conceivable discomfort. It seemed
> to me then one of the most beautiful places I have ever
> seen. So much was I impressed that when, later, I found
> myself writing a novel about someone very rich, I gave
> her a villa in Corfu, as I thought that, when I was rich,
> that was one of the first things I would buy. I still think
> so, and if enough people buy this book I shall fulfil my
> intention. It is full of lovely villas, many of them for
> sale. Before the [First World] war the harbour was much
> frequented by private yachts, and during the season the
> shores were peopled by a very gay cosmopolitan society.
> It has become less fashionable since the collapse of the
> Central Powers, but all the more habitable. Do let me
> urge you, gentle reader, if you have only borrowed this
> book from a library, to buy two or three copies instantly
> so that I can leave London and go and live peacefully
> on this island.[30]

MISSOLONGHI

> Any spot on the surface of the earth, or in its bowels,
> that holds out a prospect of gain, you will find inhabited;
> a morass that will produce rice, the crust of a volcano
> in which the vine will grow; lagunes, in which fish
> abound, are temptations which overcome the terror of
> pestilence or death. So I was not surprised at seeing
> Missolonghi, situated as it is on the verge of the most
> dismal swamp I had ever seen. The marvel was that
> Byron, prone to fevers, should have been induced to land
> on this mudbank, and stick there for three months shut
> in by a circle of stagnant pools which might be called
> the belt of death.[31]

Trelawny, Byron's companion and posthumous critic, who
arrived in Missolonghi a few days after his death in April 1824,
made the place sound as dreadful as possible. It is not quite
as damp and deadly as this. (The poet Kostis Palamas, who
came to live here as a six-year-old orphan in 1865, often refer-
red as an adult in Athens to the strange, melancholy beauty
of 'the lake strewn with islands, where the *maïstrali* [the
north-west wind, the Mistral] . . . stirs the seaweed on the
distant shore.'[32]) Missolonghi is, however, as Trelawny
says, surrounded on three sides by lagoons of stagnant
water; surprisingly, he makes no mention of the infamous
mosquitoes.

Byron himself had little to say for his final abode. 'If
we are not taken off with the sword,' he wrote to Charles
Hancock on 5 February 1824, 'we are like to march off with
an ague in this mud-basket . . . the Dykes of Holland when
broken down are the Desarts of Arabia for dryness in comparison.'[33] He had come to Missolonghi expecting to see
some military action, to find 'a soldier's grave'.[34] Instead, he
was frustrated of combat, bombarded with demands for
money from Greeks and foreign volunteers of every faction,
and finally afflicted by the doctors whose ministrations –
bleeding, principally – played at least some part in killing him.
But through it all, even when he felt so angry that he stopped
keeping a journal because 'he could not help abusing the

Greeks in it',[35] he stayed loyal to the Greek cause. This loyalty, preserved inviolate by his death, made him a popular hero in Greece, commemorated by innumerable ballads, statues, and road names. This was not a fate which could remotely have been foreseen in his days of poetry and scandal. It is difficult, as Louis MacNeice says in 'Cock o' the North', to imagine the living Byron in Missolonghi

> from his statue in the Garden of Heroes
> Among the arranged trees and the marble clichés
> And the small memorial cannon like staring infants
> With lollipops in their mouths.[36]

Missolonghi's fame was redoubled two years later by the heroic death of many of its citizens as they ran through the Turkish lines in a last attempt to break through a second siege. Others blew themselves up to avoid capture. Among those killed in the final sortie were a number of German volunteers and the Swiss editor of the radical *Greek Chronicle*, Dr Jean-Jacques Meyer. Byron had disapproved of Meyer and his newspaper, fearing that its republican sentiments would only cause more trouble for and among the already divided Greeks. He would perhaps have admired, however, the sentiments expressed in the last letter which Meyer succeeded in sending to a friend a few days before his death.

> The labours we are undergoing, and a wound in the shoulder, (a prelude to that which will be my passport to eternity,) have hitherto prevented my writing to you. We are reduced to the necessity of feeding on the most unclean animals; we suffer fearfully from hunger and thirst, and disease is added to our calamities; 1740 of our comrades are dead; the shot and shells have overturned our houses and ramparts; we are in want of firewood, and pinched with cold. It is an exhilarating spectacle to behold the ardour and devotion of the garrison amid so many privations. . . . I declare to you, that we have sworn to defend Mesolonghi foot by foot, to listen to no capitulation, and to bury ourselves in its ruins. Our last hour approaches. History will do us justice, and posterity weep over our misfortunes.[37]

EPIROS

When Byron had Childe Harold explore 'Albania' (modern Albania and Epiros) in his own footsteps, he introduced a new Greece to the great majority of his readers.

> From the dark barriers of that rugged clime,
> Ev'n to the centre of Illyria's vales
> Childe Harold pass'd o'er many a mount sublime,
> Through lands scarce noticed in historic tales.[38]

Classical Epiros had left little but a memory of its fine Molossian hunting dogs, the oracle at Dodona (undiscovered until after Byron's time), and King Pyrrhos and the costly victories named after him. These were now overshadowed by new prospects and new names – the mountain views from glistening white 'Monastic Zitsa', 'Dark Suli's rocks', Ioannina and its lake island – and by tales, ideally suited to Gothic and Romantic expectations, of the terrifying Ali Pasha, torturer and attentive host who ruled from Ioannina.

For a time, travellers included Epiros in their itineraries. Disraeli consciously followed Byron's footsteps. Edward Lear came, and painted, amongst much else, scenes mentioned by the poet or made famous by the deeds of Ali Pasha. But without classical sites (with the exception of Nikopolis, in the more accessible south) to console tourists for the toughness of the terrain, Epiros soon relapsed into alpine, poverty-stricken obscurity. The best known modern book about the region concerns not Ioannina or Arta with their exotic past, but the village of Lia, on the modern Albanian border. Nicholas Gage's story of his mother, *Eleni*, reconstructs life there in the 1940s in painstaking detail. Lia consisted, as the author (then Nikola Gatzoyiannis) knew it until he was eight, of one hundred and fifty 'crude stone huts' clinging precariously to 'the cleft between two naked granite peaks of the Mourgana mountain range'.

> The landscape in which the villagers of Lia spun out their lives like spiders clinging to a wall affected them in ways that could never be understood by those who walk on flat land. Mankind seemed an afterthought of the gods who created such mountains. The relentless

cycles of the seasons, rain and snow, sunlight and darkness, ruled the daily lives of the peasants who worked
with one goal: to wrest food out of the stony mountain
slopes, digging terraced steps on which to plant their
crops.[39]

The Greek Civil War, during the last stages of which
the Communist *andartes* maintained a tenacious hold on the
northern mountains, disrupted this simple life, and made
lethal the tensions and envies of a community in which no
privacy had ever been known. Informers were readily available
to condemn neighbours, in particular Eleni Gatzoyiannis,
the 'Amerikana', whose husband's job in America made her
family a little less poor than most. Her crime was to help her
children escape from Lia. Unable to join the escape party
herself, she was executed by Communist guerrillas in a group
of thirteen others in August 1948. Sixteen days later, taking
the remaining villagers with them, her killers fled across
the border into Albania before the advancing government
forces.

ARTA

In November 1848 a 'way-worn' Edward Lear wound into
Arta through 'dark and strange places full of mud, among
masses of building black against bright moonlight.' The
'streets', daylight confirmed, were 'gutters, or ditches, full of
mud, with a raised trottoir on each side.'[40] Lear seems not
to have been especially impressed by the great bridge across
the River Arakhthos, which Thomas Smart Hughes had pronounced 'very lofty and picturesque',[41] and which, legend
asserted, could not be completed until the master-builder,
reluctantly obeying the instructions of a magical bird, buried
his wife in the foundations.

To make matters worse for Lear, a 'nautical Turk' bound
for Prevesa requisitioned the party's horses. (The Governor
obligingly provided fresh ones.) Yet in spite of these initial
bad impressions, Lear came to admire Arta during his two
brief visits, the second in the spring of 1849.

Few places in Albania are more magnificent in aspect
and situation than Arta . . . Nothing can exceed the
venerable grandeur of its picturesque Hellenic walls, and
from the site of its ancient Acropolis, the panoramic
splendour of the view is majestic in the highest degree.

Even the muddy lanes were

less disagreeable now than heretofore, on account of the
odoriferous orange trees, all in full bloom. Arta is surrounded by gardens, and in a great degree supplies the
markets of Yannina with fruit and vegetables.[42]

This provincial garden-city had for a time, in the thirteenth
and fourteenth centuries, been the capital of the independent
Despots of Epiros; lesser members of the Komnenos dynasty
of Constantinople. One monument of this hour of glory has
continued to attract strong responses: Lear's 'very curious old
church' of Paregoritissa, the Virgin Comforter, begun in
about 1289. Sir Steven Runciman, the great historian of
Byzantium and the Crusades, confesses that he finds its blend
of Greek and Italian elements clumsy. More particularly, the
exterior 'looks like a box with handles on top.'[43] Osbert
Lancaster outrageously presses the box analogy further, much
in the style of his cartoons: 'Seen from the west it resembles
nothing so much as an old-fashioned biscuit-box crowned
with five symmetrically disposed pepper-pots and a filigree
salt-cellar.'[44]

NIKOPOLIS

Adopting a casual tone which only briefly succeeds in masking
his excitement at the success of his first expedition to Greece,
the twenty-one-year-old Byron announced in a letter to his
mother on 12 November 1809:

Today I saw the remains of the town of *Actium* near
which Antony lost the world in a small bay where two
frigates could hardly manouvre, a broken wall is the sole

remnant. – On another part of the gulph stand the ruins of Nicopolis built by Augustus in honour of his victory. . . . Last night I was at a Greek marriage, but this & 1000 things more I have neither time or *space* to describe. – I am going tomorrow with a guard of fifty men to Patras in the Morea, & thence to Athens where I shall winter.[45]

In *Childe Harold's Pilgrimage* Byron gave his more public response to Nikopolis, in the eighteenth-century 'Ruins of Empire' tradition.

Look where the second Caesar's trophies rose:
Now, like the hands that rear'd them, withering;
Imperial anarchs, doubling human woes!
GOD! was thy globe ordain'd for such to win and lose?[46]

'Imperial anarchs' of yesterday were, however, more tolerable than those of today. Thomas Smart Hughes, examining the ruins soon after Byron, was horrified to find the agents of Ali Pasha removing the marble shafts and entablature of a temple for re-use in the new palace at Prevesa: 'thus perish even the ruins of Nicopolis; and the monuments of Augustus's glory serve to decorate the dwelling of an Albanian robber.'[47]

Fortunately, whereas Ali's palace did not long survive him, a large part of Nikopolis did. On 1 May 1849 Edward Lear noted his on-site experiences:

The scattered remains of Palaio-Kastro (so the peasants call the site of Nicópolis) occupy a large space of ground; and although there are here and there masses of brick-work, which forcibly recall to my memory those on the Campagna of Rome, yet the principal charm of the scene consists in its wild loneliness, and its command of noble views over the Ionian sea as well as of the Gulf of Arta and the mountains of Agrafa. My principal object was to obtain correct drawings from the great theatre, as well as from the Stadium and the lesser theatre; but at this season of the year I found many impediments which in the late autumn of 1848 had not presented themselves.

Vegetation had shot up in the early spring to so great
a size and luxuriance, that a choice of position was difficult to find among gigantic asphodel four or five feet
high – foxgloves of prodigious size, briars and thistles of
obstinate dignity. Nor was the passing from one point
of the ruins to another, through the fields of beans and
Indian corn which cover the cultivated portions of the
soil, a light task; there were snakes too in great numbers
and size.[48]

Hughes, given time, would have set to and removed the
thistles and driven away the snakes, to judge by his ambitious
if perhaps rather idealistic plans for Nikopolis if only it could
be taken over by a 'civilized and Christian government'.

The walls, the sepulchres, the baths, the very houses are
still applicable to their former uses; churches might rise
upon the sites of temples, the gymnasium might be converted into a tennis-court, and the stadium into a riding-
school; the aqueduct might be restored, and the theatres
adapted to the representation of the modern drama.[49]

IOANNINA (YANNINA)

'There is no place in all Greece more subject to thunder-storms
than Ioánnina, none more worthy of having been the abode
of the Thunderer,' declared Captain William Martin Leake,
clinching his identification of the ancient sanctuary of Zeus at
Dodona with the modern capital of Epiros.[50] He was wrong
about Dodona, whose ruins and well-preserved Hellenistic
theatre were found thirteen miles to the south in 1873, but
Ioannina has been fit home to more than one human
'thunderer', most famously Ali Pasha between 1787 and 1822
but also Thomas Preljubović, the Serb who became Despot
of Epiros in the fourteenth century. 'Paltry is all wickedness
compared to that of Thomas,' sighed a medieval chronicler.[51]
Thomas raised excessive taxes, gave his Serbian followers
Greek women and Greek property, hanged and mutilated his
Albanian foes, blinded or sold into slavery other enemies (the

pious abbot of Metsovo was blinded *and* sold), and rejected his popular wife Maria Angelina in favour of his treacherous favourite Michael Apsaras. When Thomas was eventually murdered by his bodyguards on 23 December 1384 there were scenes of wild rejoicing in the middle of the night, as the citizens poured into the cathedral to acclaim Maria Angelina as their new sovereign.[52]

Ali Pasha was also guilty of a long list of crimes. His capture of Ioannina in 1787 and confirmation as its Pasha by the Sultan crowned years of fighting, scheming, bribing and tricking his way from a minor chieftainship in Tebelene (now in southern Albania) to the effectively independent rule of much of modern Albania and northern and central Greece. Ali maintained his reputation for ruthlessness once Ioannina had become his lair. He broke every promise, roasted rivals on spits, massacred almost the entire population of the village of Gardiki to avenge the rape of his mother and sister by some Gardikiots thirty years before, and waged systematic war on the fiercely independent people of the Suli mountains until the survivors either fled to Corfu or threw themselves over cliffs to avoid capture. Either as a moral example or, it was whispered, out of jealousy, he had his son's Christian mistress Phrosyne (Euphrosyne) and sixteen other women drowned in the Lake of Ioannina.

As the successful ruler of strategically important lands, Ali was wooed by both the British and the French. (He spurned Napoleon Bonaparte's offer of a crown and schemed, unsuccessfully, to acquire Corfu.) Travellers came mostly out of an awed fascination with the story-book ogre. Byron remembered his first audience with Ali, in the autumn of 1809, in Canto Two of *Childe Harold's Pilgrimage* (contrasting 'that aged venerable face' with 'The deeds that lurk beneath, and stain him with disgrace'[53]) and, more intimately, in a letter to his mother.

> He said he was certain I was a man of birth because I had small ears, curling hair, & little white hands, and expressed himself pleased with my appearance & garb. – He told me to consider him as a father whilst I was in

Turkey, & said he looked on me as his son. – Indeed he treated me like a child, sending me almonds & sugared sherbet, fruits & sweetmeats 20 times a day. – He begged me to visit him often, and at night when he was more at leisure.[54]

Byron's characteristically flamboyant 'garb' was 'a full suit of Staff uniform with a very magnificent sabre & c.' Thus attired, he awakened in Ali emotions probably other than paternal. But most visitors found themselves, like it or not, under Ali's spell. Charles Robert Cockerell was impressed by the 'easy familiarity and perfect good humour of his manners'; 'mighty civil', agreed Byron's companion Hobhouse.[55] He was a hospitable murderer, mesmerizing people with his light blue eyes, corpulent but dignified, thinking his own thoughts but showing kindness to visitors and expressing great interest in Revd Thomas Smart Hughes' hat as well as Byron's ears.[56]

For all Ali Pasha's villainies, Ioannina prospered under his rule. As Byron and Hobhouse rode towards the city, its 'houses, domes, and minarets, glittering through gardens of orange and lemon trees', one of the first things they saw was a human arm hanging from a tree. But the dismembered body belonged, they subsequently learnt, not to one of Ali's tribal or political enemies but to a priest turned robber-baron. Hobhouse therefore felt justified in declaring that

It is by such vigorous measures that the Vizier has rendered many parts of Albania, and the contiguous country, perfectly accessible, which were before annually over-run by robbers; and consequently by opening the country to merchants, and securing their persons and goods, has not only increased his own revenues, but bettered the condition of his subjects. He has built bridges over the rivers, raised causeways across the marshes, laid out frequent roads, adorned the country and the towns with new buildings, and by many wholesome regulations has acted the part of a good and great Prince, without perhaps a single other motive than that of his own aggrandisement.[57]

Charles Robert Cockerell was told that the number of shops had increased within living memory from five or six to two thousand.[58]

Aesthetically, much in Ioannina was not to western taste. Byron thought the palaces of the pasha and his heirs 'splendid but too much ornamented with silk & gold.'[59] Hughes also shuddered at the gilding, but was fascinated, in spite of himself, by the famous Kiosk of Ali, set in extensive gardens at the northern edge of the city.

> Its interior is divided into eight compartments, or deep recesses, diverging out of the great area, in the middle of which stands a çurious jet d'eau. This consists of a small castle built of marble surmounted by cannon, and surrounded by regular lines which play upon each other in imitation of a bombardment: between the cannon, on the parapet, stand figures of parrots, lions, and other birds or beasts, who spout water also out of their mouths as if in mockery at what is going forward: the motion of the water gives voice to a small organ attached to a pillar in the apartment. The whole may be considered an apt measure of the national taste where the curious is preferred to the beautiful, and that which can astonish a vulgar mind to what might captivate a cultivated and refined one. The recesses are splendidly fitted up with draperies of the richest silk and the most luxurious sofas.[60]

Such delights were less common after the death of Ali Pasha, following open war with his official overlord the Sultan, in 1822. He was brought down by a combination of Ottoman might, desertions from his own ranks, and a fatal unwillingness to spend money on the defensive schemes recommended by the militarily acute Colonel Napier of Cephalonia. In Napier's words,

> Love of money made and unmade him; first it made him hoard until his riches gave him power, which enabled him to increase those riches; but when the hour of danger came he would not expend his money, and so fell.[61]

Trapped on the picturesque island on the Lake of Ioannina, Ali bargained for a pardon but fell victim to the sort of trick he had so often played on his victims: a boat from the mainland brought to the wooden balcony of the monastery of St Panteleimon not the expected pardon but showers of bullets. His head was sent as a trophy to Constantinople. But the effort it cost the Ottomans to dislodge him had one important side-effect, for it was a material aid to the Greeks who had launched their great rebellion in 1821. (Epiros itself, however, did not become part of Greece until 1913.)

Ioannina continued, on the whole, prosperous. But tourists hankered after the frightening, romantic days of Ali Pasha. Fed on *Childe Harold*, the twenty-six-year-old Benjamin Disraeli was disappointed in 1830 with Ali's successor, 'the renowned Redschid'.

The Hall was vast, built by Ali Pacha purposely to receive the largest Gobelins carpet that was ever made, which belonged to the chief chamber in Versailles, and was sold to him in the Revolution. It is entirely covered with gilding and arabesques. Here, squatted up on a corner of the large divan, I bowed with all the nonchalance of St. James's Street to a little ferocious-looking, shrivelled, care-worn man, plainly dressed, with a countenance clouded with anxiety and thought.[62]

Edward Lear walked and painted happily in the squares of Ioannina with their stork-filled plane trees in 1849, safe alike from bloodthirsty pashas and the industrialization of the modern city, but could not forget Ali.

I was never tired of walking out into the spacious plain on each side the town, where immense numbers of cattle enlivened the scene, and milk-white storks paraded leisurely in quest of food: or I would take a boat and cross to the little island, and visit the monastery, where that most wondrous man Alí Pashá met his death: or sitting by the edge of the lake near the southern side of the kastron [citadel], sketch the massive, mournful ruins of his palace of Litharítza, with the peaks of Olytzika rising beyond. For hours I could loiter on the terrace of the kastron opposite the Pashá's serai, among the ruined fortifications, or near the strange gilded tomb where lies the body of the man who for so long time made thousands tremble![63]

5

THESSALY, MACEDONIA, MOUNT ATHOS

*Thessaly – Meteora – Tempe and Mount Olympos –
Macedonia – Thessaloniki – Mount Athos*

'Never go to the North,' a Greek friend told the American
writer Kevin Andrews, 'there are wolves, there are
Bulgars.'[1] Visitors to the north have usually had some
specific reason for going there. The terrain is difficult, there
are relatively few classical remains, and tradition has it that
the people are tough – according to a late eighteenth-century
Survey of the Turkish Empire, 'those of Macedonia, &c. are
robust, courageous, and somewhat ferocious.'[2]

Travellers who did venture north were rewarded by a
dramatic landscape – the extraordinary monastery-crowned
rocks of the Meteora in Thessaly, the cloud-swathed mass of
Olympos dividing Thessaly from Macedonia, Mount Athos
casting its shadow far into the Aegean. Dramatic weather was
also often encountered. Hippocrates, the 'Father of Medicine',
spent three years on Thasos, the island off Macedonia, studying
the effect of weather patterns on disease, and in the process
compiled what sounds like a long-term weather forecast.

> At the season of Arcturus prolonged heavy rain with
> winds from the north ... Winter: northerly winds;
> drought; cold spells; snow. About the equinox, severe
> storms. Spring: northerly winds; drought; some rain;
> cold spells. About the summer solstice some showers,
> and very cold until near the Dog Star. After the Dog
> Star, until Arcturus, hot summer, fierce heat, not inter-
> mittent but continuous and intense.[3]

Inland and east of Thasos, among the Thracians, the Athenian general Xenophon found that 'it was so cold that both the water and the wine would freeze in the jars. Many Greeks had their noses and ears frost-bitten.' At last the southerner understood 'why the Thracians wear the skins of foxes on their heads and over their ears.'[4]

More distinctively Greek – and as important to many Greeks as the Acropolis – are the Byzantine monuments of the north, including the early churches of Thessaloniki, once second only to Constantinople as a centre of Byzantine culture, and the notably positioned and frescoed monasteries of Athos and the Meteora. Everything about these places challenges traditional western assumptions about art: the distinctively ancient and oriental music; the pictures executed, said Lady Mary Wortley Montagu, in a 'most monstrous taste' upon a gold ground and with 'no notion either of shade or proportion'[5]; the very shape of the buildings, where an unexpected Western comparison is nevertheless helpful in Arnold Toynbee's explanation:

> The roofing of a Byzantine church is pyramidal in its general effect; but, instead of mounting from its base to its apex in smooth surfaces meeting each other at sharp angles, the Byzantine church's roofing mounts in a crescendo of billowing curves. The optical effect is wave-like, and, to a modern observer, it feels like a piece of symphonic 'classical' Western music translated into visual form.[6]

Imaginative leaps like this seem to have become common only after the 1920s. Robert Byron, one of the more successful of Byzantium's popular apologists, began at this time, especially on Athos, to examine Byzantine art on its own terms and in a context of contemporary life and worship. Only then did travellers in greater numbers begin to gaze with awe instead of puzzlement at the earthly inspirations of W.B. Yeats' spiritual Byzantium, 'the artifice of eternity', the 'sages standing in God's holy fire/As in the gold mosaic of a wall.'[7]

THESSALY

The experiences of Edward Lear as he rode from Epiros across the Pindos mountains into Thessaly could only have happened to a writer of nonsense verse. The Albanian guards at the khans – makeshift accommodation for travellers and their animals – had a tendency to demand to see passports 'which they had not the slightest idea of reading'.

> As a proof of this, on my taking out by mistake the card of a hotel-keeper at Athens, the Palíkar [proud warrior] snatched at it hastily, and after gravely scrutinising it, gave it back to me, saying, 'Good; you may pass on!' At the next guardhouse I confess to having amused myself by showing a bill of Mrs. Dunsford's Hotel, at Malta, and at another the back of an English letter, each of which documents were received as a Teskeré.[8]

Life was both more relaxed and more purposeful down in the wide Thessalian plains (the largest flat area in Greece, although even here, as one early nineteenth-century observer puts it, numerous hills 'emerge like so many islands out of their stagnant level').[9] Lear was frustrated that no canvas could capture the 'vast level extent', but inspirited by a new world full of agriculture, movement, and 'incident'. Men, women, wagon-loads of children and puppies, caravans of pack-horses, all moved among 'innumerable sheep, goats, horses, buffali, and cattle, corn or pasture land, peasants' huts, hundreds of perambulating storks.' Birds (especially those of incongruously human gait) fascinated Lear, who had started his career as a painter of parrots (*The Family of the Psittacidae*, 1832). The next day's riding revealed

> great grey cranes, too, the first I ever saw enjoying the liberty of nature. These birds seem made for the vast plains of Thessaly: how they walk about proudly by pairs, and disdain the storks, who go in great companies! Now and then there is a vulture, but there is too much society for them generally. As for jackdaws and magpies, they congregate in crowds and hover and settle by myriads.

But by the time Lear returned to Epiros ten days later, he was less enthusiastic about birds and about the charming Thessalian plains in general. On 25 May, after much rain and its attendant mire, 'The woes of Thessaly continued' at a house in the village of Nomí.

> In the middle of the night, the roof of Seid Efféndi's house being slight, a restless stork put one of his legs through the crevice and could not extricate it; whereon ensued much kicking and screams, and at the summons came half the storks in Thessaly, and all night long the uproar was portentous. Four very wet jackdaws also came down the chimney and hopped over me and about the room till dawn.[10]

METEORA

Successive visitors to the Meteora have striven to find adequate similes to describe what C.R. Cockerell called the 'curious monasteries, planted like the nest of eagles, on the summits of high and pointed rocks.'[11] 'Strange, unearthly-looking rocks are these,' said Edward Lear, 'full of gigantic chasms and round holes, resembling Gruyère cheese, as it were, highly magnified.'[12] Even Robert Curzon, seasoned explorer of the monasteries of the Middle East, moderated his habitual scepticism sufficiently to declare that

> The end of a range of rocky hills seems to have been broken off by some earthquake or washed away by the Deluge, leaving only a series of twenty or thirty tall, thin, smooth, needle-like rocks, many hundred feet in height; some like gigantic tusks, some shaped like sugar-loaves, and some like vast stalagmites. . . . Nothing can be more strange and wonderful than this romantic region.[13]

The difficulty of ascending such needles and stalagmites tested travellers' courage as much as their powers of description. Asked how the monasteries' founders had scaled the rocks in the first place, monks and nuns suggested to Patrick Leigh Fermor that, being saints, they had flown up like eagles.[14] The more conventional methods are mentioned in unemotional terms in Baedeker's *Handbook* of 1894: 'Travellers are drawn up in a net by means of a windlass to most of the monasteries; the ascent by the ladders is not recommended.'[15] Robert Curzon explains more graphically the problem with the ladders of St Barlaam's monastery:

> The lowest ladder was approached by a pathway leading to a rickety wooden platform which overhung a deep gorge. From this point the ladders hung perpendicularly upon the bare rock, and I climbed up three or four of them very soon; but coming to one, the lower end of which had swung away from the top of the one below, I had some difficulty in stretching across from the one to the other; and here unluckily I looked down, and found that I had turned a sort of angle in the precipice, and that I was not over the rocky platform where I had left the horses, but that the precipice went sheer down to so tremendous a depth that my head turned when I surveyed the distant valley over which I was hanging in the air like a fly on a wall. The monks in the monastery saw me hesitate, and called out to me to take courage and hold on; and, making an effort, I overcame my dizziness, and clambered up to a small iron door, through which I crept into a court of the monastery, where I was welcomed by the monks and the two servants who had been hauled up by the rope.[16]

The net and windlass method had its imperfections too. In 1865 the Russian Archimandrite Porfiry Uspensky, travelling among the fellow-Orthodox, was advised to pray and sing hymns as he was winched up to the Great Meteoron. Problems began to develop, however.

> As they were pulling me towards the wooden platform they turned me upside down over the abyss. I clenched my teeth in terror and almost lost consciousness. But they dragged me in to the tower, untied the net and gave

me a glass of water. I drank it and, recovering a little
from my panic, asked the abbot to lead me straight to
the church. There I fell on my knees before the icon of
the Saviour. Tears splashed from my eyes, hot tears of
gratitude to God for the salvation of my life, unnaturally
committed to the habits of a bird.[17]

Steps were finally constructed earlier this century.

Having knelt before the icon of Christ, Uspensky probably
also became aware of the presence, in frescoed form, of the
austere fourteenth-century founders of the Great Meteoron,
Saints Athanasios and Ioasaph. (Athanasios, on the north wall
of the sanctuary, is especially noticeable because he wears a
white habit instead of the usual brown or black; possibly,
Donald Nicol suggests in his history of the Meteora, this is
intended to suggest the saint's transfiguration, with garments
'exceeding white as snow' as in St Mark's Gospel.[18])
Athanasios was an ascetic so strict that, according to his early
biographer, 'The word "woman" never once passed his lips.
If he had to mention the subject he did so by allegory or
by using other terms, referring to woman either as "the
sling", which hurls the stones of sin into the souls of man,
or as "the affliction", which is the powerhouse of passion
in those addicted to the flesh.'[19] Athanasios' colleague, the
'second founder' Ioasaph, was a royal monk, descended from
Byzantine emperors and Serbian krals, as proudly declared
by his secular name John Ourosh Ducas Palaiologos. He
was briefly himself 'Emperor' of Thessaly in 1372, and his
continuing influence in (as well as on) high places obtained
for the Great Meteoron exemption from local church control
and some jurisdiction over the other rock-top communities.

Patrick Leigh Fermor in the late 1940s found the monks
of the Great Meteoron in an unhappy state, their numbers
reduced to four (three of them aged and frail), their traditional
hospitality to raki and a few walnuts, and their conversation
to the subject of *Parakmí* – decline.[20] The pressures which
would later force the nuns of St Stephanos to sell embroideries
and turn the Meteora into a centre more for tourism than
for pilgrimage were already apparent. Monastic vocations
were decreasing steadily. Funds had dwindled amid the

ravages of wars and the disappearance of contributions from the Russian faithful since 1917. In earlier times many valuable books and manuscripts had been stolen or bought at bargain price by worldly-wise visitors, the meanest of whom must have been the unsuitably named Cypriot priest Athanasios, a Catholic convert in the service of Cardinal Mazarin. Donald Nicol describes his method of arriving at monasteries disguised as an Orthodox clergyman and relieving needy monks of their books with the aid of a pair of scales: the godly tome rested on one side, and the balancing weight of small change on the other.[21]

Parakmí seemed less depressingly inevitable in Leigh Fermor's mealtime conversations, on the neighbouring rock of St Barlaam, with the shrewd but humorous and hospitable abbot, Father Christopher, and the shy, benign Father Bessarion. He became intimate with them and their church, and once joined them before dawn for the liturgy of St Demetrios' day. After the service he became much engrossed in the sixteenth-century frescoes (painted by Frangos Katellanos and George of Thebes) which, as Robert Curzon had noted, included 'a liberal allowance of flames and devils'.[22]

Over the lintel of the outer door of the narthex, the souls of the dead were being weighed in great painted scales. On one side, the righteous were conducted to paradise by angels. They floated heavenward on rafts of cloud, and the interlock of their haloes receded like the scales of a goldfish. But on the other side, black-winged fiends were leading the damned away haltered and hand-cuffed, and hurling them into a terrible flaming gyre. This conflagration, peopled with prelates and emperors, swirled them into the shark-toothed mouth of a gigantic, glassy-eyed and swine-snouted monster. Giant dolphins and herrings and carp, each one with human limbs sticking out of its mouth, furrowed a stormy sea in the background.

Below are worse horrors illustrating the texts 'The worm that dieth not' and 'Weeping and gnashing of teeth'. But the visitor's reverie was broken into by a reminder both of spiritual and (the day was just beginning) earthly needs.

> Something pressed my shoulder. Looking round, I saw the great horny hand of the abbot resting there and, above and beyond it, his eye-brows raised high. 'There you are,' he observed severely, 'Hell' (he pointed at both in turn) 'and Heaven.' His index-finger was aimed at the ascending airborne swarm. 'Let's hope *that's* where you go.' As he turned towards the stairs, I thought I could divine the ghost of a wink. 'Up we go,' the abbot continued, 'Bessarion's ready with the coffee.'[23]

TEMPE AND MOUNT OLYMPOS

Greek poetry is replete with references to the home of the Olympians, and Roman poetry with praise for the calm beauties of the nearby Vale of Tempe, later coupled by Keats with 'the dales of Arcady' as a suitable setting for the 'leaf-fring'd legend' of his Grecian urn.[24] But since few of the poets had actually been near the area, there was little to prepare verse-reading travellers for the real mountain and valley.

Tempe is certainly worth celebrating. The steep-sided valley, channelling the River Peneios, comes as a relief after the plains of Thessaly. Mr Hawkins was among those who, in the early nineteenth century, savoured the 'full but silent' river gliding by 'the Oriental plane-tree, which supports the wild-vine thickly interlaced among its branches, and dropping festoons to the surface of the water.'[25] Hawkins confessed, however, that if Ovid and Catullus had not praised the verdant vale Tempe would probably have attracted no more attention than any of the wilder valleys of western Europe. Richard Monckton Milnes (later Lord Houghton and editor of Keats) found this lack of distinctiveness positively depressing. In place of the boundless vale of the imagination he had found 'a glen of most limited dimensions.'[26] By the time Eric Newby passed through Tempe a century and a half later it had shrunk even further since,

1. Here are 'the restrained geometry, the impressive and deliberate size, the harmony and proportion and the splendid physical impact that we call classical.' Peter Levi, 1981

2. The Capuchin convent at Athens, incorporating the 'Lantern of Demosthenes'. Byron lived here in 1810–11 with 'one Friar (a Capuchin of course) and one Frier (a bandy legged Turkish cook)' and fed 'upon Woodcocks and red Mullet every day'.

3. 'Do I look like one of those emasculated fogies? Let's have a swim. I detest antiquarian twaddle. Do people think I have no lucid intervals, that I came to Greece to scribble more nonsense?' Byron, 1823

4. 'My belly was pinched, and wearied was my body . . . Yet notwithstanding of my distress, the remembrance of these sweet seasoned Songs of Arcadian Shepherds . . . did recreate my fatigated corpse with many sugared suppositions.' William Lithgow, 1614

5. The Lake Island of Ioannina: 'I would take a boat and cross to the little island, and visit the monastery, where that most wondrous man Ali Pasha met his death.' Edward Lear, 1851

6. ALI reclined, a man of war and woes:
Yet in his lineaments ye cannot trace,
While Gentleness her milder radiance throws
Along that aged venerable face,
The deeds that lurk beneath, and stain him with disgrace.
                    Byron on Ali Pasha, 1812

7. Corfu: 'Anything like the splendour of olive-grove & orange-garden, the blue of sky and ivory of church & chapel, the violet of mountain, rising from peacockwing-hued sea, and tipped with lines of silver snow, can hardly be imagined.' Edward Lear, 1857

There was an old man of Thermopylæ,
Who never did anything properly;
But they said, 'If you choose, To boil eggs in your shoes,
You shall never remain in Thermopylæ,'

8. Edward Lear in nonsense mood

9. The ruined city of Mistra: 'Sheer, beneath my feet, the silvered ruins flashed on the lead-coloured hill.' Maurice Barrès, 1900

10. The monastery of Arkadi: 'The court ran with blood, our informant said, and it was so piled with bodies that it was impossible to pass from one side to the other.' Henry Fanshawe Tozer on the massacre by the Turks in 1866 of the defenders of Arkadi (1890)

11. Theodore Kolokotronis: 'We will not submit – no, not if you cut down every branch, not if you burn all our trees and houses, nor leave one stone upon another! . . . If only one Greek shall be left, we will still go on fighting.' (1825)

12. George Psychoundakis: 'The Cretan character – warlike, proud, compulsively generous to a friend or stranger in need, ferociously unforgiving to an enemy or traitor, frugal day by day but prodigal in celebration . . .' Antony Beevor, 1991

13. 'Demanding Pater Adrianos we were ushered to the Government House, he being this year's head of the republic; very fat and benign and terribly obsequious to me, *Byron.*' Robert Byron, 1926

14. Patrick Leigh Fermor in the 'high mountains' of Crete, which 'had the austerity, the extravagance and sometimes the melancholy of the backgrounds of primitive religious paintings in Italy . . .' (1955)

15. Henry Miller and Lawrence Durrell in Corfu, 1939: 'Those who sit at home with their anthologies, their Homers and Byrons, have long grown impatient of the hackneyed eulogy. Travellers, on the other hand, know that the poet has not lived who can hackney the Greek sea itself.' Robert Byron, 1929

16. William Golding: I could hear the quiet, breathless ripple of Greek voices as he came: '*O yeros katavainei*', 'the old man descends', spoken in the wondering tones that might have welcomed Moses back from Mt Sinai . . . Peter Green, 1986

as guidebooks rarely stress, the river now 'has to share the Vale not only with a railway line but with a multi-lane highway decorated with concrete lampposts, the main road from Salonika to Athens and the Piraeus . . . jam-packed with juggernaut lorries.'[27]

Olympos is more obviously inspiring, although Newby was again disappointed, this time finding Homeric descriptions of the dulcet air and immortal joys of Olympos scant consolation as, having clambered up Mytikas, its highest peak, he squatted 'up there, enveloped in freezing cloud, with a Force 7 wind blowing, 9570 feet above the Aegean.' Homer should not have written about Olympos 'without having tried it out for himself (rather like a house agent who can write a convincing description of a house without actually seeing it).'[28]

The ever positive Revd Henry Fanshawe Tozer, on the other hand, was exhilarated by the 'masses of white cloud, swirling and seething as in a huge cauldron.'[29] When the mist does clear, the view extends as far as Athos and the great ranges of Grammos, Pindos, and Parnassos. But no physical mountain is a completely convincing home for the gods, and in ancient times 'Olympos', the name of several unconnected mountains, was as often used as a general term for the dwelling-place of the deities as for the actual peaks which divide Macedonia from Thessaly.

Nevertheless, travellers have always expected to find something divine here, if sometimes only in the way that people venture, not without a little trepidation and excitement, on to Loch Ness. And sometimes they have found the gods lingering. St Dionysos (or Dionysios), traditional founder of the monastery on the slopes of Olympos, at least overlaps with his divine namesake and predecessor. The monastery of St Dionysos, deep in its ravine, is a likely place for tales and superstitions, although not ones involving Homer's 'glittering' Olympos. An old monk explained to Henry Tozer why there were deer and wolves on Olympos, but no bears:

> Once upon a time, when St Dionysus, the founder of the monastery, was ploughing on the mountain, he was called off from his work, and forced to leave his ox with

the plough in the field. During his absence a bear came
down and devoured the ox; but the saint on his return,
discovering what had happened, seized and harnessed
the offending beast, and made him drag the plough.
After which time the bears (considering apparently that
such treatment was *un peu trop fort*) disappeared from
Mount Olympus.[30]

Another superstition with a moral concerned 'the volcanic
fire which springs up out of a hole in the side of this
mountain' shown to Charles Robert Cockerell in the spring
of 1812. His sceptical response fell on deaf Olympian ears.

My guide told me that the fire would roast eggs well,
but not if they were stolen – indeed it would not act
upon stolen things at all. The Greeks are very superstitious, and this is one of the favourite forms it takes
with them. I tried to confute him by cutting a scrap
off his turban while his back was turned and showing
him how it burned, but although he saw it consumed
it did not shake his belief in the least.[31]

MACEDONIA

Macedonia, thanks to the exploits of its kings Philip II and
his son Alexander the Great, was a name well known to early
travellers in Greece. But even in the late nineteenth century
archaeology had discovered little about its main ancient cities
at Pella, Aigai, and Philippi. Scholars even mislocated Aigai
until, in 1977, Manolis Andronikos excavated the royal tombs
near the modern Vergina and their rich artefacts, now kept
in the Thessaloniki Archaeological Museum. Peter Levi saw
the finds soon after their arrival.

The newly discovered treasure is one of the most
impressive displays in the world. There have been
arguments about whether the tomb it came from was
really Philip's, but there remains no doubt at all in my
own mind. . . . [I]t seems to me this was a king's tomb,

and the king was Philip. He was lame: the personal armour in the tomb was made at the right date and made for a lame man. There was a wreath of oak-leaves and a wreath of myrtle in blossom. The richness and grandeur of what was found with him are already a powerful evidence. But what is so moving about it all is that these things are unique both in grandeur and in beauty. The wreaths of golden leaves are blushing in a perpetual last sunlight; they speak about immortality as a king might conceive it. But the small box for his ashes is terribly small; its ornaments are terribly restrained.[32]

Such restraint was not apparent to Philip's contemporaries further south, who habitually dismissed the Macedonians as uncouth, un-Greek northerners, vulgar enough even to pronounce their king's name as 'Bilippos'. Philip loved 'debauchery and lascivious dancing', warned the great orator Demosthenes as the Macedonian troops edged nearer to Athens, and rewarded 'brigands and flatterers, and drunken men who indulge in revelry of a kind which I would rather not mention to you.'[33] Demosthenes was, of course, not the most independent of witnesses; military discipline rather than debauchery had enabled Philip to forge the army which would not only defeat Athens and such small fry, but would conquer a huge empire under Alexander. All the Athenians really knew about Macedonia beyond the plain of Aigai was, as Alexander's biographer Robin Lane Fox puts it, that it was a land of 'silver-fir forests, free-ranging horses and kings who broke their word and never died a peaceful death.'[34]

In late antiquity and the early Middle Ages, much of Macedonia outside Thessaloniki again became inaccessible to all but the hardiest of travellers. Pella and Philippi declined as the Goths approached. Gibbon describes the escape of Gothic deserters from the Roman army to the evocatively alliterative 'morasses of Macedonia' in Chapter XXVII of his *Decline and Fall*. And in 1884 Murray's *Handbook* still finds it necessary to note that, although all the shops in Thessaloniki are expensive and none good, 'The traveller who proposes going into the interior *must* lay in all stores here.'[35]

Those who did, suitably provisioned, venture out from the city, including Olympos-bound mountaineers, alpine botanists and the indefatigable Henry Tozer, found much to delight and inspire them. There were, for instance, the overhanging precipices and spectacular cascades of Edessa, hailed by Tozer as 'the Tivoli of the Balkan peninsula.'[36] Later, Byzantinists found much to reward them in places hitherto little noticed; it was in Kastoria, for instance, that Osbert Lancaster found, on the outside west wall of Panagia Koubedeliki, 'a charming Salome doing a scarf dance while balancing the charger with the Baptist's head on her own.'[37] (The perception here is the cartoonist's as much as the Byzantinist's.) But most seekers after frescoes and mosaics lingered in Thessaloniki itself, long the second city of the Byzantines.

THESSALONIKI

Being situated in great part upon the declivity of a hill rising from the extremity of that noble basin at the head of the Thermaic gulf, which is included within the Capes Várdar and Karáburnu, and being surrounded by lofty whitened walls, of which the whole extent, as well as that of the city itself, is displayed to view from the sea, it presents a most imposing appearance in approaching on that side. The form of the city approaches to a half circle, of which the diameter is described by a lofty wall, flanked with towers, extending a mile in length along the sea shore, and defended by three great towers, one at each extremity, the third overlooking the skala or landing place.[38]

The defensive structures of Thessaloniki (or Saloniki) are less complete now than when Captain William Martin Leake inspected them in the early years of the nineteenth century. But considerable sections of wall and fortress survive to bear witness to the city's long history of attacks from both land and sea.

Within the walls, by late Byzantine times, stood perhaps as many as ninety churches, great and small, their paintings and mosaics glittering in the light of sacred lamps and candles, but often rebuilt as a result of incidents like the arrival of the Saracen fleet led by a Greek renegade, Leo of Tripoli, in AD 904. With the authorities in Constantinople in disarray, the city had to rely on its own strength. John Julius Norwich takes up the story:

> The city resisted for three days, but its walls were in disrepair and its two commanders at loggerheads; the sudden death of one of them after a fall from his horse might in other circumstances have proved a blessing in disguise, but it came too late. On 29 July 904 the defences crumbled and the Saracens poured through the breach. The bloodshed and butchery continued for a full week; only then did the raiders re-embark with their priceless plunder and . . . more than 30,000 prisoners, leaving the second city and port of the Empire a smoking ruin behind them.[39]

The Emperor, also called Leo (VI), but in this case also 'the Wise', rebuilt and strengthened the fortifications and destroyed the Saracen fleet the following year.

Several sieges later, in 1185, the Normans of Sicily succeeded in breaching the walls once more. A graphic account of the siege and its aftermath by Archbishop Eustathios, famed in peacetime as a Homeric commentator, has survived. The Normans smashed whatever they could, Eustathios relates. There were rapes and murders in churches, services were disrupted by jeering, drunken 'Latins', and one barbarian sprang on to 'the holy and awe-inspiring altar and, having uncovered himself, urinated therefrom' while others made water into the crystal lamps; prostitutes 'glittered' in sacred vestments while most people were forced to wear torn rags – everything else was taken from them – and were beaten for looking either happy or unhappy. Understandably in the circumstances, the Archbishop had a low regard for Norman civilisation. Never having seen any beautiful things in their own benighted lands, he concluded they destroyed all those they found in the city.[40]

At the end of the Middle Ages Thessaloniki was successively

seized by the Turks, freed, given to Venice, and, in 1430, taken again by the Turks; they held it this time until its recapture by the Greeks in the First Balkan War in 1913. But the city's most famous betrayal occurred in AD 390, and was the work not of marauding Franks, Slavs, or Turks, nor even of the Goths who were then the main fear, but of the Emperor Theodosius himself, who often resided there. Because of the threat from the Goths a large garrison, itself consisting mainly of 'Barbarians', was stationed in the city. Among the Greek population this caused considerable resentment, the terrible consequences of which are recounted by Edward Gibbon in *The Decline and Fall of the Roman Empire*:

> Botheric, the general of those troops, and as it should seem from his name, a Barbarian, had among his slaves a beautiful boy, who excited the impure desires of one of the charioteers of the circus. The insolent and brutal lover was thrown into prison by the order of Botheric; and he sternly rejected the importunate clamours of the multitude, who, on the day of the public games, lamented the absence of their favourite, and considered the skill of a charioteer as an object of more importance than his virtue.

The mob, emboldened by the absence of part of the garrison on campaign in Italy, murdered Botheric and his principal officers and dragged their bodies through the streets. The 'fiery and choleric' Theodosius responded rapidly. The citizens were invited, 'in the name of their sovereign', to games at the Hippodrome.

> As soon as the assembly was complete, the soldiers, who had secretly been posted round the Circus, received the signal, not of the races, but of a general massacre. The promiscuous carnage continued three hours, without discrimination of strangers or natives, of age or sex, of innocence or guilt; the most moderate accounts state the number of the slain at seven thousand, and it is affirmed by some writers, that more than fifteen thousand victims were sacrificed to the manes [spirit] of Botheric.

Subsequently Theodosius was coerced by his mentor St Ambrose to do public penance, 'stripped of the ensigns of royalty', in Milan Cathedral.[41] Doubtless this was little consolation to the survivors in Macedonia. Minimal traces of walls, entrances, and seating are all that now indicate the position of the huge Hippodrome off Ipodromiou Street. But the Propylaia or entrance porch survived into the nineteenth century, when it was known in Ladino, the language of the Jews of Thessaloniki, as *Las Incantadas*, 'or "the enchanted women", from the eight caryatides which stand in the upper part of the structure, and were supposed to have been petrified, by the effect of magic.'[42]

Pitted against all these horrors rides St Demetrios, spear levelled against the (usually infidel) enemy, in the icons and frescoes of the city. Demetrios, an army officer, was martyred for his faith in AD 306 under the Christian-hating Emperor Galerius. (The Arch of Galerius, emblem of victory over his more secular foes in Mesopotamia, still stands near Odos Egnatia; the Rotunda, intended as his mausoleum, was transformed by Theodosius the Great into the church of St George.) Miraculous appearances of Demetrios, striving beside the Thessalonians, were reported in times of fire, famine and invasion; at an early date he became their patron saint, and the basilica of St Demetrios was founded to house his tomb. Imposing in size and atmosphere, internally recalling 'rather the stately Norman churches of Sicily than the usual Byzantine forms',[43] finely refurbished or rebuilt after each reconquest of the city and the great fire of 1917, this church belongs to Byzantine Christendom at its most self-confident. Probably its most admired features now are the seventh-century mosaics which survived the fire. Here the saint stands protectively with his hand on a child's shoulder, proudly between the grave, solid figures of the founders of his church, supportively with an aged deacon, its rebuilder. 'Thoughtful and grave,' says Osbert Lancaster in one of his more serious moods, 'but not severe, strictly frontal in their pose, these saints, bishops and donors seem to possess an intense inner life of their own as they gaze down detached, but not wholly indifferent, on the worshipper and the tourist.'[44]

For much of the Middle Ages, however, pride of place was reserved for the Kiborion, the resplendent shrine (*kiborion*, 'cup', refers to its rounded canopy) which was believed to cover the grave of the saint. The authors of the medieval *Miracles of St Demetrios* describe, in awed detail, a vision of the Kiborion and its contents:

> Entering the church he [the unnamed dreamer] saw the sacred receptacle and beautiful edifice which stands in the middle of the church on the left-hand side, six-sided in plan with six columns and as many little walls made of tested sheets of silver, with a roof, also six-sided, rising circularly and winding round a vault, and having above a sphere, beneath which in a circle are wonderful patterns from lilies, and, on the top, a cross.

Thus inspired, the dreamer was enabled to see, within the shrine, the saint's silver couch-shaped reliquary and 'at its head a golden throne decorated with precious stones upon which was seated the famous warrior of Christ, Demetrios, as he is portrayed on the icons.'[45]

The Kiborion had been destroyed by the Saracens in AD 904 and subsequently rebuilt. According to Archbishop Eustathios in 1185 the Normans attacked it with axes; 'they themselves deserved to be dealt with in the same way. They pulled off the silver adornments all around it, removed the golden crown which encircled the head, and even carried off one of the feet, as if trying thus to delay the swift-footed punishment which the saint might justly inflict upon them.' But a formidable eunuch commander in the service of the King of Sicily rode into the church wielding an iron mace and drove off the desecrators.[46]

By the nineteenth century the church had long been a mosque, the Kiborion was gone (its base was discovered after the fire of 1917) and the relics had been translated to Italy for safe-keeping, whence they returned only in 1980. The devout turned instead, with the tacit allowance of the mosque authorities, to the traditional site of the saint's original burial in the crypt. This humbler shrine was given short shrift by Murray's *Handbook* of 1884:

It is very doubtful if this is a tomb at all; it appears to be merely a loose slab of marble, prettily carved in low relief. Under this slab is plain black earth, in which may be observed a hole, due to the constant burrowing of pious Greeks, who repute the soil from this tomb a sovereign remedy in various maladies. Among the uneducated classes, a pill of earth from this spot is administered to children as regularly as codliver-oil in western countries. It is needless to observe that the stock of miraculous mould is kept up artificially, else it had long since been exhausted.[47]

No doubt Murray's pilgrims would have been equally unimpressed by the monk Ignatius' rapt account of how the mosaic Vision of Ezekiel came to adorn the apse of the much smaller church of Osios David in the Upper Town. It was secretly commissioned, says Ignatius, by the Emperor Galerius' Christian daughter, Theodora. When the mosaicist arrived for work one day, he found that a miraculous complete work had replaced his unfinished picture. For fear of her parents, Theodora had the vision covered over; it survived the princess and the destruction of the building, and was uncovered centuries later, amid earthquake and storm, as a special final favour to an old Egyptian monk.[48] In fact the mosaic is later than Galerius' time – it probably dates from the late fifth or early sixth century – but it was indeed bricked over to escape destruction during the ascendancy of the Iconoclasts in the eighth and ninth centuries. (Later, more prosaically, it was plastered over when the church became the Suluca Mosque.) Miraculous or not, the Vision of Ezekiel is one of the most vibrant mosaics of the Early Christian period. It represents, as Ignatius excitedly explains, Christ stepping on a cloud and riding on the wings of the wind, as sung by David (in Psalm 104). At the corners of the cloud appear the winged signs of the four Evangelists – man, eagle, lion, and bull – and the prophets Ezekiel and Habbakuk standing on either side, 'outside the cloud, amazed.'[49] The figure of Ezekiel is a particularly dramatic rendering of religious ecstasy, a gold-haloed old man leaning forwards, 'palms level with his ears'[50] in what for a moment looks like a transfigured reminder of a child's gesture of contempt. There are also a river god and multicoloured fish. But the eye wanders inevitably back to the figure of Christ; although this is Ezekiel's vision, as R.F. Hoddinott says in his lustrously illustrated book on early Byzantine churches, the spirit is entirely New Testament. 'His expression of an understanding seemingly beyond human comprehension combines a sublime detachment from the world of material strife and temptation with an infinite compassion.'[51]

There are many other churches, mosaics, and wall-paintings in Thessaloniki. There are, for instance, the mosaic martyrs, victoriously robed, hands outspread, completely convinced, who stare out from the dome of the Rotunda. Hoddinott describes their golden background,

against which [in an estimated 36 million tesserae] golden pillars, arches, friezes and cupolas gleam and sparkle with the light of many coloured jewels; rich curtains and the bright plumage of birds adding further exotic touches. It is Oriental rather than Occidental splendour, and, yet, with all the magnificence, there is a restraint which indicates an Orient that has felt the influence of Hellenism.[52]

From the fifteenth century, however, Turkish culture began to stamp its presence on the city. Most churches became mosques, and the White Tower was rebuilt to guard the sea approaches. The Tower's name results, it is said, from a deft piece of actual as well as metaphorical whitewashing designed to break its reputation as 'The Bloody Tower' following the execution of rebel janissaries there in 1826. (A later event which happened nearby was the murder, during the Civil War, of the CBS correspondent George Polk. His body was found, trussed and shot through the head, in Saloniki Bay not far from the Tower on 16 May 1948. Exactly who killed Polk and why was an issue which divided Greek society for many years afterwards and has never been entirely satisfactorily resolved.[53])

From the sixteenth century it was, however, Jewish rather than Christian or Turkish culture which contributed most to the distinctive atmosphere of Saloniki. There had been Jews in the city since Roman times (the Book of Acts takes St Paul to 'Thessalonica, where there is a synagogue of the Jews'), but it was after the mass expulsion of unconverted Jews from Spain by Ferdinand and Isabella in 1492 that numbers grew rapidly until they made up between a third and a half of the population. The Sephardic Jews continued to speak Ladino, based on the medieval Castilian Spanish of their ancestors (but written in Hebrew characters), and dressed distinctively, the men in 'dark dresses and turbans', the women with their hair 'tied up in long, caterpillar-like green silk bags, three feet in length' according to Edward Lear.[54] While in the 1160s Rabbi Benjamin of Tudela had reported that in Thessaloniki 'the Jews are oppressed, and live by silk-weaving',[55] from the sixteenth century their numbers had afforded them unusual freedoms. When David Ben-Gurion, later the first Prime Minister of Israel, arrived in the city as a student in 1911, he was amazed by the breadth of opportunity available to Jews.

Unlike Plonsk [his birthplace, in present-day Poland], which was a gentile city with Jewish quarters, Salonika seemed in many ways to be a wholly Jewish city. There were lots of Jewish manual labourers and Jews in other occupations which, in Plonsk as in most cities of the Diaspora, were always associated with non-Jews. Only in Palestine had I seen Jews with picks and shovels. Yet here I was in Salonika, in the Diaspora, and all around me were Jews who worked with their hands. Almost all the stevedores and other port workers in this very important harbour town were Jews.[56]

Jews in Thessaloniki, reported H.G. Dwight for the *National Geographic* in 1916, 'hold their heads up as do their co-religionists in no other city in Europe – down to the very boatmen in the harbour.'[57] But there were signs of bad times to come. Ten years later, Israel Cohen reported for the *Jewish Chronicle* on the damage sustained by the Jewish community following the fire of 1917 and the massive influx of Greek refugees following the compulsory exchange of Greek and Turkish populations in 1922. Rebuilding after the fire was slow and, Cohen's informants said, directed more to the needs of Greeks than of Jews. In 1926 'the once-famous Ghetto' was still a mass of charred ruins, 'a sombre succession of collapsed walls, battered buildings, mounds of bricks and heaps of rubbish and rubble.'[58] With the arrival of the refugees, Jewish power and influence in the city began to decline; the Jews became a minority, their 80,000 remaining steady while according to one count the population of Thessaloniki jumped from 190,000 to 500,000 in a matter of months. 'Anti-semitism', Cohen was told, 'is slowly but surely advancing here.' The final, much more terrible blow came less than twenty years later when the Germans deported at least 50,000 of the Jews of Thessaloniki to Auschwitz.

MOUNT ATHOS

Athos, the Holy Mountain, feels like a walled world – a paradise or a prison. Many of the monasteries have the external appearance of a towered and turreted fortress, even, at the Great Lavra for example, a fortress-town with the church and cruciform refectory well within the protecting walls. Originally (the monasteries date mostly from between the tenth and fourteenth centuries) there was a practical need for such precautions owing to the frequent raids of Arab pirates. Cannon were to be seen on monastery walls until the Turks removed them in the 1820s. In the absence of artillery, today the Holy Mountain is protected from the outside world by complicated admission procedures, semi-independence from the state including tax exemptions, rigid monastic discipline, uncompromising attitudes towards the non-Orthodox, and a ban on women.

Such separateness has attracted the sort of monks encountered by Sir Paul Rycaut, the Levant Company's consul in Smyrna during the reign of Charles II: 'for the most part good simple men of godly lives, given greatly to devotion and acts of mortification', not only 'real and moral good men, but such also as are something touched with the spirit of God.'[59] It is unreasonable to expect, however, that monks in every monastery and every period can fulfil such expectations.

No doubt equally unreasonable, if entertaining, is Edward Lear's bout of alliteration at the expense of 'these muttering, miserable, mutton-hating, man-avoiding, misogynic, morose, & merriment-marring, monotoning, many-mule-making, mocking, mournful, minced-fish & marmalade masticating Monx. Poor old pigs!'[60] The American Ralph Harper, an Anglican priest, was more deeply wounded by what he experienced on Athos in 1985. A man of liberal views, interested in existentialism and Buddhism as well as Christianity, he enjoyed good-natured hospitality at some of the religious houses, but was saddened and angered by what happened when he tried to attend services at Philotheou and Grigoriou. At Philotheou, when he entered the church at daybreak, 'Monks converged on me and hissed, "No! Out!".' An American Orthodox monk explained to Harper before breakfast that he had been excluded because 'you are a heretic, and do not have the Apostolic Succession.' At Grigoriou he was able to watch a service through bars; he thought of prisons, physical and mental.[61]

Harper attributes his treatment to a tightening of discipline in recent years at Athos, with many houses which used to be idiorrhythmic (loose communities meeting chiefly for worship) becoming cenobitic (close communities under the rule of an abbot). Certainly the earlier travellers, amongst whom the best known are Hon. Robert Curzon in the 1830s and Robert Byron in the 1920s, did not report similar encounters. But there have always been tensions between Athos and the outsider. It is so Orthodox, so strict, so male, that many have been moved to mirth, complaint, or mystification, if not always to reactions as extreme as that of General Pangalos, briefly republican dictator of Greece in 1926, who suggested that the monasteries should be converted into casinos.

An aspect of Athos which has forcibly struck those admitted from the world is the exclusion of women. 'Tell me,' wailed the civil governor seconded from Paris to Karyes, where he received Robert Byron, 'Is there a woman in the world? Shall I ever dance again?'[62] Ninety years earlier Robert Curzon met a monk with no memory of women, let alone Paris. A 'magnificent-looking man of thirty or thirty-five

years of age, with large eyes and long black hair and beard'
who worked on an outlying farm of the (idiorhythmic)
monastery of Xeropotamou, he had lost his family in a
massacre – he no longer knew exactly where – and early been
enrolled at the monastery school.

> He did not remember his mother, and did not seem quite
> sure that he ever had one; he had never seen a woman,
> nor had he any idea of what sort of things women were,
> or what they looked like. He asked me whether they
> resembled the pictures of the Panagia, the Holy Virgin,
> which hang in every church. Now, those who are con-
> versant with the peculiar conventional representations of
> the Blessed Virgin in the pictures of the Greek Church,
> which are all exactly alike, stiff, hard, and dry, without
> any appearance of life or emotion, will agree with me
> that they do not afford a very favourable idea of the grace
> or beauty of the fair sex; and that there was a difference
> of appearance between black women, Circassians, and
> those of other nations, which was, however, difficult to
> describe to one who had never seen a lady of any race.
> He listened with great interest while I told him that all
> women were not exactly like the pictures he had seen,
> and that they differed considerably one from another, in
> appearance, manners, and understanding; but I did not
> think it charitable to carry on the conversation farther,
> although the poor monk seemed to have a strong inclina-
> tion to know more of that interesting race of beings from
> whose society he had been so entirely debarred.[63]

Not only women but all female creatures were (and are)
forbidden on the Holy Mountain. As one Dr Hunt reported
in the early years of the nineteenth century, this 'whimsical
regulation' meant that all dairy products had to be imported
to the peninsula from neighbouring Thasos, Lemnos, or
Macedonia.[64] But Curzon, sceptical as ever, and victim in his
time to many a bedbug and flea, discovered that the law of
gender exclusion 'is infringed by certain small and active
creatures who have the audacity to bring their wives and large
families within the very precincts of the monastery.'[65]

Food, like cohabiting bugs, was of immediate practical importance to visitors exhausted from hard journeys between monasteries and disoriented by the change from their daily rhythms. But meals frequently left them as unsettled as when they arrived. If we can believe Robert Byron, who has a gift for humorous exaggeration, his meal at the monastery of Grigoriou began with 'a disintegrated and nameless fish' (meat is forbidden the monks) and continued with cod 'salted after it had rotted in the summer sun', macaroni 'embalmed in the juice of goats' udders curdled to a shrill sourness; water-melon, ghastly pink like some spongy segment of a body delved from the intestines of a dog-fish; and accompanying all, like a rasping bassoon in a band of village oboes, thick resinated wine tasting of pine-needles and reducing the human mouth to the texture of a cat's.'[66]

Robert Curzon's predicament at the Great Lavra had been more awkward. With the growing horror of the traditional Briton offered a hospitable frog's leg or sheep's eyeball, he watched as the kindly abbot prepared him a special breakfast with his own hands.

'This,' said he, producing a shallow basin half-full of a white paste, 'is the principal and most savoury part of this famous dish; it is composed of cloves of garlic, pounded down, with a certain quantity of sugar. With it I will now mix the oil in just proportions, some shreds of fine cheese (it seemed to be of the white acid kind, which resembles what is called caccia cavallo in the south of Italy, and which almost takes the skin off your fingers, I believe) and sundry other nice little condiments, and now it is completed!'

Presumably the cheese was *feta*. Tension mounted, with the guest wondering 'Who could have expected so dreadful a martyrdom as this?' But the only chance of seeing what he had come to see was to eat up.

'Now,' said the agoumenos [abbot], crumbling some bread into it with his large and somewhat dirty hands, 'this is a dish for an emperor! Eat, my friend, my

much-respected guest; do not be shy. Eat; and when you
have finished the bowl you shall go into the library and
anywhere else you like; but you shall go nowhere till
I have had the pleasure of seeing you do justice to this
delicious food, which, I can assure you, you will not
meet with everywhere.'

Improvising desperately, Curzon claimed that, sadly, this was
a fast-day for Englishmen. The abbot admired the scruples of
the 'excellent and virtuous young man.' But, he was delighted
to explain, 'to travellers all such vows are set aside.' The
visitor was obliged to take a gulp, 'the recollection of which
still makes me tremble.' But then, with true Jeevesian timing
and aplomb, his servant intervened: 'he said "that English
gentlemen never ate such rich dishes for breakfast, from
religious feelings, he believed; but he requested that it might
be put by, and he was sure I should like it very much later
in the day".' Saved, Curzon was allowed to head for the
library and heard no more of the dreaded dish.[67]

Yet it was also at the Great Lavra that in 1677 John Covel,
afterwards Master of Christ's College, Cambridge, had set
to and enjoyed meals of 'excellent fish (severall ways), oyl,
salet, beanes, hortechockes, beets, chees, onions, garlick,
olives, caveor, Pyes of herbs' and 'exquisite' oranges. There
was 'good wine (a sort of small claret), and we alwayes
drank most plentifully.' In fact, according to Covel, 'He is
no Greek that cannot drink 20 or 30 plump glasses at a
setting.'[68] Perhaps he was either less fastidious or more
drunk than his later compatriots.

Most travellers hardy enough to penetrate monastic Athos
before this century were determined to take back something
more substantial than stories about food and ignorant or
holy monks. They came questing for manuscripts and early
books, which they felt justified in taking away as gifts,
bargain purchases, or loot, on the – sometimes convincing –
grounds that the monks took no interest in their contents
or their preservation. Curzon saw himself only half ruefully
as 'a sort of biblical knight-errant' who 'had entered on
the perilous adventure of Mount Athos to rescue from the
thraldom of ignorant monks those fair vellum volumes, with

their bright illuminations and velvet dresses and jewelled clasps, which for so many centuries had lain imprisoned in their dark monastic dungeons.'[69] He went about his business honourably in the main, negotiating purchases where the fathers had some little experience of bargaining, donating to church funds where they had none. Nevertheless it is difficult not to think of Lord Elgin, especially since it was again the British Museum (now British Library) collections which were later enriched by the contents of Curzon's bulging saddlebags.

Robert Byron, not searching for books but for his beloved Byzantium, saw more in the churches than many outsiders. Amid frescoes in the afternoons, 'half stupefied with the heat, the incense, and the midday meal,'

> the beholder develops an unconscious familiarity with the different cycles of iconography that prevail upon the Mountain: the alert ass of the Passion in this arch; the oxen lowing to the new-born Christ in that; in the south transept, geometric rays of Christ transfigured, distorting to the curve of the terminal vault; opposite, in the north, Christ treading delicately the grave-tops of purgatory; over the entrance-door, the Virgin stretched in the rigid pallor of her assumption, Christ gathering to himself her soul in the guise of a little child; behind the painted wooden crucifix that surmounts the *eiconostasis*, itself so deeply and minutely carved as to resemble some giant creepered wall petrified to gold, glimpses of Pentecost and the Ascension; they all become imprinted on the mind; till, with any change, the attention, hitherto subconscious, is suddenly aroused.[70]

More spectacular, like a living fresco, was the ceremony of the Elevation of the Cross which Robert Byron saw at Xeropotamou, involving an unusually large (thirteen-inch) fragment of the cross.

> Within the corona, itself a ring of flames, the central chandelier rose in a mountain of light. Beneath stood a stool, caparisoned in brocade. And on it, at this moment, borne aloft from out the *eiconostasis*, was placed the

casket containing the Cross. From his throne, at the back of which I stood, stepped a bishop in a full red cope falling in folds from his shoulders and fastened at the ankles. From his head streamed the black veil which all the monks were wearing. In his hand was his staff, with the twin serpents' heads of ivory. There joined him two deacons in copes of green and gold; and two others in black. All but he carried candles. And, forming a circle, they began to pace slowly round the relic, while the singing swelled from soft accompaniment to the attack. Rhythm of chant and paces, that intrinsic rhythm independent of 'time,' caught the beholders from their human frames. The voices were no longer nasal. Once and again, a hundred and a thousand times, the *Kyrie eleison*, in limitless plurality, beginning deep and hushed, mounted the scale with a presage of impending triumph – to die off and begin again.[71]

6

THE AEGEAN ISLANDS

Tenos – Syros – Mykonos – Delos – Naxos – Paros – Antiparos –
Santorini – Chios – Lesbos – Skyros

'Good God, Ellen, the Grecian Archipelago! Cant you see it
in your mind's eye, a group of exquisite islands in a turquoise
setting? Ugh! Cold, storm, sleety grey, pitching & roll-
ing, misery, headaches, horrors of universal belchings!'[1] So
Bernard Shaw wrote to Ellen Terry, safe on dry land among
the theatres of London, when he crossed the Aegean during
a Mediterranean cruise in October 1899. The moods of
the Aegean (combined with donkey problems) had even as
passionate a Graecophile as Patrick White, delayed on
Santorini, vowing an end to island-hopping and declaring
that 'Greece is only for Greeks and masochists.'[2]

From the Bronze Age to the early nineteenth century piracy
was an even greater hazard than storms. The corsairs preyed
on passing shipping from innumerable creeks and coves, and
dominated many of the smaller islands as does the fierce pirate-
chief Lambro in the Second and Third Cantos of Byron's *Don
Juan*. Nevertheless, Byron's contemporaries were already
discovering the delights of 'exquisite islands in a turquoise
setting', and it is on the pirate isle itself, on whose 'breaker-
beaten coast' the young Juan is shipwrecked, that Byron
grants his hero an idyll beyond the dreams of modern sun-
seekers. Lambro's daughter, Haidée (from a Greek word for
'sigh') finds him on the beach and, in a nearby cave, nurses
him back to health. Fortified by 'eggs, fruit, coffee, bread,
fish, honey,/With Scio [Chios] wine, and all for love, not
money,' Juan is soon well enough to learn some Greek from
his hostess and, naturally, to become her lover. When not

thus engaged he can, like modern visitors to Cycladic beaches, refresh himself with a dip; but 'Juan, after bathing in the sea, came always back to coffee and Haidée.'[3]

Byron laughs tolerantly at young love, but also envies it. While their creator was still smarting from the scandal of his divorce from Annabella Milbanke, the lovers are able to wander together, undistracted by otherwhere and otherwhen, in the purple twilight of the island summer.

> They looked up to the sky, whose floating glow
> Spread like a rosy ocean, vast and bright.
> They gazed upon the glittering sea below,
> Whence the broad moon rose circling into sight.
> They heard the wave's splash and the wind so low,
> And saw each other's dark eyes darting light
> Into each other, and beholding this,
> Their lips drew near and clung into a kiss.[4]

Once Haidée's father is safely out of the way, plundering some vessels bound for Chios, the idyll becomes a non-stop party. It is at this party that the song about 'The Isles of Greece', once so much anthologized, is sung to the revellers by a travelling bard. But the song laments the modern failure to emulate the courage of the heroes of Marathon and the intensity of 'burning Sappho'; the singer is himself unheroically willing to provide suitable songs for patrons of any political persuasion so long as the price is right; and the idyll is about to come to an ugly end. Lambro returns and surprizes the lovers together. Juan is cut down and bundled off to be sold as a slave in Constantinople (the beginning of a series of more cynical affaires). Haidée dies, after a few days, of shock and fever.

In the 1920s the poet's distant relation, Robert Byron, associated the sea and its isles with a different longing from that of Juan and Haidée. For him this is the essential home of a people in quest of the divine.

> As the sapphire and the aquamarine from the turquoise, so differ the waters of the Aegean from the flat blue of the Mediterranean whole. Sail from Italy or Egypt. And

as the rose-tinted shores of islands and promontories rise incarnate from the sea, a door shuts the world behind. Earth's emotion diffuses a new essence. Who are we to cut the water and cleave the air with prow and funnel?

Those who sit at home with their anthologies, their Homers and Byrons, have long grown impatient of the hackneyed eulogy. Travellers, on the other hand, know that the poet has not lived who can hackney the Greek sea itself. How lies it apart? What magnet of our stifled love holds this blue, these tawny cliffs and always the mountains framing the distance? Why does the breeze blow with a scent of baking herbs which the misty shores echo in their colours? What is this element, hybrid of air and water, physical as a kiss, with which the night enfolds us? The islands float past, forming and reforming in good-bye, gleaming golden white against the sharp blues, or veiled in the odorous haze of evening.[5]

TENOS

Tenos was for centuries a poor, rather bleak place. As Byzantine power declined in the late Middle Ages, pirate raids became ever more frequent and ever more successful. The ruling Venetian family, the Ghisi, built the fortified Exombourgo on a mountain 1800 feet high and with three steep sides, still difficult of access. The Teniots could, if the dreaded ships were sighted in time, flee to join their rulers in Exombourgo in time of peril, but this did not prevent the harrying of coastal and other settlements. In 1700 Joseph Pitton de Tournefort, botanist to Louis XIV, found fine plants to study here, but little to eat: 'We were reduced to make pottage with Sea-Snails'.

It was the only Ragou this Island supply'd us with; for we had neither Nets, nor Hooks for fishing; and the Goat-herds taking us for Banditti, durst not come near us, tho our sailors, who knew not where to look for fresh Water, had display'd all the white Rags they could muster up, as a Token that we were peaceable Folks.[6]

Relief from such 'sorry fare' came on Ikaria, where Tournefort and his companions were able to feast on red partridges 'of a wonderful beauty', tough but, by comparison with sea-snails, 'as delicious as those of *Perigord*.'[6]

The fortunes of Tenos revived thanks to an event which, according to different viewpoints, was either providential or suspiciously convenient. In 1822, with the War of Independence in its first fraught year and Greeks in need of all possible encouragement, a certain Sister Pelagia was led by a dream to the place of concealment of a miraculous icon of the Virgin. The grand church of the Panagia Evangelistria was built on the site of the discovery; after the war, a degree of prosperity came to Tenos with the great numbers of pilgrims who, particularly on 15 August, the feast of the Assumption of the Virgin, come to seek aid through the icon. James Theodore Bent, the Victorian explorer, archaeologist, and early anthropologist, arrived outside the church on the eve of the festival in 1884:

> It was a fine starry night, and the thousands of little oil lamps which decorated the church and its steeple rivalled the lights of the celestial hemisphere in their twinklings. Patience, assisted now and again by an ingenious push, enabled us to get inside and witness the weird sights in the church.[7]

Bent found many people 'grovelling on their knees' in the main body of the church and crowds with 'their beds, their carpets, and their cooking utensils' in the gallery. Penetrating the stifling but especially sacred crypt-like lower church he came across

> three blind men, holding on to one another, groaning and striking their breasts; behind them was a sinister form, which barked, as it were, not able to speak, and wriggled at my feet like a fish. Further on was a poor girl, in the last stage of consumption, leaning for support on her sister . . . An old man on all fours hindered our progress; and close to him a madman stood, still for the time being, but ominously so. A damsel stretched

on the knee of her mother was relating, like Ophelia, in subdued and mysterious voice, some secret of her distraught brain, whilst her mother offered up a never-ceasing prayer to the all-healing Madonna for the recovery of her child's intellect.[8]

Early the following morning

The sea of men rolled beneath me, for I had secured a seat for the occasion on a balcony; and as it went past it looked like a carpet sparkling with every colour – gold-embroidered tunics, snow-white *fustanellas*, gorgeously embroidered skirts and vests from Asia sparkling with gold and silver coins, rich furs, and the more humble green and blue dresses of the islanders, mingled with a tinge of gaudy parasols and tall hats from the more civilized Athens. It was a sight to rivet and dazzle one.

"Ερχεται, 'ερχεται!' (It comes!) was heard on all sides in a dull murmur; the procession was coming, and the crowd solemnly divided so as to make a passage for the priests. On the steps of the sanctuary the priests were marshalled, in rich vestments, carrying banners round the holy εικων; then as a breath of wind disturbs a pool so did the advent of the procession disturb the almost breathless crowd below. Everyone made the sign of the cross and lowered his head in silence as it passed; and then when it was gone the murmur and the noise again increased – the sacred ceremony was over.[9]

Mussolini's Italy could scarcely have chosen a more provocative action than to torpedo the cruiser *Elli* in Tenos harbour on the day of the festival, 15 August 1940. Hostilities did not actually break out until the end of October, but the determination which the Greeks would show in repelling the Italian invasion and resisting the German occupation was immediately made manifest. Lawrence Durrell reached Tenos an hour after the attack:

I saw a new expression on the Greek countenance – a silent, enraged resolution which boded ill for the enemy.

The whole town had been stirred like a beehive, and it buzzed with indignant life. In the harbour, the divers were busy about the patch of oil, and a corvette had appeared to help. Strangely, there was no weeping, no public lamentation, as there is so often. The uncanny silence showed me that the weight of this mortal insult went right to the depths of the Greek heart and could only be expunged now by war.[10]

SYROS

On Syros there was no sleep for Joseph Pitton de Tournefort, 'not in the night-time, because of the universal Din made by the Hand-mills each Man works at to grind his Corn; nor in the day-time, because of the Rumbling made by the Wheels for spinning of Cotton.'[11] The royal botanist was, however, positively delighted to be disturbed by such worthy, such 'laborious' people, particularly no doubt because almost all of them were Roman Catholics with a special relationship with France. In 1537, when the Turks took Syros, François I succeeded in negotiating the right to protect Catholic religious institutions. Dealing with 'the Turk' excited self-righteous anger among other European powers, but was of real benefit to the islanders who were left mostly to themselves by their conquerors.

But Syros became famous as a shipping centre not through French assistance or native industriousness but because of the commercial skills of the thousands of refugees from the Turkish devastation of Chios and Psara who arrived in the early 1820s. The port of Ermoupoli ('the town of Hermes', patron of trade) was built by the Orthodox newcomers while Catholics continued to occupy the poorer upper town of Ano Syros with its many convents. Ermoupoli became a port of call on many Mediterranean routes, and as such often gave mid-nineteenth-century travellers their first taste of the Levant. Herman Melville arrived here on 2 December 1856 *en route* for Constantinople. He had earlier visited northern Europe and, more hazardously, sailed the Pacific in the whaling voyages which had nourished *Moby Dick*, but Syros was something new and exotic. The exotic becomes rather mannered in his later poem where eastern figures lounge 'with gold-shot eyes,/Sunning themselves as leopards may.'[12] Fortunately, however, a journal entry preserves his original excitement:

> Went ashore. New & old Town. Animated appearance of the quay. Take all the actors of operas in a night from the theaters of London, & set them to work in their fancy dresses, weighing bales, counting cod-fish, sitting at tables in the dock, smoking, sauntering, – sitting in boats &c – picking up rags, carrying water casks, bemired &c – will give some notion of Greek port. Picturesqueness of the whole. Variety of it. Greek trousers, sort of cross between petticoat & pantaloons. Some with white petticoats and embroidered jackets. Fine forms, noble faces. Mustache &c. – Went to Old Town. From the water looks like colossal sugarloaf. White houses. Divided from new town by open lots. Climbed up. Complete warren of stone houses or rather huts, built without the least plan. Zig-zag. Little courts in front of each, sometimes overhead, crossing the track. Paved with stone, roofs flat and m'cadamized.[13]

Melville moved on to Constantinople, but returned to Syros in order to take ship for Egypt and the Holy Land. Again he reflected on the operatic quality of life in Ermoupoli, but this time he sounds more dubious about its value:

> Went ashore to renew my impressions of the previous visit. The Greek, of any class, seems a natural dandy. His dress, though a laborer, is that of a gentleman of leisure. This flowing & graceful costume, with so much of pure ornament about it & so little fitted for labor, must needs have been devised in some Golden Age. But surviving in the present, is most picturesquely out of keeping with the utilities.[14]

Appropriately costumed or not, the Greeks of Ermoupouli were in a position to attract commerce. But the opening of the Corinth Canal in 1893 led to Piraeus rapidly supplanting Ermoupoli as a commercial port and it became, until the growth of the tourist industry at least, as purely picturesque as it looked.

MYKONOS

Mykonos has become one of the most popular tourist destinations in Greece, an island where large numbers of air-travellers seek to fulfil the longing of Shirley Valentine, in Willy Russell's play, for 'just two weeks of sun, sand, taramasalata an' whatever else takes our fancy.'[15] It is difficult now to imagine the poor, bare isle which the Venetian Senate put up for auction in June 1391.

> Notice is given to the inhabitants of Crete, of Coron, and of Modon, Venetians, allies or subjects, that in the month of December, in Venice, the islands of Tenos and Mykonos will be sold to the highest bidder; the agreed sum will be payable over a period of ten years.[16]

No bids were recorded, and the Venetians were forced to appoint a succession of governors who, to survive, made the island poorer by their extortion. A second attempt to dispose of the dubious assets had the same lack of success in the mid-fifteenth century. When Venice lost Mykonos to the Turks in 1540 it was a military rather than a material set-back.

When Lawrence Durrell first knew Mykonos, in 1940, it was in many ways more like the unsellable Venetian outpost than the much-sold island he returned to in 1976. But his love even for Mykonos Town was untarnished, because 'There is nothing quite like this extraordinary cubist village, with its flittering, dancing shadows, and its flaring nightmare of whiteness', the labyrinth of curling streets 'hazing-in all sense of direction until one surrenders to the knowledge that one is irremediably lost in a village hardly bigger than Hampstead.'[17]

On a more mystic note, Durrell claims that no amount

of tourist chatter and litter can forestall the island's effect on strangers:

> Its exemplary purity of tone and line will hush them, its island wind alarm their sleep, its black seascape nudge their nerves with the premonition of things as yet unformed and unformulated in their inner natures; perhaps the very things they have come here to experience.[18]

Shirley Valentine has a taste for plainer language, but her island has something of the effect which Durrell describes. She starts as an unfulfilled Liverpool housewife of forty-two who addresses the kitchen wall since no one else will listen. Then she escapes, not daring to tell her hidebound husband that she is leaving, to pursue her dreams on a Greek island. In the play, Russell does not specify the island beyond one brief mention of a ticket for 'Cor'[fu], but his 1989 screen adaptation was filmed on Mykonos. Shirley begins to rediscover her own identity partly thanks to the mealtime conversation at her hotel. Dougie and Jeanette from Manchester tell her all about 'the price of the new extension, the colour of the microwave an' the contents of the Hoover' before the first course.

> It's a good job it wasn't soup – I would've put me head in it an' drowned meself. It wasn't until we got to the main course that they even acknowledged we were in Greece. And then I wish they hadn't bothered. Everything was wrong – the sun was too hot for them, the sea was too wet for them, Greece too Greek for them. They were that type, y'know, if they'd been at the last supper they would have asked for chips.[19]

Shirley seethes with sympathy for the Greek waiter who must endure these complaints, explodes at the entire room with a defence of Greeks who were 'buildin' roads an' cities an' temples' when the English were 'runnin' round in loincloths an' ploughin' up the earth with the arse bone of a giraffe' and later lets off a culinary bombshell on the unsuspecting Jeanette. Dougie wants to know what he is eating:

> 'Hey mate. What is this?' An' he points to his plate. The waiter says to him, 'Et ees calamares Sir.' 'Yeh but what I'm askin' y',' Dougie says, 'What I'm askin' y', is what is it?' 'Erm . . . eet's calamares, sir, eet's er a type of er . . . feesh.' Well Dougie looks at his plate an' he's not convinced. 'It don't look much like fish to me,' he says. 'My wife's got a very delicate stomach. She's very particular about what she eats. Are you sure this is fish?'

The waiter reassuringly insists. Shirley, however, wants to appear more sociable after her outburst:

> Well, what I said was, 'The squid's very nice, isn't it?' The pair of them stopped eatin' an' looked at me. 'Pardon me?' Jeanette said. 'The squid,' I said, pointin' to her plate. 'The squid, the octopus, it's quite nice really isn' . . . ' Well it was funny the way Jeanette fainted. Y' know sort of in slow motion.[20]

Shirley's relationships with islanders are more successful. Costas, from the seaside taverna, takes her out in his boat, makes love to her and, more importantly, treats her as an attractive woman and an attractive human being. Costas and the relaxed atmosphere of life on the island give back to Shirley her sense of identity, so that when in the film her husband finally arrives to try to bring her home she can declare, from her shoreside table, 'Hello. I used to be the mother. I used to be your wife. But now, I'm Shirley Valentine again. Would you like to join me for a drink?'[21]

DELOS

> Mount Cynthos is an ugly, bare, sugar-loaf mound, rising about three hundred and fifty feet above the sea-level in the centre of the island, affording a scanty pasturage for goats; the rest of the island is tolerably

fertile, and is let to a few shepherds. . . . There are
a few huts scattered about and a wooden shanty, where
two old men live to guard the ruins from the descent
of European pirates, who will go there in yachts and
steal what they can find. All around stretches a vast
sea of ruins, recalling Pompeii in extent and complete
annihilation; you wander through houses with mosaic
pavements, pillared halls with cisterns below, and the
richness of marble wherever you turn is most striking,
and in the brilliant sunlight almost dazzling. Much of
the lychnites vein from Mount Marpessa of Paros has
found its way here.[22]

The anxiety of James Theodore Bent about 'European pirates'
was well founded. Greeks seeking good marble for building
on nearby islands did some damage to the ancient buildings,
but it was outsiders who arrived with the manpower to
render this place, desolate for the most part since its sacking
by Rome's enemy Mithridates of Pontus in 88 BC, even
more so.

The plunder began in earnest in the seventeenth century,
when the grandees of England, France, and Venice desired
their agents to furnish them with collections of classical
sculpture. In 1625 Sir Thomas Roe, British Ambassador in
Constantinople, was able to report some promising information to his patron the Duke of Buckingham. Apparently the
Patriarch of Constantinople had told Roe about 'Delphos'
(Apollo's sacred places Delos and Delphi were habitually
confused), 'a small, despised, uninhabited island, in the Arches
[Archipelago], a place anciently esteemed sacred, the burial
of all the Greeks, as yet unbroken; where, he tells me, are
like to be found many rare things . . . they may take without
trouble or prohibition whatsoever they please, if any man
of judgment to make the choice.'[23] Sir Kenelm Digby put
this advice into practice when he was privateering in the
Mediterranean three years later. Digby was a colourful parti-
cipant in English cultural and political life from the 1620s
to the 1660s, a diplomat, author, alchemist, religious contro-
versialist, and propounder of the doubtful claims of his
wound-curing 'Powder of Sympathy'. His successes against

Venetian ships were applauded at home, but had diplomatic ramifications and threatened the livelihood of Levant merchants. Pillaging Delos seemed a simpler undertaking, as Digby explains in his *Journal*:

> I went with most of my shippes to Delphos, a desert iland, where staying till the rest were readie, because idlenesse should not fixe their mindes upon any untoward fansies (as is usuall among seamen), and together to avayle myselfe of the conveniencie of carrying away some antiquities there, I busied them in rolling of stones downe to the sea side, which they did with such eagernesse as though it had been the earnestest businesse that they came out for, and they mastered prodigious massie weightes; but one stone, the greatest and fairest of all, containing 4 statues, they gave over after they had bin, 300 men, a whole day about it. . . . But the next day I contrived a way with mastes of shippes and another shippe to ride overagainst it, that brought it downe with much ease and speede.[24]

Digby also reports on the huge statue of Apollo, already 'broken in two peeces about the wast' which 'weigheth att least 30 tonnes.' It is much worn but 'the yieldinges of the flesh and the muscular partes are visible, so that it is still a brave noble piece, and hath by divers been attempted to be carried away, but they have all failed in it.' Some time later in the century an anonymous adventurer, said to be either English or Venetian, again tried to remove the colossal statue. Failing in this attempt, 'he brake off its head, arms, and feet, and carried them with him.'[25] (Part of a hand and the toes of one foot are now in the British Museum, while the huge base and fragments of torso remain on the site.)

But the denuding of Delos (halted in Bent's time before it became entirely naked) has made it all the more poetically ancient. Survivors such as the five archaic lions take on a significance which they must surely have lacked among the standing buildings and the grander statues. They contribute, now, to the atmosphere suggested in Constantine Trypanis' poem 'Delos', an atmosphere of 'Hard silence sliding down

marble flutes,/Stone silence, locking the lion's jaws.'[26]
Visitors today may, of course, find such quiet hard to come
by. Lawrence Durrell took the precaution of illegally camping
on the island, where he and his wife swam by moonlight,
listened to the slither of snakes and lizards, and prowled
among the ruins.

> There was a hole in the barbed wire which gave access
> to some proconsular villa, built by some long dead
> Roman magistrate. The tessellated floor had a fish or
> dolphin design, I don't remember which now; but the
> salt and dust had dried over it and obliterated it. At any
> rate (we did not need the torches we had brought; you
> could have read a Greek newspaper by the moon's light),
> I filled a pail with seawater and swished it over the floor
> and suddenly the whole design printed itself like a
> photograph does in a developing-tray. I still remember
> the way the eyes emerged, even though I do not recall
> if they were dolphin's or fish's. Fish, I think.[27]

In fact Durrell was looking at the bulging eyes of the leaping
dolphins, probably Hellenistic rather than Roman, which gave
their name to the House of the Dolphins.

Patrick White was on Delos in May 1958. His daylight
impressions make a suitable companion-piece for Durrell's
moonlit Delos. On 15 May he wrote to Gwen and David
Moore:

> A long rocky barren island covered with yellow grass and
> thistles, but at the same time masses of pink convolvulus,
> purple statice, yellow sea-poppies and the common field
> red, as well as a little flower resembling the gentian.
> The air full of a sound of what could have been deafening
> larks. Cisterns full of green water and enormous, green,
> coupling frogs. Crimson dragonflies above the water,
> intent on the same game. And all through it, the remains
> of what must have been a great city, columns, temples,
> mosaics (fabulously beautiful ones that one wants at
> once for a house of one's own), with down by the sea,
> propped up against stones, the marble torso of a giant

Apollo, worn down by the weather to a texture of cuttlefish.[28]

NAXOS

In 1204 a group of western European or 'Latin' knights, supposedly participating in the Fourth Crusade, seized Constantinople and partitioned its empire. The Cyclades fell to Venice, but the Republic preferred to delegate its power in the area to private citizens on condition that they did not work against Venetian interests. A highly suitable candidate presented himself in Marco Sanudo, a bold adventurer but also the nephew of Doge Enrico Dandolo. Sanudo in turn established his nominees as lords of some islands, but reserved for the capital of his new Duchy of the Archipelago the large and fertile Naxos, associated since antiquity with Dionysos and the fruits of the earth. (It was thanks to Dionysos, the French traveller Thévenot was told in the early 1660s, that 'the inhabitants of Nixia are so great Drunkards.' The god had first come to the island in order to rescue and marry Ariadne, abandoned by that 'perfidious wretch Theseus'.)[29]

Sanudo and his followers took possession of the island after a brisk five-week siege. The victorious new Duke then embarked on an ambitious building programme. In the town of Naxos he built the partly surviving stout citadel, the cathedral, and the ramparts. In the countryside the towers of the Italian landowners bore witness to their domination. But Sanudo was careful not to offend Greek sensibilities too far; himself a Catholic, he nevertheless handled the Orthodox clergy tactfully.

Francesco III Crispi, 'the Mad Duke of Naxos', was a more passionate man than Marco. His story is told by the great historian of the Latins in the Levant, William Miller, drawing on the *Diarii* of Marino Sanudo or Sanuto, of the earlier ducal family. On 15 August 1510, Francesco, recently released from protective custody by the Venetians, was with his wife Taddea Loredano:

Having inveigled the duchess to his side 'by songs, kisses, and caresses,' he seized his sword and tried to slay her.

The terrified woman fled, just as she was, in her night-dress, out of the ducal palace, and took refuge in the house of her aunt, Lucrezia Loredano, Lady of Nio [Ios]. Thither, in the night of Saturday, August 17, her husband pursued her; he burst open the doors, and entered the bedroom, where he found the Lady of Nio and her daughter-in-law, to whom he gave three severe blows each. Meanwhile, on hearing the noise, the duchess had hidden under a wash-tub; a slave betrayed her hiding-place, and the duke struck her over the head with his sword. In the attempt to parry the blow, she seized the blade in her hands, and fell fainting to the ground, when her miserable assailant gave her a thrust in the stomach. She lived the rest of the night and the next day, while the duke fled to his garden, whence he was induced by the citizens to return to the palace.[30]

Next, back at the palace, Francesco attempted to stab his son Giovanni, who escaped the duchess's fate only by jumping from a balcony. The Naxiots subsequently suceeded in removing their wayward ruler to Santorini; thence he was sent to face higher Venetian justice on Crete, where he died of a fever in August 1511, almost exactly a year after the original murderous attack.

PAROS

On landing at Paroikia, the chief town of Paros, you immediately come in contact with the speciality of the place: the little jetty on which you land is made of marble, marble pillars for mooring boats to are jotted here and there, and you realise before long that Paros is nothing but one huge block of marble covered with a thin coating of soil.[31]

Since Bent wrote, in the 1880s, the marble has become less immediately apparent – Paroikia, like other Cycladic settlements, sparkles mostly with thickly applied whitewash – but is still very much in evidence. The castle – a monument, says Bent, to Frankish vandalism – incorporates the drums of ancient marble pillars. And the light, reflective, near-translucent stone, some of it again borrowed from ancient temples, some quarried afresh in the contrastingly dark and damp tunnels of Marathi, also contributes to the splendour of the oldest and largest church in the Cyclades, the Panagia Ekatontapiliani, probably founded in the sixth century. Niketas Magistros, author of an apocryphal *Life of St Theoktiste of Lesbos*, saw the church in something approaching its pristine glory when, in AD 911, he came to Paros as a member of a Byzantine expedition against Arab-held Crete. 'The craftsman finished the stone with such skill that the wall looked as if it was covered with fine linen. It gleamed with such a fluid sheen that it outshone the brilliance of pearls.'[32]

The present church has evolved through a gradual process of accretion, collapse (earthquake damage was at its most severe in 1773) and restoration. But through the centuries it has remained crucial to the Parian sense of identity. 'Ekatontapiliani' – 'Hundred Gates' – may well be a corruption of 'Katapoliani' or 'Below the Town', but local tradition prefers the gates or doors and declares that ninety-nine of them are known but the hundredth will be discovered only when the Greeks regain Constantinople. (Counting the ninety-nine would require some ingenuity.) With more immediate prospects in mind, love-sick maidens were, according to Bent, heard to cry 'By the Hundred Gates of Paros may I win whom I love!'[33]

There have, however, been times when there were few Parians to swear by their church. In the time of Niketas Magistros the island was all but deserted as a result of persistent Arab raids. His Saint Theoktiste, a young nun who escapes the Arabs' clutches, lives on Paros for thirty-five years in solitude before she finally meets a visiting huntsman, tells him her story, and expires. A second period of depopulation was caused by the the advent of the Lesbos-born Ottoman admiral Kheir-ed-Din Barbarossa in 1537. Between 1536 and 1538 he terrorized the Aegean, expanding the dominions of Suleiman the Magnificent, slaughtering those who resisted, but above all enslaving the islanders, enough to provide an army of new oarsmen for the Turkish galleys and to cause, it is said, a glut in the slave-market at Constantinople. He took about 6000 prisoners from both Paros and Aigina and 3800 from Skiathos, and removed all six hundred inhabitants of Anaphi, the small island to the east of Santorini. Such deeds won Barbarossa his western reputation as a piratical villain and treacherous renegade (which was unfair, since he had never in fact been a Christian). Equally, and perfectly justifiably, he went down in Turkish and North African history as inspired resuscitator of an ailing fleet and bold champion of Islam. Indeed Kheir-ed-Din means 'Defender of the Faith'. (His given name was Khizr; 'Barbarossa' derives from the red beard of his elder brother, Aruj.)[34]

One of the 6000 Parian slaves was Cecilia Venier, daughter of a former Venetian lord of the island. She was more fortunate than most, since she was destined for the imperial harem and ended her days as the influential Sultana Nur Banu, mother of Sultan Murad III. By this time her native island was slowly reviving. But for centuries many of the smaller islands remained deserted or under-populated, places such as Lambro's isle becomes at his death, 'all desolate and bare,/Its dwellings down, its tenants passed away' while 'No dirge, except the hollow sea's,/Mourns o'er the beauty of the Cyclades.'[35]

ANTIPAROS

The cave at Spilaion was, traditionally, the only reason for visiting Antiparos. The most noticeable visitor was undoubtedly Charles-François Olier, Marquis de Nointel, who travelled in great pomp through Greece in the 1670s, both to satisfy his own curiosity and to demonstrate the power and glory of King Louis XIV, the Sun King whose light could illuminate even the obscurer parts of the eastern Mediterranean. Tournefort describes the bizarre and spectacular scenes sponsored by the temporarily troglodytic Nointel:

Monsieur the Marquis *de Nointel*, Ambassador of *France* to the *Porte*, pass'd the three *Christmas* Holydays in this

Grotto, accompany'd by above five hundred Persons, as well his own Domesticks, as Merchants, Corsairs, or Natives, that were curious to follow him. A hundred large Torches of yellow Wax, and four hundred Lamps that burnt night and day were so well placed, that no Church was ever better illuminated. Men were posted from space to space, in every Precipice from the Altar [a roughly pyramidal formation] to the opening of the Cavern, who gave the signal with their Handkerchiefs, when the body of J.C. was lifted up; at this signal fire was put to 24 Drakes, and to several Patereroes that were at the Entrance of the Cavern: the Trumpets, Hautbois, Fifes, and Violins, made the Consecration yet more magnificent.[36]

Even superstition seems to have bowed before Nointel's munificence: 'The Natives themselves durst not go down into it before he came to *Antiparos*; he encouraged them by *Largesses*.'

SANTORINI (THERA)

Fynes Moryson, a Fellow of Peterhouse, Cambridge, who spent much of the 1590s travelling in Europe, passed Santorini with some trepidation.

They report, that this Iland, and another of the same name (both of little circuit) were in our age cast up in the middest of the Sea, with an eruption of flames and of Brimstone, and that they are not inhabited, but are commonly called the Divels Ilands, because many ships casting anchor there, and fastning their Cables upon the land, have had Cables loosed by spirits in the night, and so suffered shipwrack, or hardly escaped the same.[37]

Volcanoes, vampires – the preferred form taken by Moryson's 'spirits' – and strangeness are the traditional themes of writing about Santorini.

This is an extraordinary island, or group of islands. The first stage in a geological sequence which is still, unpredictably, in process was marked by the massive eruption which shattered the ancient round island in about 1450 BC. Old Burnt Island (Palaia Kameni) formed from 198 BC onwards. Small Burnt Island appeared in 1573 and gave rise to Moryson's idea of two new islands, but was later to be incorporated into New Burnt Island (Nea Kameni), gradually formed as a result of successive eruptions between 1707 and 1941. Today this island is often called simply Volcano Island; near the crater, the ashy remains of lava still smoke. Visitors, including those as unlikely to credit vampires as the rational James Theodore Bent, found the resulting landscape 'hideous, yet fascinating'. Santorini's cliffs are 'all in strata of twisted and contorted volcanic lava, red, green, and black' opposite 'the active centres of the volcano, the three [now two] hideous islands, steaming with smoke and streaked with sulphur.' On the Volcano Island

> . . . the aspect of everything is infernal beyond descrip-
> tion. . . . All is black, save a few bright coloured stones
> and streaks of sulphur; huge blocks of lava and broken
> volcanic bombs lie about everywhere.
> The ascent, though only four hundred feet high, is
> anything but easy, owing to the ashes, which give way
> beneath the feet, and the jagged promontories of red
> and black lava rocks which have to be passed. On the
> summit there are extensive lava fields, in parts too hot
> to be touched, and on which we were told we could
> have had poached eggs, if we had had any with us. Out
> of fissures in the mountain smoke was pouring pretty
> freely, the sulphurous flames of which gave us some
> idea of what the inhabitants of Santorini must have
> suffered when enveloped for days in it at the time of
> the [1866] eruption. Large patches of bright yellow
> sulphur adorned this extraordinary spot. No wonder
> it excites awe in those who live near it! The sailors
> who rowed us home . . . [told] us wonderful tales of their
> reminiscences of the eruption. The Hephaestus, as they
> call it, is to them a terrible unknown foe; the inward
> groanings to them are the furious battle-cry of an
> infernal deity.[38]

François Richard, a Jesuit priest, was an awestruck witness of the activities of this 'infernal deity' in 1650. He wrote, in Greek verse, of Hellish peals of thunder, the growling sea, the clouds on fire and strange fiery shapes of snakes, spears, and 'whirling blazing torches', huge flying boulders, the temporary blindness of the islanders, and the blackening of all gold and silver objects.[39] Another odd phenomenon, fit to breed vampire stories, was that, as Bent puts it in his summary of Richard, 'asphyxiated people revived just as their friends were mourning for them and preparing for their funeral, so that the priest had to return home with his stole and his cross unused.'[40] Another Jesuit, Father Tarillon, described the no-less-terrifying fireworks of 1707. He watched rocks emerge from the fiery sea, and the rock of Skaros undulating amid loud explosions, doors banging open as the people ran to the churches.[41] (Skaros, which had been the capital of Santorini's various Italian rulers during the Middle Ages, was gradually abandoned in favour of the modern capital, Phira.) A cooler – more chilling – account was compiled by British officers on three ships sent to lend assistance during the eruption of 1866:

> On the 22nd a curious phenomenon displayed itself. A dense column, which had its form as clearly defined as if it had been a mass of dark purple basalt, rose slowly out of the volcano into the air. It was about 600 ft. in diameter, and ascended to a height of 4000 ft. It appeared as if a central column of fire glowed with a lurid colouring through a dense covering of ashes mingled with smoke. For some time it preserved its columnar structure without yielding to the wind, but as the heavy matter fell the smoke began gradually to disperse.
>
> The inhabitants of Thera are greatly alarmed, and ships have been sent to enable those to escape who desire to quit the island. The danger, if not really great, is magnified by its uncertainty. The force that casts up islands of lava from the depths of the sea may topple down the town of Thera [Phira] from the summit of the precipice where it stands, 1000 ft. above the level of the sea, into the gulf below.[42]

So far Phira has not toppled down, despite a major earth-quake in 1956 and intensive tourist development since then. The quieter lanes which survive near the Catholic convents in the Upper Town continue to give some impression of the tranquil place which Bent suspected would make, if only there were a few trees for shelter, 'an inviting residence in the summer.'[43]

The ancient Therans preferred the other side of the island – Akrotiri where, long after Bent's time, were uncovered the vital, elegant Minoan-period frescoes now in the National Museum in Athens, and the mountain fastness of Ancient Thera, high above the dark volcanic sands of Kamari. There the threat from the infernal enemy seems less.

CHIOS

When he came to Chios William Lithgow, the widely travelled Jacobean Scot, duly inspected the reputed 'sepulchre of Homer', but reserved his enthusiasm for the island's abundant vegetable life.

The levell, or lower parts of the Ile . . . aboundeth so in Oranges and Lemmons, that they fill Barrels and Pipes with the juyce thereof, and carry them to Constantinople, which the Turkes use at their meate, as we doe the Verges [or verjuice – a sour tasting fruit-juice]. [Chios] is of circuite an hundreth miles, and famous for the medicinable Masticke that groweth there on Trees: I saw many pleasant Gardens in it, which yeeld in great plenty, Orenges, Lemmons, Apples, Pears, Prunes, Figges, Olives, Apricockes, Dates, Adams Apples [limes], excellent hearbes, faire flowers, sweete Hony, with store of Cypre and Mulbery-trees, and exceeding good silke is made here.[44]

The most important of all these was the mastic, a gum extracted from the lentisk trees in the south of Chios. It could be used as an ingredient in varnish, as a jelly, or added to drinks. Its most important use was for Turkish ladies, from the Sultana downwards, to chew. 'The effects which they find by it are,' says Bernard Randolph, a merchant whose account of the islands was published in 1687, 'that it carryes away the flegme, cleanses and prevents the aking of the teeth; and causes a sweet breath.'[45]

Chiot women, if one is to believe Lithgow, kept busy not by chewing gum but by selling themselves to strangers. They are, he assures the reader, with evident relish for any shock or titillation he may occasion, 'much given to Venery' and their husbands are their pandars. They charge a gold Sequin, 'nine Shillings English', for a supper and 'a belly full of sinfull content.'[46] Whether Lithgow chose to avail himself of this facility he does not record. Probably it was the fantasy of a man who was, tradition has it, so unfortunate in his sexual relations that he turned to travel: four Lanark men who found him with their sister mutilated his ears so that he became 'Cut-lugged Willie'. Nevertheless, Chiots did have a widespread reputation for gaiety and open-heartedness. Their way in life was eased by an unusually relaxed attitude on the part of the Turks, who were happy to leave the islanders to their own devices so long as the mastic and profits from other produce continued to flow into Constantinople. Bernard Randolph, not one to fantasize, reports that 'In the summer time every evening the marine is full with all sorts of people with musick, singing, and dancing, and none offer to molest them.'[47]

Molestation did occur, on a terrible scale, when Chios joined the Greek struggle for independence. Most Chiots had little inclination to insurrection – their life was more comfortable than that of most Greeks and the Turkish mainland was dangerously close – but were drawn in by their poorer neighbours from Samos, who had less to lose. A contingent of Samians terrorized Turks on Chios and laid siege to the citadel. The Turkish response, in April and May of 1822, was rapid. Once the Captain Pasha's ships were sighted, hostages from the old ruling families like the Argenti were hanged in the citadel. The gardeners from the mansions of such families were forced to reveal any valuables buried in the grounds, and then strangled. When the confiscated goods arrived on the mainland, they 'enticed over' what one survivor called 'a horde of these barbarians thirsting for Christian blood and plunder.'[48] The *Spectateur Oriental*, a newspaper based in Smyrna, relayed to the French-speaking world descriptions of the streets of Chios town, strewn with corpses, lined with ransacked, blazing buildings, and loud with the roar of cannon, the report of firearms, and 'wild screams as every passion was unleashed.'

At dawn on 12 April, according to the *Spectateur*, the acting French consul, Charles Alexandre Digeon, agreed to shelter the 1500 people, mainly but not all Roman Catholics, who were clamouring at his door. Swearing to save them or die in the attempt, he rushed out into the street, sabre in one hand, white flag in the other, and was immediately surrounded by a crowd of Turks. '*FRANÇAIS*,' he shouted, '*Français, je suis le Consul de France et ami du Pacha.*' The astonished marauders took him to the Pasha, who granted his request to spare the lives of those who, having played no part in the rising, had placed themselves under the protection of France.[49]

No doubt there were other, unrecorded acts of individual heroism and mercy. But few Greeks were as fortunate as those saved by Digeon. At least 25,000 people were slaughtered in a matter of days. Many more were enslaved or became refugees. Philip Argenti, great-great-grandson of one of the murdered hostages, points out that in 1822 the population of Chios slumped from about 120,000 to 30,000; in 1928 (depleted additionally by the earthquake of 1881) it had not risen beyond 76,000.[50] Even the precious mastic villages, to the reported fury of the Sultana, suffered some damage. Chios remained Turkish until 1912. Nevertheless, the massacre had a crucial effect in canvassing foreign support for the fledgling Greek cause. Greeks had massacred Turks, but there had been nothing on this scale. In France Delacroix painted one of his best-known pictures to illustrate the Chiots' plight. In England Revd Thomas Smart Hughes foresook the informed, observant manner of his earlier *Travels* to dash off, in three days, his impassioned *Address to the People of England ... Occasioned by the Late Inhuman Massacres in the Isle of Scio.* Hughes dwells particularly on the fate of the women and children, whose joyous song and garlanded dance once welcomed 'the return of spring or the gathering of the purple vintage.'

> Where are ye now, ye fairest flowers of Homer's rocky isle? plucked up and withered! gone into slavery worse than death, if death could be ten times repeated! sold, after the most horrible pollution, at a price less than cattle in a market to Asiatic barbarians and to African Moors. Gracious God! a tenth part of these atrocities in an unenlightened age, would have aroused all the gallant spirits of Christendom to avenge their wrongs! and shall we not only sit by tamely, while they are perpetrated, but suffer them to be extended, as far as in us lies, to future generations and the most distant ages?[51]

Here was a general appeal to virility, racism, and religion. While the British government continued to refuse to interfere directly in what it considered to be the internal affairs of another nation, individuals clearly were moved by this outcry. Once news of events on Chios spread, there was a considerable increase not only in numbers of volunteer soldiers and helpers joining the Greek rebels from Europe and America, but in the amount of cash donated. Revd Hughes set a good example by announcing that any profits from the sale of his pamphlet 'shall be religiously applied to that sacred cause.'

LESBOS

The misadventures of Jan Struys, a Dutch soldier who served with the Venetians, included, as the title-page of the English version of his memoirs has it, 'Ship-wrack, Robberies, Slavery, Hunger, Tortures, with other Incommodities and Hardships.' But July 1657 was an interlude of blessed calm on the island of Lesbos, where

> The South- and North-sides are Champain Land; but the East and West for the most part hilly and montanous, affoarding rich Quarries of white and black Marble; and about the Center of the Land it is woody, and mostly

grown over with Cypres Trees. The arable part of the Land which is tilled, is of a good Soil, and affoards plenty of Corn, of which they make two sorts of bread, the one they call *Trachana* and the other *Bouchourt*, either of which is more durable than our Ship Biscake. They make an excellent sort of red Wine, which the *Turks*, notwithstanding the voice of their *Alchoran*, greatly covet and swallow when they can have it. The Pastures swarm with all kinds of Cattel [livestock] both great and small.[52]

It was also as a soldier that Sir (then Captain) Compton Mackenzie was on Lesbos in July 1915. Mackenzie, already author of *Sinister Street* and later of *Whisky Galore* and much else, was detailed to the island during the Gallipoli campaign. His brief was to decoy the Germans into sending a submarine to Lesbos in the belief that a major new British encampment was being planned there. While he travelled around making deliberately conspicuous enquiries, Mackenzie got to know and love the landscape of the island. But it was the bugs he remembered most vividly.

In my bedroom [were] innumerable juvenile bugs, partially traluscent [*sic*] creatures as bright as rubies which scurried about over the sheets like animated cayenne pepper. My arms and legs and shoulders and neck looked every morning as if they had been rubbed with a nutmeg-grater.

Adult bugs might have succumbed to blows with a hammer, but with 'infant buglets' there were special difficulties.

A single blow might have obliterated a hundred, but such vicious and esurient atoms could have incarnadined the multitudinous seas, and against their myriads what was a hammer? They percolated the mosquito-net as easily as claret; they seemed to rise from the mattress like a crimson dew.[53]

Lesbos has been home or host to public figures as colourful as the buglets and as various as the landscape. Most famously there is the poet Sappho, born at Eresos in the mountainous west of the island, renowned equally, at least in legend, as a suicide for heterosexual love (leaping, however, from the cliffs of the Ionian island of Leukas) or a fervent exponent of homoerotic 'Lesbian' love, in either case Byron's 'burning Sappho' of 'The Isles of Greece'.

The primitive painter Theophilos Hajimikhail or Papa-mikhail (1873–1934), called usually plain Theophilos, led a quieter life. An impoverished, eccentric wanderer who had originally trained as a plasterer, he painted in bold colours on rags, wood, and walls, first in Smyrna, for many years in the Pelion villages of Thessaly, and in his last years, more often on canvas, back on his native Lesbos. His subjects include fishermen, olive-gatherers, strong-men, and scenes from ancient myth and the War of Independence. Revalu-ation – aesthetic and financial – came some years after his death; in 1965 a Theophilos museum was opened in Varia, his birthplace, to the south of Mytilene. Among his earlier apologists was George Seferis, who, in a lecture introduc-ing the first Theophilos exhibition in Athens in 1947, began his exposition of primitivism with a story about one of the canvases now at Varia. Theophilos was painting a baker at work:

> When he came to putting in the baker's rake, instead of following the laws of perspective and making it horizontal, he drew it perpendicular, showing the whole breadth of its surface; then, in the same way, he drew a loaf of bread on the rake. A clever man came past and said to the painter, 'That loaf of bread is going to fall down, the way you've painted it.' Without bothering to turn his head, the painter replied, 'Don't worry. Only real loaves fall down; the painted ones stay put, and in a picture one ought to show everything.'[54]

Dame Freya Stark in the early 1960s descended, *en route* for Turkey, on the expatriate community living in hitherto sleepy Molyvos (also called Mithimna). The great traveller disrupted the writing and drinking schedules of Peter Green, novelist and classical scholar then working on a story about Sappho,

The Laughter of Aphrodite, and his guest William Golding. (Golding regularly consumed bottles of 'Fix', the beer named after King Otho's brewmaster Fuchs, and became known, says Green, as '*O Vasilevs Phix* – King Fix, the Lord of the Liquid Feast'.) Green had met Stark and knew that she had 'a knack of talking people into things.'

> This, as things turned out, was an understatement. She arrived, she dazzled, she waved a casual hand to indicate that suitable lodging should be found for her. Greeks whom I had never before seen move except during an earthquake rushed to oblige. Then it was my turn. '*Peter, I know* I can rely on you to find a little man with two donkeys for me to go to Ephtalou at six o'clock sharp tomorrow morning, *can't* I?' 'Of course, Freya.' So that was how she'd worked it through the Valley of the Assassins. 'And Mr Golding – would you by any chance be free to drive me into Mytilene about noon on Monday?' Free, King Fix or not, was what Bill assured her he'd be. A house was found, the donkeys materialized, trips were taken.[55]

Mytilene and Molyvos in summer are perhaps unconducive to great spiritual experiences. Golding found his elsewhere, Green remembers:

> We had been exploring in and around Aghiassos, a high town among mountains, with a strange dialect and a miracle-working icon of the Blessed Virgin, a place of pilgrimage in mid-August, a numinous centre of strong and primitive belief. While we drank in the taverna Bill climbed the long narow street of stepped cobbles that led up to the great chestnut forest above the town. He wanted, he said, to get the feel of the place. It was almost dark by the time he got back, stepping down the street lost in a far away reverie, hair and beard blowing in the breeze, immensely dignified, somewhere private and quite different. And I could hear the quiet, breathless ripple of Greek voices accompanying him as he came: '*O yeros katavainei*', 'the old man descends', spoken in

the wondering tones that might have welcomed Moses back from Mt Sinai with the Tablets of the Law.[56]

SKYROS

Skyros, in the windswept Northern Sporades, became by chance the burial-place of Rupert Brooke. Ships and men were massing on Lemnos in the spring of 1915 for the ill-fated Gallipoli assault. So crowded was Moudros Bay that Brooke's detachment was directed to wait instead off Tris Boukes in the far south of Skyros. Between manoeuvres Brooke and some fellow officers rested on shore in a small olive grove which, the others remembered, he particularly liked. Three days later he died of blood-poisoning on a nearby hospital ship at the age of twenty-seven. The details of the interment are given in a letter to Edward Marsh from W. Denis Browne:

> We buried him the same evening in the olive grove I mentioned before – one of the loveliest places on this earth, with grey-green olives round him, one weeping above his head: the ground covered with flowering sage, bluish grey & smelling more delicious than any other flower I know. The path up to it from the sea is narrow & difficult and very stony: it runs by the bed of a dried-up torrent. He was carried up from the boat by his A Company petty officers, led by his platoon-sergeant Saunders: and it was with enormous difficulty that they got the coffin up the narrow way. The journey of a mile took two hours. . . . First came one of his men carrying a great white wooden cross with his name painted on it in black: then the firing party, commanded by Patrick; & then the coffin followed by our officers. . . . Think of it all under a clouded moon, with the three mountains around & behind us, and those divine scents everywhere. We lined his grave with all the flowers we could find & Quilter set a wreath of olive on the coffin. The funeral service was very simply said by the Chaplain and after the Last Post the little lamp-lit procession went once again down the narrow path to the sea.[57]

Brooke's 'corner of a foreign field' was undoubtedly more agreeable than Gallipoli where Browne himself was killed and buried less than two months later.

In English tradition Brooke was remembered first as a patriot and martyr, later as a gilded, doomed youth who did not live to see the horrors of trench warfare which made grimmer, more powerful poets out of combatants like Wilfred Owen. On Skyros, Patrick Leigh Fermor tells us, a different picture has lingered. Leigh Fermor's friend Tanty Rodocanaki once met an old shepherd at Brooke's tomb:

> 'I see you are admiring the grave of O Broukis,' he said. 'He was a great poet. We are glad to have him with us. He was a good man.'
>
> Intrigued by the conviction of his tone and curious to discover how much he knew, Rodocanaki asked him what he thought of his poetry.
>
> 'I've never read any of it, I'm sorry to say,' the shepherd answered. 'I'm not strong on letters and foreign languages. But you could tell he was a great man. You see that old olive tree over there? That was his tree.'
>
> 'How do you mean?'
>
> 'He used to sit under it every day and write poetry.'
>
> Reluctant to contradict, Rodocanaki asked him if he was sure they were talking about the same person.
>
> 'Of course I am! O Broukis used to wander about the woods in silence, the very picture of an old-fashioned English gentleman.'
>
> 'What did he look like?'
>
> 'Magnificent, sir,' the shepherd answered. 'Tall, dignified, flowing hair, burning eyes and a long white beard.'[58]

CRETE, THE DODECANESE
AND RHODES

*Herakleion – Knossos – The Villa Ariadne – Mount Ida – Gortys
and Phaistos – Southern Crete – Rethymnon – Arkadi – Khania –
Patmos – Kos – Rhodes*

In myth Crete is the birthplace or childhood home of
Zeus and the land of his son or companion King Minos,
who became unwilling stepfather of the dreaded Minotaur.
Daidalos built the Labyrinth to contain the monster, and
Ariadne provided Theseus with the sword to slay him and
the thread to trace back through the maze. Later travellers
came seeking some foundation for these stories, some trace
of the ninety rich cities with which Homer credits the island.
Drawn no doubt to the archetypal pattern of the man's
overcoming of the fearsome man-beast in the dark, they
looked particularly for the Labyrinth. They found it most
often in what were actually disused ancient quarries in the
hills near the Roman city of Gortys. The enterprising late-
eighteenth-century group led by Claude-Étienne Savary followed legendary example by 'proceeding with the thread of
Ariadne, and fastening it at different distances lest it should
break'; even so,

> We walked with precaution in the doublings of this vast
> Labyrinth, amid the eternal darkness that reigns through-
> out it, and which our torches could hardly dispel. Thus
> situated, the imagination raises up phantoms; it figures
> to itself precipices under the feet of the curious, monsters

placed as centinels, and, in a word, a thousand chimeras which can have no existence.[1]

Nineteenth-century Minos-hunters turned their attention more often to Knossos, where walls and great storage-jars were first uncovered by the suitably named Cretan merchant Minos Kalokairinos in 1878–9. Like Schliemann at Troy and Mycenae (Schliemann himself seriously considered buying the land and digging here), the excavators of Knossos – principally Sir Arthur Evans from 1900 – gave myth a local habitation and a name. Evans called the site the Palace of Minos, the term 'Minoan' was coined, and visitors continued to think about Theseus and labyrinths as well as ancient frescoes and washing arrangements. All over the island new discoveries were made, including the palaces at Phaistos and Mallia; Herakleion museum filled with snake-goddesses, bulls, and double axes, and in 1910 Saki had his MP, Arlington Stringham, quip during a debate at the House that 'the people of Crete unfortunately make more history than they can consume locally.'[2] Father Ronald Knox, later known for his translation of the Bible, asked punningly, 'Give the probable date of the first person who thought of describing the civilization of Knossos as "a poor thing, but mine own".'[3]

Many visitors, intent on Minoans or Minotaurs, knew little of the island's later inhabitants or its remoter areas. It was the Second World War which did most to change this, by allowing Allied soldiers first-hand experience of that indomitable Cretan spirit which fired generations of rebels against the island's Venetian, Turkish, and now German occupiers, and of the mountains which made such resistance possible. Antony Beevor, in *Crete: the Battle and the Resistance*, observes that

> The Cretan character – warlike, proud, compulsively generous to a friend or stranger in need, ferociously unforgiving to an enemy or traitor, frugal day-by-day but prodigal in celebration – was, of course, strongly influenced by the landscape of dramatic contrasts in which the islanders lived. . . . From sub-tropical vegetation with banana trees, carobs and orange groves, a

mountain village, only fifteen kilometres away as the crow flew, but probably sixty on foot, seemed to exist in a different world and a different climate.[4]

The best known fictional account of the withdrawal of the Allies from Crete in 1941 was provided in *Officers and Gentlemen* (1955) by Evelyn Waugh, who had been intelligence officer with the commando force controlled by Colonel Robert Laycock. 'Layforce' landed in southern Crete in May 1941 having been informed that the island was largely in the hands of Allied forces. Instead, they found them retreating in confusion. Guy Crouchback, in the novel, witnesses scenes of cowardice, desertion, 'gunners without guns', mismanagement and utter weariness. But the reality was somewhat less unrelievedly depressing – Beevor points out that Waugh's fictional account should be seen 'more as a projection of a personal sense of disillusionment than as an objective depiction of events'[5] – and a different and more positive story emerges from accounts of the bravery, humour, and camaraderie of the men of the SOE (Special Operations Executive) who worked behind enemy lines after May 1941, and of the many Cretans who supported them in the face of cruel reprisals by the occupiers.

SOE veterans remember groups of straightforward *andartes* or guerrillas in the tradition of resistance to the Turks, breathing 'blood and slaughter and garlic in the best Cretan style' and bold individuals like Kapetan Antonis Grigorakis, known as Satanas because 'nobody but the devil himself could have survived the number of bullets he had in him.'[6] George Psychoundakis told his own story in *The Cretan Runner* (1955), an account of his survival – against the odds – as a 'runner' for the British, scrambling away from enemy bullets and suspicions, carrying messages and heavy weights from cave to cave, hiding wirelesses and wireless-operators. Alongside the Cretans were those SOE men and the like who became, by immersing themselves in the life, dialect and sufferings of the island, honorary Cretans. Their manner was often no less extravagant than that of the real inhabitants. John Pendlebury was killed in 1941, but his memory took on the colour of legend. Patrick Leigh Fermor remembers how

his florid handsome face, his single sparkling eye [he
would leave his glass eye on his bedside table in Herakleion to indicate his absence on guerrilla missions] . . .
his slung guerrilla's rifle and bandolier and his famous
swordstick brought a stimulating flash of romance and
fun into that khaki gloom.[7]

Leigh Fermor himself, who worked with Psychoundakis
and seems to have met almost all the Cretan and British heroes
chronicled by Antony Beevor, was a notable doer in occupied
Crete before he emerged as a writer.

Nikos Kazantzakis, Crete's most famous novelist, com-
mented on the favourable reaction of foreign readers to a
section of his passionate tale of the nineteenth-century rebel-
lions, *Freedom and Death*: 'Crete seems to them now like a
world of giants, where people still live with the intensity
they had when they first issued from God's hands.'[8] Fiction
helps to give this impression, but fact often seems to confirm
it.

HERAKLEION

'Mealy-ruiny, earthquaky, odious' was Edward Lear's verdict
on Herakleion in 1864. It was full of bugs, and lacking in
pictorial prospects.

> The walk round the walls this morning: utter ruin and
> mishmash *qua* town and forts, but much picturesqueness
> *qua* distance. . . . It is hardly possible to make any draw-
> ing of any part of the city, which lies low sloping to
> the sea, and is of uniformly flat-topped houses, broken
> mosques and palms here and there. . . . Altogether a
> nastier and less interesting Turkish town I was never
> in.[9]

Visiting Candia (the Venetian name for Herakleion; the
traditional Greek name is Kastro, Fort) was even less pleasant two hundred years earlier, when this last outpost of
Venetian rule in Crete held out against its Turkish besiegers
for twenty-one years from 1648–69. The ramparts around

which Lear walked and the Venetian Fortress with its lions of St Mark guarding the old harbour are extant reminders of this period. (Under the Turks the fortress became, less gloriously, the wave-beaten dungeon, brooded on by Kazantzakis' Kapetan Mikhalis in *Freedom and Death*, where so many Cretans 'gasped out their lives' in chains.[10]) It was from the battlements of the fortress, on 19 June 1669, that the weary remnants of the garrison saw the Papal banner of the crossed keys fluttering over forty French ships. Other European powers were reluctant to aid their old rivals the Venetians, but now, belatedly, Louis XIV had given this relief force his qualified blessing. So it was amid scenes of wild joy and ringing of bells that the five thousand volunteers were welcomed ashore. They found a city of desolation, according to Reaux de la Richardière, one of their officers.

> The streets were covered with cannon-balls and shot, with splinters of bombs and grenades. There was no church, no building, whose walls had not been breached and almost ruined by the cannon-fire. None of the houses were anything, now, but sad hovels. Everywhere there was a bad smell. Whichever way you turned you encountered soldiers who had been killed, wounded or maimed.

The reinforcements, led by the Dukes of Beaufort and Navailles, took the Turks by surprise just before dawn on 25 June, driving them out of their entrenchments. But this success was short-lived: some barrels of powder having accidentally been blown up, panic spread among the French. They retreated towards the city, leaving the Duke of Beaufort and many scions of noble French houses among fifty killed; the Turks displayed their heads in triumph before the walls. The remaining French sailed home in August. Realizing that further resistance was now useless, the Venetian leader Francesco Morosini salvaged what he could from the wreckage: he succeeded in exchanging the keys of Candia for the right of his garrison and the surviving citizens to depart peacefully.[11] So ended the Venetian presence in Crete after four and a half centuries. (A quarter of a century later Morosini, as Doge of Venice, temporarily reconquered much of southern Greece, but not Crete. One of his less enviable achievements was the accurate shelling of the Turkish gunpowder store in Athens, the Parthenon.)

Before the siege, Candia made a better impression on visitors. It was, the English traveller Fynes Moryson found in 1596, a fine city whose houses were 'built of stone, with a low roofe, after the manner of Italy, and the streets thereof are faire and large.'[12] And in spite of the siege and the later massacres and uprisings, in spite of earthquakes, fires, aerial bombardment in 1941, and rapid tourist development from the 1960s, substantial traces of this proud Renaissance town (helped by skilful restoration in some cases) survive in the centre of Herakleion. There are the fortress and the ramparts, the great arches of the *Arsenali* where galleys were built and refitted, the elegant portico of the Basilica of St Mark, and the Loggia or meeting-place of the native and colonial magnificoes noticed by Bernard Randolph in 1687 as 'a very stately building of white Marble, with several works in *Basso Relievo*.'[13] (The original seventeenth-century building, largely demolished in 1904, was splendidly rebuilt in 1968.) Such buildings were the setting for public ceremonials like the reading of proclamations, the annual acclamation of the Doge of Venice and the Doge of Candia (elected every two years), or the Doge's regular outings 'in great pomp and preceded by thirty musicians.'[14] These displays were ideal opportunities for members of the ruling class to indulge their taste for luxury in dress. According to Jan Struys, a Dutch mercenary in Venetian service in 1656–7, even when they were buried the noblewomen of Candia were 'dressed up as if they were going to a ball, adorned with pearls round their necks, on their heads and even on their slippers, their fingers covered with diamonds, their aprons of silk trimmed with fine lace.'[15]

Candia was a cultural as much as a social and political centre. Its most famous progeny was El Greco – Dominikos Theotokopoulos – who worked in the city before leaving for Venice and Toledo in 1567. The striking fusion of eastern and western precedents in his work is apparent also, if less dramatically, in the icons of his contemporary Mikhalis Damaskinos, several of which are displayed in the church of

St Katherine of Sinai. This church – a quiet contrast to the
grand nineteenth-century Cathedral of St Minas nearby – is all
that remains of the Mount Sinai Monastery School, first
founded by exiles from Constantinople after its fall in 1453.
Damaskinos was probably a student here, as, traditionally,
was El Greco and, more certainly, the greatest writer of
the Cretan Renaissance, Vitsentzos Kornaros, or Vicenzo
Cornaro (1553–1613 or 1614), son of a noble Veneto-Cretan
family, landowner, health inspector, and author of the long
verse romance *Erotokritos* (*c.*1595–1613).

Erotokritos is the story of the vicissitudes of the heroic
Rotokritos and Princess Aretousa, who arrive eventually, by
way of heartache, exile, tournament, battle, and near-death,
at their desired union and happy rule as King and Queen of
Athens (an Athens as unlocalized as that ruled by Theseus in
A Midsummer Night's Dream). Like the Cretan paintings of the
period, *Erotokritos* absorbed Western influence rather than
being overwhelmed by it. It is based loosely on an Italian
translation of a French romance, but written in confident
Cretan Greek and in distinctively Greek fifteen-syllable metre.
Despite purists' disdain for the Cretan locutions, the poem
was recited and read throughout Greece long after the fall of
Candia had ended the Cretan Renaissance. For many it had
become less a love story than a focus of nationalist feeling,
with the sufferings of hero and heroine analogous to those
of enslaved Greece.

One of the most solid reminders of Venetian Crete, in
the square now called Venizelou, has changed little since
Richard Pococke observed in 1739 'In the piazza there is
a fine fountain . . . the lower basin is adorned with excellent
bass reliefs, the upper basin is supported by four lions, and
had in the middle a fine statue [of Poseidon] by the same
hand, which the Turks destroyed.'[16] The reliefs, of tritons,
nereids, visored helmets, are much decayed now, but the
proud, hoary lions (fourteenth-century themselves, incorporated in the fountain in 1629) look like survivors,
unconcerned at their incongruity amid the parked motorbikes
and the restaurant tables. The atmosphere was rather more
formal in 1629, when the fountain was inaugurated with true
Venetian magnificence. Governor (Provveditor General)

Francesco Morosini (uncle and namesake of the man who surrendered the city forty years later), the scheme's originator, reported that

> On the feast day of our blessed patron St Mark, water
> was to be seen flowing into the square of Candia from
> eight mouths or pipes, and at that point it was blessed
> by Monsignor the Archbishop with the Latin clergy, and
> by the Protopappas with the Greek clergy, in the
> presence of innumerable people and with applause from
> all the citizens and the army to the glory of the Divine
> Majesty and of the Most Serene Republic.[17]

Probably the audience had little choice but to applaud La Serenissima, but the fountain did provide much needed water.

When the Turks took Candia the lions continued to spout. The Pasha could look down at them from the windows of his (formerly the Duke's) palace. By the late nineteenth century he could also rejoice in the presence of a large plane tree from which captured rebels were hanged. In periods of turbulence innocent victims of rampaging gangs also died in this way, as in the scene described by Kazantzakis in his semi-autobiographical *Report to Greco*:

> I looked up towards the plane tree and uttered a cry.
> Three hanged men were swinging there, one next to
> the other. They were barefooted, dressed only in their
> nightshirts, and deep green tongues were hanging out
> of their mouths. Unable to endure the sight, I turned
> my head away and clung to my father's knees. But he
> grasped my head with his hand and rotated it toward
> the plane tree.

The boy asks who killed the men, and gets the answer 'Liberty, God bless it!'[18] The square now has several small plane trees. The palace, together with Kazantzakis' gallows tree, has disappeared.

Kazantzakis himself, although he spent much of his life away from Crete, is buried in Herakleion. The grave is high on the ramparts at the Martinengo Bastion, the huge bulwark built by Michele Sammicheli of Verona as the Turkish threat increased in 1538. (A more detailed memorial is the reconstruction of Kazantzakis' study in the Historical and Ethnographic Museum.) A tall wooden cross surmounts a stone incised with his words 'I hope for nothing. I fear nothing. I am free.' The sense of freedom is enhanced by the long views across Herakleion, once suffering, still sometimes claustrophobic, to the sea and to the mountains, Iouktas and Stroumboulos.

KNOSSOS

Extensive excavation by Sir Arthur Evans and his successors has transformed the area since Edward Lear noted, in May 1864, that

> The site of Knossos possesses water and trees and plenty of *aïdhónia*, [nightingales], but except scattered masses of brickwork, little remains. The place however with its green hillside slopes and corn has a pretty aspic.[19]

The 'aspic' must always have been pretty, but Knossos must have been a much busier place in Minoan times. In *The King Must Die* Mary Renault imagines the huge palace of Minos, which

> crowned the ridge and clung to its downward slopes, terrace after terrace, tier after tier of painted columns, deep glowing red, tapering in towards the base, and ringed at head and foot with that dark brilliant blue the Cretans love. Behind them in the noonday shadow were porticoes and balconies gay with pictured walls, which glowed in the shade like beds of flowers. The tops of tall cypresses hardly showed above the roofs of the courts they grew in. Over the highest roof-edge, sharp-cut against the deep blue Cretan sky, a mighty pair of horns reared towards heaven.[20]

Most of the details here are inspired by Evans' part-restoration or 'reconstitution' of Knossos, complete with 'deep glowing red' columns. (Renault was so affected by her brief but revelatory encounter with Knossos in 1954 that when the ship carrying her tour-party arrived at its next port of call, Santorini, she stayed aboard, remaining 'lost in spirit in Minos' labyrinth'.[21]) Evans' decisions remain controversial. The Art Deco influence has often been noticed, and it has even been argued that the restorations and interpretations are distorting because the 'Palace' was in fact a temple or necropolis.[22] Evans was less of a romantic and much more of a scholar than Schliemann, but in one passage from his monumental *Palace of Minos* he confesses, a little hesitantly, the dreams which the reconstruction was fulfilling for him:

The Grand Staircase as thus re-compacted stands alone among ancient architectural remains. With its charred columns solidly restored in their pristine hues, surrounding in tiers its central well, its balustrades rising, practically intact, one above the other, with its imposing fresco of the great Minoan shields on the back walls of its middle gallery, now replaced in replica, and its still well-preserved gypsum steps ascending to four landings, it revives, as no other part of the building, the remote past. It was, indeed, my own lot to experience its strange power of imaginative suggestion, even at a time when the work of reconstitution had not attained to its present completeness. During an attack of fever, having found, for the sake of better air, a temporary lodging in the room below the inspection tower that has been erected on the neighbouring edge of the Central Court, and tempted in the warm moonlight to look down the staircase-well, the whole place seemed to awake awhile to life and movement. Such was the force of the illusion that the Priest-King with his plumed lily crown, great ladies, tightly girdled, flounced and corseted, long-stoled priests, and, after them, a retinue of elegant but sinewy youths – as if the Cup-Bearer and his fellows had stepped down from the walls – passed and repassed on the flights below.[23]

Murkier imaginings are also possible at Knossos. Dilys Powell, who knew Knossos intimately as the wife of the archaeologist Humfry Payne in the 1930s, felt 'the pall of history pressing bloodstained and heavy on summer days' and 'as I clambered about the reconstructed passages something sacrificial in the air; one half-expected a roll of drums.'[24] Evelyn Waugh reflected that

I do not think that it can be only imagination and the recollection of a bloodthirsty mythology which makes something fearful and malignant of the cramped galleries and stunted alleys, these colonnades of inverted, conical pillars, these rooms that are mere blind passages at the end of sunless staircases; this squat little throne, set on a landing where the paths of the palace intersect; it is not the seat of a law-giver nor a divan for the recreation of a soldier; here an ageing despot might crouch and have borne to him, along the walls of a whispering gallery, barely audible intimations of his own murder.[25]

But Knossos has more often struck writers as a happy place, its many courts not so much labyrinthine as luxuriant. It grew, says Kazantzakis, 'slowly, like a living organism, a tree. It was not built once and for all with a fixed, premeditated plan; it grew by additions, playing and harmonizing with the ever-renewed necessities of the times.'[26] Henry Miller felt that 'here through long centuries reigned an era of peace.'[27] Knossos is humanized especially by the bright 'pictured walls' which reproduce the original frescoes as displayed (in considerably reconstructed form) in the Archaeological Museum in Herakleion. Waugh may be right that the modern painters 'have tempered their zeal for accurate reconstruction with a somewhat inappropriate predilection for covers of *Vogue*'.[28] But Kazantzakis was unaware of or unperturbed by such scruples as he celebrated these

large almond-shaped eyes, cascades of black tresses, imposing matrons with bare breasts and thick voluptuous lips, birds – pheasant and partridge – blue monkeys,

princes with peacock feathers in their hair, fierce holy
bulls, tender-aged priestesses with sacred snakes wrapped
around their arms, blue boys in flowering gardens. Joy,
strength, great wealth; a world full of mystery, an
Atlantis which had issued from the Cretan soil. This
world looked at us with immense black eyes, but its lips
were still sealed.[29]

THE VILLA ARIADNE

Sir Arthur Evans, who brought up this Atlantis, was
possessed of considerable private means. This enabled him,
in 1905, to build a substantial house from which to preside
over the digging. The Villa Ariadne, approached by a quiet
lane off the Herakleion road at the edge of the village of
Knossos, remains as described by Dilys Powell, who lived
there in the 1930s after Evans' retirement and return to
England.

> The polygonal blocks of sand-coloured stone outlined in
> mortar, the flat roof against the background of pine
> trees, the dark shutters and the half-basement, the sense
> of suffocation, stubbornly Victorian in the Mediterranean
> landscape.[30]

Here Evans lived in what Piet de Jong, who worked at
Knossos from 1922 and was later Curator there, described to
Powell as 'feudal state'. The great man personally supervised
pay-day for his workforce each Saturday from the steps of the
Villa. (There was extra payment for finds duly declared.) More
exotically, de Jong remembered 'a train of donkeys bringing
snow from Mount Ida for the sherbet.'[31]

Later occupiers of the Villa Ariadne included, between 1941
and 1944, successive Wehrmacht Divisional Commanders.
On 26 April 1944, as he was driven home from headquarters
at Arkhanes, General Karl Kreipe was ambushed and kidnapped by Patrick Leigh Fermor, W. Stanley Moss – who
later published his account of the incident in *Ill Met by
Moonlight* – and several Cretans. One of these was Miki

Akoumianakis, whose father, Manolaki, had been Sir Arthur
Evans' chief assistant in the excavation of Knossos; soon
after receiving the mistaken information that Miki had died
in action in Epiros, Manolaki was himself killed leading
a desperate charge against an enemy position on the ridge
opposite Knossos.[32]

The abduction was intended to strike a blow at German
morale on the island (the original target had been Kreipe's
notoriously brutal predecessor, General Müller); it was
followed up by 'a whispering campaign that Kreipe had
planned his own escape. Handbills were stuck up round
barracks with the words: "*Kreipe Befehl: Wir Folgen!*" –
"Kreipe give us the order: we are following!" – a skit on
the Nazi slogan "*Führer Befehl: Wir Folgen!*"'[33] The escapade
itself had its farcical elements. Moss remembered that having
been bundled into the back of the car, 'The General kept
imploring, "Where is my hat? Where is my hat?" The
hat of course was on Paddy's head.' With Leigh Fermor
thus attired, the party drove through the crowded streets
of Herakleion and a number of checkpoints, at one of which
wary guards were brushed aside with the confident cry
'*Generals Wagen!*' They abandoned the car, a brand new Opel,
a few miles from Panormos on the north coast, leaving a
letter of explanation for the Germans insisting that no
civilians had been involved in the mission and therefore
reprisals against the local population would be unjustified,
and concluding 'P.S. We are very sorry to have to leave
this beautiful car behind.'[34] Kreipe was then smuggled up
into the mountains on foot, a gruelling journey hampered
by a fall in which the general injured his shoulder, and
eventually taken off to Egypt by boat from the beach at
Rodakino, with his captors, on 14 May.

MOUNT IDA

Intimate knowledge of Ida or Psiloritis, the White Mountains,
and lesser heights, was essential to the success of the Cretan
resistance network. 'The high mountains' where Leigh
Fermor and Psychoundakis lived

had the austerity, the extravagance and sometimes the melancholy of the backgrounds of primitive religious paintings in Italy (though no Italian softness) or the vertigo of those insane and toppling crags – steel grey on purple, or ice blue on asbestos white – that surround the saints and martyrs on the ikons of Byzantium.[35]

In 1700 Joseph Pitton de Tournefort, botanist and physician travelling in the name of Louis XIV, was less impressed. In search of botanical specimens, he and his party ascended Psiloritis. Unexcited at the possibility of seeing 'the Sea, South and North' from the highest point on the island (2456m), he concluded that the fame of the peak was ill-deserved:

This celebrated Mount *Ida* exhibits nothing but a huge overgrown, ugly, sharp-rais'd, bald-pated Eminence; not the least shadow of a Landskip, no delightful Grotto, no bubbling Spring, nor purling Rivulet to be seen: there is indeed one poor sorry Well with a Bucket, to keep the Sheep and Horses from perishing with Thirst. All the Cattel bred on it, are a few scrubby Horses, some Sheep and starveling Goats, which are forc'd to brouze on the very Tragacantha; a Shrub so prickly, that the *Greeks* call it Goats-thorn.

The whole party was fed up. They were finding flints rather than uncommon flowers. Plants simply could not grow in this nightmarish region of 'bottomless Quagmires, and deep Abysses fill'd with Snow ever since the Reign of King *Jupiter*, the first of the Name.' (Jupiter or Zeus was associated with Ida.) Tournefort and his followers were 'scarce able to draw one Leg after the other.' Nature needed some help, and it came in the form of the good wine which made possible a bracing departure from the usual eastern recipe for sherbet:

We fill'd our Cups with clean crystalliz'd Snow-Drops; and here and there a Lay of Sugar between: on this we pour'd a quantity of excellent Wine; and then shaking the Cups, the whole presently dissolv'd. We did our

selves the honour to drink the King's Health and wish
his Majesty long Life and Happiness: after which, we the
more manfully clamber'd up to the very point of this
Rock, steep as it was. Whither would not one go, with
such good Wine, and commanded by so great a Prince?

Even today only fairly serious hill-walkers are likely to reach
the summit, with or without sherbet à la Tournefort.[36]

GORTYS AND PHAISTOS

Serious archaeological interest in Gortys or Gortyna, the
Roman capital of Crete, followed Federico Halbherr's
discovery, in 1884, of the twelve incised columns of the early
Greek law-code now preserved in the Odeion. Continuing
excavation has imposed a degree of order on the rambling,
grassy site, rendering it somewhat less confusing than when
Tournefort saw it.

These Ruins show indeed how magnificent a City it once
was, but 'tis impossible to look on 'em without concern:
they plough, sow, feed Sheep among the Wrecks of a
prodigious quantity of Marble, Jasper, Granate-Stone,
wrought with great curiosity: in the room of those great
Men who had caus'd such stately Edifices to be erected,
you see nothing but poor Shepherds, who are so stupid
as to let the Hares run between their legs, without
meddling with them; and Partridges bask under their
very noses, without offering to catch 'em.

Some of the stone, Tournefort found, had been put to
use in Agii Deka, 'a Village within two Musket-shot of
these ruinous Fragments, where the Garden-Gates are of two
antique Columns, between which they place a Hurdle of
Wood for a Door.'[37]
The road from Gortys to Phaistos continues through
Tournefort's 'finest and fruitfullest Plain of all *Candia*', the
Messara. Phaistos is notable as much for its setting as for
the Minoan ruins, as Henry Miller concluded during one
of his leisurely excursions from Herakleion.

I descended the broad steps of the levelled palace and glanced here and there automatically. I hadn't the faintest desire to snoop about examining lintels, urns, pottery, children's toys, votive cells and such like. Below me, stretching away like an infinite magic carpet, lay the plain of Messara, girdled by a majestic chain of mountain ranges. From this sublime, serene height it has all the appearance of the Garden of Eden. At the very gates of Paradise the descendants of Zeus halted here on their way to eternity to cast a last look earthward and saw with the eyes of innocents that the earth is indeed what they had always dreamed it to be: a place of beauty and joy and peace. In his heart man is angelic; in his heart man is united with the whole world. Phaestos contains all the elements of the heart; it is feminine through and through.

Such flights of the imagination perhaps owe something to Miller's meal with the custodian, at which

I believe the wine was called *mavrodaphne*. If not it should have been because it is a beautiful black word [*mavros* means black] and describes the wine perfectly. It slips down like molten glass, firing the veins with a heavy red fluid which expands the heart and the mind. One is heavy and light at the same time; one feels as nimble as the antelope and yet powerless to move.[38]

SOUTHERN CRETE

According to Jan Struys the air of Crete 'is temperate enough, but on that side facing *Africa* is something hot, and rendered unwholesom by southerly Winds: for which reason most of the Towns are built on that side of the Island which lies next to the *Archipelago*'.[39] Certainly Crete's conquerors made little impact on the rocky southern coast. The Sphakians in the south-west (like the Maniots in the southern Peloponnese) were so independent-spirited that they were, claimed the Dutch traveller Olfert Dapper in the seventeenth century, 'almost wild.'[40] When George Psychoundakis needed to cross the Samaria Gorge, he found himself in danger not from Germans but from the local 'wind-boys' or outlaws, although this did not prevent him from marvelling at these 'spectacular regions: enormous trees, planes, cypresses and pines with strong and gigantic trunks, and crystal springs streaming down on all sides.'[41]

There is one striking reminder of outside influences at Frangokastello – the 'Castle of the Franks'. Michael Llewellyn Smith described its present state in his book about Crete, *The Great Island*:

Frangokastello in its lonely eminence seems untouched by subsequent history, totally foreign. From a distance the castle seems perfect, unscarred. The golden, honey-coloured stone glows and traps the light. Only when you approach can you see that the weather-beaten, battered lion of St. Mark, who stands guard over the southern door, is protector of a ruin. The roof has gone. Lizards bask on the sun-baked stone. Coarse grasses and pungent herbs have wedged themselves into the fissures and taken possession of the Franks' preserve.[42]

The castle was built by the Venetians in the fourteenth century to protect Sphakia from the depredations of the corsairs. Here in 1828 the rebel leader, Hadzimikhalis Daliannis, made his last stand against the Turks, and according to legend still charges across the plain with his men one morning every May. His end was happier than that of the Sphakian rebel leader of 1770, Daskaloyiannis, who was flayed alive in Herakleion. But Daskaloyiannis ('Teacher John') also entered folk mythology, in this case through the verses of the bard Barba Pantzelios, written down in 1786 and commemorating his bold denunciation of the 'lawless pashas', his faithful determination to fix the cross to the gate of Khania, and his heroic endurance.

Zorba the Greek, called by Kazantzakis himself *The Life and Adventures of Alexis Zorbas*, is set in an unspecified area of the south coast. Kazantzakis and Zorba's original, a Macedonian workman and adventurer, George Zorbas, really embarked on their unsuccessful lignite-mining scheme at Prastova in Mani, but the change of location reflects both the author's Cretan roots and the needs of the novel. The south-Cretan setting, with its empty sea or rocky solitude on the one hand and fruitful land of oranges and figs on the other, enacts the narrator's struggle to escape from 'pen-pushing' and abstraction into sensual engagement. On remote white sands, beneath the stars, between two worlds, the Boss and Zorba eat and argue and Zorba expounds the earthy philosophy expressed most famously in his 'clever and impetuous' dancing after the mining venture has ended in spectacular disaster:

> He pounded on the pebbles with his bare feet and clapped his hands. 'Boss,' he said, 'I've dozens of things to say to you. I've never loved anyone as much before. I've hundreds of things to say, but my tongue just can't manage them. So I'll dance them for you! Here goes!'
>
> He leaped into the air and his feet and arms seemed to sprout wings. As he threw himself straight in the air against that background of sea and sky, he looked like an old archangel in rebellion. For Zorba's dance was full of defiance and obstinacy. He seemed to be shouting to the sky: 'What can you do to me, Almighty? You can do nothing to me except kill me. Well, kill me, I don't care! I've vented my spleen, I've said all I want to say; I've had time to dance . . . and I don't need you any more!'[43]

RETHYMNON

Rethymnon has had its periods of intense activity. The vast hill-top enclosure of the Venetian fortress, with its ruined churches and mosques, was once populous, and in the sixteenth century the city below boasted, like Candia and Khania, its own Accademia. It was an important Turkish centre, with fine public buildings like the surviving mosque and tall minaret of Nerantzes. Now tourism flourishes. But the most eloquent tribute to Rethymnon, *The Tale of a Town* (1938), by the art historian and novelist Pandelis

Prevelakis, was written during one of its least prosperous periods. After years of economic recession, the shopkeepers sat in their doorways chatting with each other to 'beguile the slow passing of time and forget the lack of business with all the advantage of enjoying the scented sea air.'

The economic problems resulted not only from the Great Depression, but from the Treaty of Lausanne which in 1923, when Prevelakis was fourteen, enforced the exchange of populations by which over a million Greeks left Turkey and 350,000 Turks left Greece. The social and psychological consequences, as well as the economic, were severe on both sides. Much of *The Tale of a Town* is an elegy for the Turkish community which had moulded the atmosphere and appearance of the old town. One section describes the life of the important Turks who spent the days on their estates in the country but kept their wives in Rethymnon 'on account of the frequent Christian risings.' Every evening they would ride proudly up to the castle before the closing of the Great Gate. At this stage they were haughty and grim-faced. But later, having dined with their womenfolk, 'their eyelids drooping with repletion', they would go to the Turkish café by the harbour to relax.

They bowed to each other, with hand across the breast, and went to sit, each in his appointed place, up there on the platform. It was a fine piece of carpentry, that platform, built of cypress-wood which after years of wear shone like amber. Above it burned the two hanging lamps, their glass chimneys protected by a tin shade, and below it, like the sea menacing a ship, seethed the common mob, some bareheaded, others in turban or fez and most of them barefoot. The boys brought the nargilehs properly prepared and with lowered eyes set them down before each client and applied to the tobacco the lighted coal which they took from a little brazier, no bigger than a cup, made for this purpose. Then the Turkish grandee, with ineffable bliss, coiled the tube round the neck of the nargileh, to keep it from trailing, raised the amber mouthpiece to his lips and sank into a gentle torpor, like a grub into the rose he is devouring.

With the nargilehs arrived, too, the professional story-teller who was to relate that evening's story.[44]

This was one way of enjoying life in a town where, Edward Lear complained in 1864, there was 'little to do.'[45] .

ARKADI

The road from Rethymnon to the monastery of Arkadi leaves the coastal plain to climb past crumbling farm walls, slopes thick with olives, and hill-top villages, and on up to the dusty plateau where the most famous incident of all the Cretan insurrections took place.

When Tournefort visited Arkadi in 1700 there were one hundred monks in the monastery and a further two hundred 'out-liers' tending nearby farms. The farm produce included grapes for wine-making. Tournefort counted 'no less than 200 Butts of Wine' in the handsome cellar; 'the best Piece is mark'd with the Superior's name, and no body dare touch it without his leave.'[46] In 1864 Lear found the wine very good if too sweet, but was pleased with his meal and his host, Abbot Gabriel,

who is a man of the world, was very jolly and pleasant and apologized, unnecessarily, for the supper, owing to its late coming: stewed pigeons, three sorts of salad, a dish of honey, cherries, beans, cheese, etc. etc.

As usual on this expedition Lear had some problems locating the toilet, but slept well, rose early to draw, and was off at 6.10. 'I like Gabriel' he concluded.[47]

Two and a half years later, Abbot Gabriel Marinakis proved himself more than a jolly host. Like some of his predecessors, he was prepared to use the monastery as a base for anti-Turkish activities. In the autumn of the insurrection year 1866, a large Turkish force advanced on the monastery, which was occupied by monks, resistance fighters, and local people. Marinakis refused to surrender, and a fierce siege began. There were to be many impassioned and understandably hagiographical accounts of the Cretans' sacrifice; Revd Henry Fanshawe Tozer, visiting in March 1874 when much of the monastery was still in ruins, tells a plainer but no less affecting tale. One of the survivors told him how, after cannon had blown in the entrance gate, the Turks

> forced their way in at the point of the bayonet, and commenced an indiscriminate massacre, in which 300 souls perished. The court ran with blood, our informant said, and it was so piled with bodies that it was impossible to pass from one side to the other. Simultaneously with this attack in front, another band of Turks made an assault from behind, where there was a postern; but close to it the powder magazine was situated, in a chamber over which numbers of monks and women and children were congregated together. As soon as the besiegers were close to the postern, the Christians set fire to the powder, and blew up all this part of the building, involving their friends and their enemies in common ruin. Large pieces of the shattered wall remain outside the new wall, and though most of the Turks were buried where they fell, yet the bones of others might be seen lying on the ground. In the midst of the massacre six-and-thirty Christians took refuge in the refectory, but they were pursued and all killed, and their blood still stained the walls. About sixty others collected together in a corridor, and begged for quarter, as having taken no part in the insurrection, and the lives of these were spared. The monastery was then fired, and many sick and helpless persons perished in the conflagration.[48]

Constantine Giaboudakis, probably following the Abbot's instructions, fired the pistol shot which blew up the 'gunpowder room', kept still as an unroofed shell. (The Abbot himself was killed by a Turkish bullet.) Other relics of the fighting are the refectory and its bullet-riddled door, and the skulls displayed in the ossuary.

The much-chronicled explosion not only gave Crete more martyrs but forcefully called the attention of the Western European public to the plight of the islanders. As Victor Hugo wrote in the Trieste newspaper, *Clio*, on 8 March 1867, Arkadi had battled like a fortress, but died like a volcano.

KHANIA

> The appearance of the town was striking, as its irregular wooden buildings rose up the hill sides from the sea, interspersed with palm-trees, mosques, and minarets. There was no mistaking that we were in Turkey. The whole place is surrounded by a Venetian wall of great massiveness, and the harbour is enclosed by extensive moles.[49]

So observed Henry Tozer, arriving by sea at Khania in 1874. Like Rethymnon, Khania retains much of this Turkish appearance. The Turks had taken the city, in 1645, after a siege of only two months, in spite of all the precautions noticed thirty years before by William Lithgow, who found Khania

> exceeding populous, well walled, and fortified with Bulwarkes. It hath a large Castle, containing ninety seaven Pallaces, in which the Rector and other Venetian Gentlemen dwell. There lye continually in it Seaven Companies of Souldiers who keepe Centinell on the walles, guard the gates and Market places of the Citie: Neither in this Towne nor Candia, may any Countrey Peasant enter with weapons (especially Harquebuzes) for that conceived feare they have of Treason.

Lithgow had one of his more dramatic adventures in Khania. A French Protestant, one of a group of four who had 'killed a young Noble Venetian, about the quarrell of a Courtezan' and been condemned to the galleys, was allowed ashore with a keeper and 'carrying an yron bolt on his legge.' Lithgow, meeting his co-religionist, felt sorry for him and hastily resolved on a plan to help him. The following day he succeeded in getting the keeper very drunk, and in smuggling the Frenchman away, disguised in a gown and veil provided by Lithgow's 'Landresse', to 'a Greekish convent on the South side of the land.' But as Lithgow went towards the city walls, rejoicing at a good deed done, he was met by two English soldiers who had come to warn him that 'all the Officers of the Galleys, with a number of Souldiers were in searching the City, and hunting all over the fields for me.' Various well-disposed English and French soldiers somehow conveyed him though the gates and even – or so Lithgow claims – at one point fought off armed challengers and 'deadly wounded two of the Officers.' Finally he reached the sanctuary of the Italian monastery where he was staying, and there boldly outfaced the questions of the 'Generall of the Galleys.'[50] He was less fortunate in Malaga in 1620, when he was imprisoned and racked on allegations of spying and heresy.

Renaissance Khania, like Candia and Rethymnon, had its Accademia for the cultivation of literature in Italian, and there were frequent opportunities for the less erudite to indulge in the traditional Venetian delights of theatre, music and masquerade. In 1594, for instance, a great joust was preceded by festivities which turned the harbourside into a very different place from that later dominated by the sober Mosque of the Janissaries or the current lines of fish restaurants.

The high point of the entertainment, in more senses than one, was announced by a melody so sweet that the spectators fell instantly silent; and into the harbour-side square trundled Mount Ida, complete with rocks and dittany [Ida's famous medicinal herb], and drawn by torch-bearing satyrs. Around the mountain hunters, hawks and dogs were engaged in chasing birds and hares. On its summit sat a handsome young shepherd, white-clad and garlanded, watching his sheep: he sang some verses in Greek. 'But Fortune always mingles the bitter with the sweet', and the mountain suddenly burst open to reveal a horrible one-eyed monster as big as a lion, snaky-tailed, scaly-backed, with huge claws, long teeth and a mouth that breathed fire.[51]

Nearly four hundred years later Edward Lear encountered less spectacular goings-on. For him as for most visitors to

Crete at this time, Khania was the port of arrival and departure. Its 'detestable' streets gave him no pleasure, and dinner, pipes and coffee with the Pasha and 'tother cove' (the visiting Pasha of Rethymnon) were a sorry trial which allegedly included 'Twenty dishes, and only one wine.' Perhaps Lear busied himself mentally on such occasions with literary compositions such as the lines he had published eighteen years before in *A Book of Nonsense*:

> There was a young person of Crete
> Whose toilette was never complete;
> She dressed in a sack, spickle-speckled with black,
> That ombliferous person of Crete.

When free of the pashas he did, however, succeed in producing some fine drawings and watercolours of the city. He worked from the ramparts, a café gallery, nearby hills, and finally, from the boat bound for Syros as sunrise began to turn the water pinkish-purple, he painted the great and smaller domes of the Janissaries' mosque and the mansions beyond. From the ramparts Lear had also immortalized one of those views of the mountains – in this case the 'wondrous' White Mountains 'contrasted with the deep velvet green-grey of the hills and green of the plain' – which have solaced, harboured, or defeated so many Cretans and so many outsiders.[52]

With the exception of Rhodes and Kos, most of the southeast Aegean islands grouped as the Dodecanese are small and rocky. At one time they were remote and little visited by outsiders other than corsairs. Hardy merchants like Bernard Randolph in the late seventeenth century might pause briefly as he did on Karpathos, roughly half-way between Crete and Rhodes, where

> The inhabitants are very poor, and seldom free from the visits of the Privateers. Any ships which put in here may have all provision very cheap; Partridges at half a dollar a hundred alive . . . Here the Mountains are most Marble, and to those that come from the South, they make

a glorious shew, the Sun shining upon them. Not a quarter of the island is inhabited.[53]

Travellers driven by mere curiosity were rare. A century after Randolph was on Karpathos, Claude-Étienne Savary was rather shocked by his encounter with Symi, to the north of Rhodes. The sparseness of vegetation made sponge-diving, in spite of the hazards of the bends or of being devoured by 'monsters of the deep', the islanders' only possible livelihood. Sunk deep in poverty, they 'have a reserved and melancholy air' and 'appear absorbed in their own wretchedness.' The inhabitants of Kasos were more interested in the alien.

Europeans rarely land in this solitary island, and the inhabitants, accustomed to see nothing but bald heads, wrapped round with shawls, long robes fastened with sashes, and venerable beards, could not but view with astonishment a foreigner with long plaited hair, without mustachios, and wearing a cocked hat, and short coat, that came no lower than his knee. They appeared greatly struck with the contrast.[54]

By the late nineteenth century foreigners were less of a rarity even on the smaller islands. But Patmos was still off the steamer routes; Revd Henry Fanshawe Tozer 'engaged a good-sized decked vessel' to sail there from Samos, while Revd Dr Arthur Penrhyn Stanley (later famous as Dean Stanley), chaplain to Edward, Prince of Wales on his tour of Egypt and the Holy Land in 1862, was able to take advantage of 'our homeward voyage in H.M. Yacht Osborne' to take in 'this sacred spot'.[55] (Bertie's responses to the sacred spot are not recorded.) A steamer did call at Leros. Its arrival, Tozer discovered when he was sitting 'in an upper room belonging to a very dirty *café*,' was 'the fortnightly excitement of the island,' signalled by a terrific shout 'from every side, as if the whole population of Leros had risen in insurrection.'[56]

PATMOS

Patmos owes its fame to the statement by the writer of the Apocalypse – traditionally St John the Evangelist – that he 'was in the isle that is called Patmos, for the word of God' when he received his revelation. Henry Tozer, controlling his Protestant scepticism at the cave chapel of the Apocalypse, explains that

> In one part of the roof a rent is pointed out, where the rock was broken at the commencement of the Revelation, and from a somewhat deeper cleft in this the Divine voice is said to have proceeded; nor does the process of identification stop here, for a hole in the wall close by this is believed to have been the place where St. John's head lay.[57]

It was perhaps with some relief that Tozer moved on to the great Monastery of St John, whose foundation by St Christodoulos in 1088 was a matter of fact. The ascetic but influential saint had been some time searching for a suitable home for a small community of monks when the Emperor Alexios Komnenos granted him Patmos in the huge charter or chrysobul which is one of the most treasured items in the monastic library. From the practical point of view, Patmos did not seem a good choice. The imperial commissioner charged with handing over the island reported as follows:

> Having visited all parts of the island of Patmos, we found it deserted, uncultivated, completely covered with impenetrable thickets of brushwood and hawthorn, entirely arid as a consequence of the lack of water. In the whole island indeed we found no running water and no spring water, with the exception of a few small wells, which, in any case, rarely yield sufficient water . . . Moreover what arable land there is is enclosed and as it were strangled by long chains of mountains. All the rest of the island is mountainous country, rough and unuseable; in the arable part itself, there are scarcely 160 measures capable of being ploughed; all the rest must be

broken up with pickaxe and mattock, and watered by
the blood and sweat of the farmer. . . . Of trees we
saw not the slightest trace, apart from about twenty
desiccated pear-trees.[58]

Confronted by these problems and by the ever-present risk
of attack by corsairs, the monks, after initial attempts to
establish a monastery, abandoned Patmos and sailed to the
greater safety and comfort of Euboia. There Christodoulos
died in 1093. But the saint had insisted that his followers
should return to Patmos. 'Surprisingly, they did', as A.R. and
Mary Burn cannot resist saying in their guide to historical
sites, *The Living Past of Greece*.[59]
The monks brought the saint's body back with them
and, by dint of determination, imperial support, lay aid,
and the construction of water cisterns, succeeded in building
their monastery. Within a century it was one of the
wealthiest and most powerful in the Byzantine Empire.
The rich library and treasury began to be built up. Abbot
Theoktistos, who died in 1157, once had to buy off the
corsairs, but the monastery became increasingly fortress-like.
Its grey, martial bulk still dominates Patmos. Tozer was
struck by how 'closely and strangely packed together' the
fortress-monastery is.

Its staircases are quite a puzzle, and passages occur in
the most unexpected places, and diverge in a variety of
directions. The court round which it is built is very
irregular in shape, and several pointed arches are thrown
across it to strengthen the buildings on either side:
within it are numerous cisterns for storing water and
troughs for washing. The upper part is a wilderness of
chimneys, bells, domes, and battlements. A pavement of
tiles or flags covers the flat roof, or rather roofs, for
different parts have different levels, and the communi-
cation between these is made by steps constructed at
various angles. Among them the domes of chapels
project at intervals.[60]

KOS

> Though *Rhodes* exceeds it in bigness, this doth that
> as much in beauty; most part of it being low land, in
> comparison to the other Islands about it. Here are woods
> of Cyprus trees, of a great many years standing, and the
> *Turks* are so pleased with them that they will not suffer
> them to be cut down.

Bernard Randolph's personal observation confirmed for
English readers the existence of the shaded paradise of the
seventh Idyll of the poet of Kos, Theocritus.

One large tree in particular, Randolph goes on to say, the
Turks made 'their place of recreation in hot weather, there
being several shops for Barbers, and where Coffee and Sherbett
is sold.'[61] The tree – the great plane near the Castle of the
Knights – is so old that legend has made it the one under
whose already flourishing boughs Hippocrates, the 'Father of
Medicine', taught his disciples. Compton Mackenzie enjoyed
the shade during a brief time ashore on Kos in April 1917:

> Asclepius, the guardian demigod of Cos, must have
> breathed long life into that plane tree whose branches
> weighed down by age are held up by marble columns.
> The tree is not tall. No doubt the sea winds have kept
> its stature low, but the girth of the trunk is prodigious,
> and the amount of space it covers is at first incredible.
> One looks at every supporting column in turn, expecting
> to find it masks the trunk of another tree.

Mackenzie, in need of some permanence in a world where
war continually emphasised transience, cannot resist believing
that the tree is 2,500 years old. (The accurate figure, still not
unimpressive, is about six hundred.) 'The Colossus of Rhodes
has long been overthrown. Of the Heraeum at Samos a single
column remains. The temple of the Ephesian Artemis is level
with the earth. The plane tree of Hippocrates . . . has outlived
them all.'[62]

On returning to Kos forty years later while preparing to
make a series of films about Greece for the BBC, Mackenzie

was sad to find that the tree, now cut back, no longer seemed such a wonder.[63]

RHODES

> Nestling in the natural amphitheatre where once stood the white buildings and temples of the ancient town, the Crusader fortress with its encircling walls and crumbling turrets looks for all the world like a town in pen and ink, situated upon the margins of some illuminated manuscript: the medieval dream of a fortress called Rhodes which the mist has invented for you.[64]

As Lawrence Durrell's description suggests, the city of Rhodes is still dominated by traces of the medieval might of the Order of St John: the fortified Palace of the Grand Masters, the great stone hospital, the gigantic ramparts.

This Rhodes is largely a modern restoration and even in many places a modern creation. The lavish interior of the Palace, its floors adorned with mosaics transferred from Kos, is very much a creation (1937–40) of the Italian Governor whose residence it became, designed to impress on Rhodes and the world his own and Mussolini's glory. (Italy held the Dodecanese from 1912.) The whole medieval upper storey had been accidentally blown up, in 1856, by gunpowder stored in the Church of St John of the Collachium. But the city had been battered and rebuilt before – most extensively after the long and fierce sieges of 304 BC, 1480, and 1522, and following several major earthquakes. Use or sale of materials from the unsuccessful siege-machines of 304 BC enabled the construction of the Colossus at – but not, as poets and painters have imagined, astride – the harbour entrance.

The stalwart resistance of the Knights to the Turkish onslaught of 1480 was chronicled by the Vice-Chancellor of the Order, Guillaume Caoursin. Since the fall of Constantinople in 1453 Europe had watched the seemingly irresistible advance of the Turks with increasing unease, and was eager for reassurance. As a result, there was a substantial market, in these early days of printing, both for Caoursin's

Latin text and for translations including that into English (1482) by John Kay, who styled himself Poet Laureate to King Edward IV. It must have been with mingled horror and relief that readers or hearers of the chronicle learnt how close the Turks had come to victory. Following a parley in which the Knights defied the besiegers to do their worst, 'with great bombards, guns, engines, and all other such instruments of war, they vexed and grieved the Rhodians and proposed to prove if the deeds of the Rhodians should accord with their great words.' To this onslaught they added psychological warfare in the evenings: they approached the much-holed walls 'with their taberettes and made songs of mirth', which the Rhodians in turn tried to drown out with 'trumpets and clarions'. The Turks also let it be known that they had made ready eight thousand stakes with which to impale their opponents if they failed to surrender. At dawn on 27 July the Janissaries captured the Tower of Italy and the Turks entered the city. Grand Master d'Aubusson was wounded in five places. Disaster seemed inevitable. A miracle was needed, and, according to Caoursin, was vouchsafed: at the very point where the fighting was most fierce

> the Turks saw properly in the midst of the clean and bright air, a cross all of shining gold, and also saw a bright virgin, which had in her hands against the host of the Turks a spear and a shield, and in that sight also appeared a man clothed in poor and vile array [St John the Baptist, patron of the Order], which was accompanied with great number of fair and well-be-seen men in arms, as if he would come down to the help of Rhodes.

Suitably full of 'wonder and fear', the Turks decided to withdraw; in honour of the miracle, 'many of them forsook their false belief and were christened in the city of Rhodes.' And so, concludes Caoursin, 'Rhodes was and is preserved and kept from the Turks captivity.'[65]

The defenders of 1522, led by Grand Master Philippe Villiers de l'Isle Adam, fought no less stalwartly and prayed no less devoutly than those of 1480. But many Knights were absent, embroiled, in their home countries, in the struggle between the Emperor Charles V and Francis I of France; the Turks, led first by the son-in-law of Suleiman the Magnificent and then by the Sultan himself, operated a more effective blockade of the harbour while attacking from land; and the townspeople finally prevailed upon the Grand Master to capitulate rather than wait for the sacking of the city. The Knights were allowed to depart with dignity for Crete on 1 January 1523. From 1530 they were established in a new base in Malta, which they successfully defended from another great Turkish siege in 1565.

In the centuries between the departure of the Knights and the modern restoration of their domains, travellers found a quiet, crumbling city whose atmosphere was so conducive to idleness, Thackeray maintained in 1844, that most visitors wouldn't move 'though we had been told that the Colossus himself was taking a walk half a mile off.'[66] (The fragments of the Colossus, felled by an earthquake in 224 BC, had themselves lain idle for nearly nine hundred years until Arab invaders sold the bronze covering and deposited the rest in the harbour in AD 654.) Parts of the Palace were used, before the explosion of 1856, as a prison and later as a coffee-house. 'The grand hospital' of the Knights, reported Murray's *Handbook*, 'is now a public granary.'[67] Chateaubriand felt, however, that less had changed in the Street of the Knights (Odos Ippoton), which slopes up from the Hospital to the Palace:

> At every step Rhodes offered me traces of our customs and memories of my homeland. I found a little France in the middle of Greece. . . . I went up a street still called Street of the Knights. It is lined with Gothic houses; the walls of these houses are studded with Gallic devices and the coats of arms of our historic families. I noticed the crowned fleurs-de-lis, as fresh as if they had just come from the sculptor's hand. The Turks, who everywhere have mutilated the monuments of Greece, have spared those of chivalry: Christian honour has astonished Turkish courage, and the Saladins have paid respect to the Coucis [a noble French family].[68]

Possibly the French connection concealed from Chateaubriand the extent of the decay of the Houses of the 'Tongues'. (The Knights had been divided into the language or dialect groups of Spain, England, Germany, Auvergne, Provence and France.) Murray's *Handbook* bemoaned the disfiguring of the windows by 'the wooden lattices placed before them by the Turks to conceal the ladies of the harems' and lamented that the surface of the street itself was now in 'a melancholy state of dilapidation.'[69]

Amid such scenes Thackeray mused ironically on time, change, the 'chivalrous relics', and what had succeeded them:

The Turks, who battered down chivalry, seem to be waiting their turn of destruction now. In walking through Rhodes one is strangely affected by witnessing the signs of this double decay. For instance, in the streets of the knights, you see noble houses, surmounted by noble escutcheons of superb knights, who lived there, and prayed, and quarrelled, and murdered the Turks; and were the most gallant pirates of the inland seas; and made vows of chastity, and robbed and ravished; and, professing humility, would admit none but nobility into their order; and died recommending themselves to sweet St. John, and calmly hoping for heaven in consideration of all the heathen they had slain. When this superb fraternity was obliged to yield to courage as great as theirs, faith as sincere, and to robbers even more dexterous and audacious than the noblest knight who ever sang a canticle to the Virgin, these halls were filled by magnificent pashas and agas, who lived here in the intervals of war, and, having conquered its best champions, despised Christendom and chivalry pretty much as an Englishman despises a Frenchman. Now the famous house is let to a shabby merchant, who has his little beggarly shop in the bazaar; to a small officer, who ekes out his wretched pension by swindling, and who gets his pay in bad coin.[70]

Among the present occupants of the houses are the Italian

Vice-Consulate, the Ministry of Culture, and the Price Control Police.

The landscape as well as the much-used stone of Rhodes attracts attention. There is the 'gnarled, rock-hewn' country around Lindos, as described by Durrell.[71] Savary found lower parts of the interior, during a period of neglect imposed by Turkish taxes and monopolies, carpeted with wild roses and perfumed with the scent of flowering myrtle.[72] For Lamartine 'Rhodes emerges like a green bouquet from the midst of the waves; the light and graceful minarets of its white mosques rise above its forests of palms, carobs, sycamores, planes, and fig-trees.'[73] Let us return with Lawrence Durrell, however, for a last afternoon in the city:

> By the post of England on the medieval walls – so broad that six horsemen could gallop abreast upon them – we spend the afternoon lounging. We can overlook the whole town from here, as well as the shrill private lives of a dozen families who live directly under the towering walls, in gardens picked out with palms and bushes of red hibiscus. A windmill turns, creaking, and from the invisible market-place rises the surf of human bartering – the vibration of business. On the wall itself two armies are fighting with wooden swords – a dozen children in paper hats against half a dozen bareheaded ones. They are not Knights and Saracens, as one might think, but British and Germans. The battle sways forwards and backwards. Nobody dies or is hurt, though one of the shock-troops has started crying. Their shouts marry the thin keening of the swifts by the walls, darting against the blue. High up against the sun an eagle planes above us, watching history plagiarising itself once more upon these sun-mellowed walls.[74]

REFERENCES

PREFACE

1. Percy Bysshe Shelley, *Hellas* (1822), in *The Poetical Works of Percy Bysshe Shelley*, ed. Thomas Hutchinson, London, 1905, p. 447.
2. John Cam Hobhouse, *A Journey Through Albania and Other Provinces of Turkey in Europe and Asia*, London, 1813, Vol. I, pp. 301–2.
3. Karl Baedeker, *Greece: Handbook for Travellers*, London, 1889, p. xiv.
4. William Eton, *A Survey of the Turkish Empire*, London, 1798, p. 334.
5. *The Diaries of Evelyn Waugh*, ed. Michael Davie, London, 1976, p. 276; Martin Seymour-Smith, *Robert Graves: his Life and Work*, London, 1982, p. 513; Henry Miller, *The Colossus of Maroussi*, London, 1991 (1941), p. 9.
6. Edmund Wilson, *Europe Without Baedeker*, London, 1986 (1948), pp. 236–7.

ATHENS

1. Patrick Leigh Fermor, *Roumeli: Travels in Northern Greece*, London, 1966, p. 116.
2. Demetrios Sicilianos, *Old and New Athens*, trans. Robert Liddell, London, 1960, p. 256.
3. James Stuart and Nicholas Revett, *Antiquities of Athens*, Vol. II, London, 1787, p. 24.
4. Sebastiano Ittar, 'Fête with a Tightrope Walker by the Theseum', in Fani-Maria Tsigakou, *The Rediscovery of Greece: Travellers and Painters of the Romantic Era*, London, 1981, p. 146.
5. Sicilianos, *Old and New Athens*, p. 161.
6. *The Diaries of Evelyn Waugh*, ed. Michael Davie, London, 1976, p. 274.
7. Arnold Toynbee, *The Greeks and their Heritages*, Oxford, 1981, p. 244.

8.   William Lithgow, *The Totall Discourse of the Rare Adventures & Painefull Peregrinations*, Glasgow, 1906, p. 67.

9.   John Addington Symonds, *Sketches and Studies in Italy and Greece*, London, 1898, Vol. III, p. 341.

10. Kostis Palamas, 'Athens' in *Απαντα*, Vol. III, Athens, 1962-9, p. 15.

11. *Letters of George Gissing to Members of his Family*, ed. Algernon and Ellen Gissing, London, 1927, pp. 295-6.

12. Edward Lear, letter of 3 June 1848, quoted by Tsigakou, *The Rediscovery of Greece*, p. 127.

13. Symonds, *Sketches*, Vol. III, pp. 345-6.

14. Isadora Duncan, *My Life*, London, 1988 (1928), pp. 95-102.

15. Aristophanes, *Lysistrata*, l. 265.

16. Michael Akominatos Khoniates, *Works*, ed. Lambros, Athens, 1879-80, Vol. II, p. 12.

17. Ibid., Vol. II, p. 259.

18. Ibid., Vol. I, p. 105.

19. Sir George Wheler, *A Journey into Greece*, London, 1682, p. 363.

20. Gustave Flaubert, letter to Louis Bouilhet, 10 February 1851, in *Correspondance*, ed. Jean Bruneau, Paris, 1973, Vol. I, p. 752.

22. *The Letters of George Gissing to Eduard Bertz 1887-1903*, ed. Arthur C. Young, London, 1961, p. 89.

23. Alphonse de Lamartine, *Voyage en Orient*, ed. Lotfy Fam, Paris, 1960, pp. 283-4.

24. William Makepeace Thackeray, *Notes of a Journey from Cornhill to Grand Cairo*, ed. Sarah Searight and Briony Llewellyn, Heathfield, 1991 (1846), p. 48.

25. Robert Byron, *Europe in the Looking Glass*, London, 1926, pp. 155-6.

26. Peter Green, 'King Fix: Bill Golding in Greece', in *William Golding: the Man and his Books. A Tribute on his 75th Birthday*, ed. John Carey, London, 1986, p. 49.

27. Flaubert, *Correspondance*, Vol. I, p. 752; Byron, *Europe in the Looking Glass*, p. 156; H.V. Morton, *In the Steps of St. Paul*, London, 1936, p. 269.

28. Quoted in Robin A. Fletcher, *Kostes Palamas: a Great Modern Greek Poet*, Athens, 1984, p. 181.

29. Morton, *In the Steps of St. Paul*, pp. 268-9.

30. Lamartine, *Voyage en Orient*, p. 279.

31. Peter Levi, *The Hill of Kronos: a Personal Portrait of Greece*, London, 1991 (1981), p. 21.

32. *The Autobiography and Journals of Benjamin Robert Haydon*, ed. Malcolm Elwin, London, 1950, pp. 78–9; W. Sharp, *Life and Letters of Joseph Severn*, London, 1892, p. 32.

33. George Gordon, Lord Byron, *English Bards and Scotch Reviewers* (1809), ll. 1029–30.

34. Lord Byron, *The Curse of Minerva* (1811), l. 204.

35. For Benizelos' letter see William St Clair, *Lord Elgin and the Marbles*, Oxford, 1983 (1967), p. 213.

36. Francesco Morosini, quoted by Richard Stoneman, *Land of Lost Gods: the Search for Classical Greece*, London, 1987, p. 83.

37. David Watkin, *The Life and Work of C.R. Cockerell*, London, 1974, pp. 6–7.

38. Charles Robert Cockerell, *Travels in Southern Europe and the Levant, 1810–1817: the Journal of C.R. Cockerell, R.A.*, ed. Samuel Pepys Cockerell, London, 1903, p. 262.

39. Virginia Woolf, *A Passionate Apprentice: the Early Journals 1897–1909*, ed. Mitchell A. Leaska, London, 1990, p. 323.

40. John Boardman, *Greek Sculpture. The Classical Period: a Handbook*, London, 1985, p. 161.

41. Brian de Jongh, *The Companion Guide to Mainland Greece*, revised by John Gandon, London, 1989, p. 30.

42. Wheler, *Journey into Greece*, p. 364.

43. Woolf, *Passionate Apprentice*, pp. 325–6.

44. Harold Macmillan, *War Diaries: Politics and War in the Mediterranean January 1943–May 1945*, London, 1984, pp. 655, 614.

45. Alistair Horne, *Macmillan 1894–1956*. (Vol. I of official biography), London, 1988, p. 234.

46. Evelyn Waugh, *Labels: a Mediterranean Journal*, London, 1974 (1930), pp. 149, 150, 152–4.

47. Quoted by John Freely, *Strolling Through Athens: a Guide to the City*, London, 1991, p. 262.

48. Thackeray, *Journey from Cornhill*, p. 50.

49. Mary and David Hogarth, *Scenes in Athens*, c. 1900, quoted by Tsigakou, *Rediscovery of Greece*, p. 149.

50. Victor Seroff, *The Real Isadora*, London, 1972, p. 227.

51. Evelyn Waugh, *Diaries*, ed. Michael Davie, London, 1976, pp. 274–5; Robert Byron, *Europe in the Looking Glass*, pp. 159, 170; John Pearson, *Façades: Edith, Osbert and Sacheverell Sitwell*, London, 1978, p. 251; Edmund Wilson, *Europe Without Baedeker: Sketches Among the Ruins of Italy, Greece and England*, London, 1986 (1948), p. 238.

52. Macmillan, *War Diaries*, p. 617.
53. Leigh Fermor, *Roumeli*, p. 117.
54. Andromache Schliemann Melas, *Reader's Digest*, July 1950, p. 48.
55. Carl Schuhhardt, *Schliemann's Excavations*, trans. Eugénie Sellers, London, 1891, pp. 15–16.
56. Sicilianos, *Old and New Athens*, pp. 203–6.
57. *Callas as They Saw Her*, ed. David A. Lowe, London, 1987, pp. 22–5.
58. Levi, *The Hill of Kronos*, p. 27.
59. Diana Cooper, *The Light of Common Day: Autobiography*, London, 1984 (1959), p. 186.
60. Eugenia Fakinou, *Astradeni*, trans. H.E. Criton, Athens, 1991, pp. 175–6.
61. Karl Baedeker, *Greece: Handbook for Travellers*, London, 1894, p. 80.
62. Ibid., p. 80.
63. Mary and David Hogarth, *Scenes in Athens*, quoted by Tsigakou, *The Rediscovery of Greece*, p. 150.
64. Evliya Chelebi (Muhammad Zilli Ibn Darvish), *Narrative of Travels*, 1834.
65. Gustave Flaubert, *Voyages*, ed. René Dumesnil, Paris, 1948, Vol. II, p. 397.
66. Hugh William Williams, *Travels in Italy, Greece, and the Ionian Islands*, Edinburgh, 1820, Vol. II, p. 363.
67. Thomas Smart Hughes, *Travels in Sicily, Greece and Albania*, London, 1820, pp. 311–12.
68. Wheler, *Journey into Greece*, pp. 397–8.
69. '*Famous in my time: Byron's Letters and Journals*, Vol. II, ed. Leslie A. Marchand, London, 1973, pp. 37, 27, 11–14.
70. John Cam Hobhouse, *A Journey Through Albania and Other Provinces of Turkey in Europe and Asia*, London, 1813, Vol. I, p. 291.
71. Lord Byron, 'Maid of Athens, ere we part' (1810).
72. '*Famous in my time*', p. 13.
73. Wheler, *Journey into Greece*, p. 411.
74. Levi, *The Hill of Kronos*, p. 26.

ATTICA AND CENTRAL GREECE

1. *Dictionary of Greek and Roman Geography*, ed. William Smith, London, 1856, p. 415.

2. *The Letters of George Gissing to Eduard Bertz 1887–1903*, ed. Arthur C. Young, London, 1961, p. 87.
3. David Marr, *Patrick White: a Life*, London, 1991, pp. 333–4. (To Gwen and David Moore, 23 April 1958.)
4. *Don Juan*, Canto III, lxxxvi, in George Gordon, Lord Byron, *Poetical Works*, ed. Frederick Page and John Jump, London, 1970, pp. 695–6.
5. *'Famous in my time': Byron's Letters and Journals*, Vol. II, ed. Leslie A. Marchand, London, 1973, pp. 30–1.
6. George Giannaris, *Mikis Theodorakis: Music and Social Change*, London, 1973, p. 67.
7. See Demetrios Sicilianos, *Old and New Athens*, trans. Robert Liddell, Athens, 1960, pp. 42–6.
8. Ibid., p. 87.
9. Richard Chandler, *Travels in Greece*, Oxford, 1776, p. 185.
10. [Sir George Ferguson Bowen,] *Handbook for Travellers in Greece*, London, 1900, p. 457.
11. Brian de Jongh, *The Companion Guide to Mainland Greece*, revised by John Gandon, London, 1989, p. 80.
12. Richard Stoneman, *Land of Lost Gods: the Search for Classical Greece*, London, 1987, pp. 152–3.
13. Edward Daniel Clarke, *Travels in Various Countries of Europe, Asia and Africa*, Part Two, Section Two, London, 1814, pp. 772–90.
14. Bernard Shaw, *Collected Letters 1898–1910*, ed. Dan H. Laurence, London, Max Reinhardt, 1972, p. 112.
15. Samuel Johnson, *A Journey to the Western Isles of Scotland*, ed. Mary Lascelles, New Haven and London, 1971, p. 148; Samuel Taylor Coleridge, *Table Talk*, ed. Carl Woodring, Princeton, 1990, Vol. I, p. 413 (4 August 1833).
16. *Dictionary of National Biography 1941–50*, p. 805.
17. Ethel Smyth, *A Three-Legged Tour in Greece*, London, 1927, p. 45.
18. Joslyn Francis Pennington, Lord Muncaster, *Greece: Journal of Lord Muncaster 11th April–7th May, 1870*, 1870.
19. Jan Morris, *The Venetian Empire: a Sea Voyage*, London, 1990, pp. 52–3.
20. John Julius Norwich, *A History of Venice*, London, 1982, pp. 350–1.
21. Roald Dahl, *Going Solo*, London, 1986, p. 143.
22. Alphonse de Lamartine, *Voyage en Orient*, ed. Lotfy Fam, Paris, 1960, p. 267.

23. *Travels in Southern Europe and the Levant, 1810–17: the Journal of C.R. Cockerell, R.A.*, ed. Samuel Pepys Cockerell, London, 1903, pp. 51–2.

24. *Letters of Samuel Gridley Howe During the Greek Revolution*, ed. Laura Richards, London, 1907, pp. 305–6.

25. William St. Clair, *That Greece Might Still Be Free*, Oxford, 1972, p. 345.

26. Henry Miller, *The Colossus of Maroussi*, London, 1991 (1942), p. 55.

27. Lawrence Durrell, *The Greek Islands*, London, 1978, p. 265.

28. George Seferis, *A Poet's Journal: Days of 1945–1951*, trans. Athan Anagnostopoulos, Cambridge, Mass., 1974, pp. 53, 38, 82.

29. Alexander Kinglake, *Eothen: or Traces of Travel Brought Home from the East*, Oxford, 1982 (1844), p. 63.

30. George Finlay, *History of the Greek Revolution*, Edinburgh, 1861, Vol. I, pp. 37–8.

31. *History of Modern Greece From 1820, to the Establishment of Grecian Independence*, London, 1823, p. 77.

32. John Fowles, *The Magus: a Revised Version*, London, 1977, p. 51.

33. Robert Byron, *Letters Home*, ed. Lucy Butler, London, 1991, p. 68.

34. Ibid., p. 67.

35. Hugo von Hofmannsthal, *Selected Prose*, trans. Mary Hottinger and Tania and James Stern, London, 1952, pp. 167–8.

36. E.M. Forster, *A Room With a View*, Harmondsworth, 1955 (1908), pp. 222, 219.

37. Rose Macaulay, *Pleasure of Ruins*, London, 1953, p. 313.

38. Hugh William Williams, *Travels in Italy, Greece, and the Ionian Islands*, Edinburgh, 1820, Vol. II, p. 247.

39. Oliver Taplin, *Greek Fire*, London, 1989, p. 28.

40. Peter Levi, *The Hill of Kronos: a Personal Portrait of Greece*, London, 1991 (1981), pp. 65–6.

41. Taplin, *Greek Fire*, pp. 27–8.

42. Charles Ricketts, *Pages from a Diary in Greece*, ed. Paul Delaney, Edinburgh, 1978, pp. 36–7.

43. Stephen Spender, *Journals 1939–1983*, ed. John Goldsmith, London, 1985, p. 115.

THE PELOPONNESE

1. Book VIII, section 334, in *The Geography of Strabo*, Vol. IV, ed. and trans. Horace Leonard Jones, London, 1927, p. 11.

2. *The Marble Threshing Floor: a Collection of Greek Folksongs*, ed. Ellen Frye, Austin, Texas, 1973, p. 24.
3. W.H. Humphreys, *Journal of a Visit to Greece*, London, 1826, pp. 310–11.
4. William Lithgow, *The Totall Discourse of the Rare Adventures and Painefull Peregrinations*, Glasgow, 1906, p. 63.
5. *Home Letters Written by the Late Earl of Beaconsfield in 1830 and 1831*, ed. Ralph Disraeli, London, 1885, pp. 97–8.
6. *The Iliad* II. 570, trans. Martin Hammond, London, 1987, p. 77.
7. Odysseus Elytis, 'Drinking the sun of Corinth . . .', in *Selected Poems*, trans. Edmund Keeley and Philip Sherrard, London, 1981, p. 27.
8. Shakespeare, *Henry IV, Part One*, II. iv.
9. Sir George Wheler, *A Journey into Greece*, London, 1682, p. 441.
10. Lord Byron, *The Siege of Corinth*, 1816, l. 1020.
11. Hon. Frederick S.N. Douglas, *Essay on Certain Points of Resemblance Between the Ancient and Modern Greeks*, London, 1813, p. 21.
12. Heinrich Schliemann, *Ithaque, Le Peloponnèse, Troie*, Paris, 1869, pp. 91, 92–3.
13. *Cook's Continental Time Tables, Tourist's Handbook, and Steamship Tables*, London, 1903, pp. lvii, 269.
14. Osbert Lancaster, *Classical Landscape with Figures*, London, 1975 (1947), p. 112.
15. Stephen Spender, *Journals 1939–1983*, ed. John Goldsmith, London, 1985, p. 115.
16. Heinrich Schliemann, *Briefwechsel*, ed. Ernst Meyer, Berlin, 1958, Vol. II, p. 68.
17. Heinrich Schliemann, *Mycenae: a Narrative of Researches and Discoveries at Mycenae and Tiryns*, London, 1878, p. 290.
18. Deuel, *Heinrich Schliemann*, p. 228.
19. Ibid., p. 256.
20. Andromache Schliemann Melas, *Reader's Digest*, July 1950, p. 48.
21. Henry Miller, *The Colossus of Maroussi*, London, 1960 (1941), pp. 91–2.
22. Roger Lancelyn Green and Walter Hooper, *C.S. Lewis: a Biography*, London, 1974, p. 272.
23. Pausanias, II. xxv. 8, ed. and trans. W.H.S. Jones, London, 1918, Vol. I, p. 383.
24. Schliemann, *Mycenae*, p. 3.
25. Heinrich Schliemann, *Tiryns: the Prehistoric Palace of the Kings of Tiryns*, London, 1886, p. 3.

26. Schliemann, *Briefwechsel*, Vol. II, p. 192.
27. Schliemann, *Tiryns*, p. 52.
28. Lady Bourchier, *Memoir of the Life of Admiral Sir Edward Codrington*, London, 1873, Vol. I, p. 380.
29. Ibid., p. 409.
30. See C.M. Woodhouse, *Capodistria: the Founder of Greek Independence*, London, 1973, pp. 349–50 and passim; Richard Clogg, *A Short History of Modern Greece*, Cambridge, 1986, pp. 67–8.
31. George Finlay, *History of the Greek Revolution*, Edinburgh, 1861, Vol. II, pp. 245–6.
32. Osbert Lancaster, *Classical Landscape with Figures*, London, 1975 (1947), pp. 121–2.
33. David Marr, *Patrick White: a Life*, London, 1991, pp. 420–1.
34. *Peter Hall's Diaries: the Story of a Dramatic Battle*, ed. John Goodwin, London, 1983, p. 165.
35. Thucydides, *The Peloponnesian War*, I. 10.
36. Henry Blount, *A Voyage into the Levant*, London, 1636, p. 105.
37. François-René de Chateaubriand, *Travels in Greece, Palestine, Egypt, and Barbary*, trans. Frederic Shoberl, London, 1811, Vol. I, p. 152.
38. Ibid., pp. 156–64.
39. Maurice Barrès, *Le Voyage de Sparte*, Paris, 1906, p. 193.
40. Karl Baedeker, *Greece: Handbook for Travellers*, Leipzig and London, 1894, p. 274.
41. Barrès, *Le Voyage de Sparte*, pp. 186–7.
42. Ibid., pp. 202–3.
43. J.A. Buchon, *Recherches historiques sur la principauté française de Morée*, Paris, 1845, p. 88.
44. Patrick Leigh Fermor, *Mani: Travels in the Southern Peloponnese*, London, 1984 (1958), p. 230.
45. Photis Kontoglou, trans. Philip Sherrard, *The Pursuit of Greece*, London, 1964, p. 95.
46. Barrès, *Le Voyage de Sparte*, pp. 214–15.
47. Jan Morris, *The Venetian Empire: a Sea Voyage*, London, 1990, p. 121.
48. Buchon, *Recherches historiques*, pp. 91–3.
49. Kevin Andrews, *The Flight of Ikaros: a Journey into Greece*, London, 1959, p. 53.
50. Lewes Roberts, *The Marchants mappe of Commerce*, London, 1638, p. 205, quoted by Spencer, p. 71.

51. Gérard de Nerval, *Oeuvres complètes*, ed. Jean Guillaume and others, Paris, 1984, Vol. II, pp. 234, 240.
52. Charles Baudelaire, 'Un Voyage à Cythère', in *Les Fleurs du mal* (1857), *Oeuvres Complètes*, ed. Marcel A. Ruff, Paris, 1982, p. 117; Victor Hugo, 'Cérigo', in *Les Contemplations* (1856), *Poésie*, Vol. I, Paris, 1972, p. 729.
53. Wheler, p. 47.
54. Finlay, *History of the Greek Revolution*, Vol. II, p. 243.
55. Peter Greenhalgh and Edward Eliopoulos, *Deep into Mani: Journey to the Southern Tip of Greece*, London, 1985, p. 36.
56. Leigh Fermor, *Mani*, p. 88.
57. Greenhalgh and Eliopoulos, *Deep into Mani*, p. 153.
58. Leigh Fermor, *Mani*, p. 98.
59. Ibid., pp. 141–2.
60. Pliny the Elder, *Natural History*, Book XXXV.
61. Judith Swaddling, *The Ancient Olympic Games*, London, 1980, p. 7.
62. Lancaster, *Classical Landscape*, p. 141.
63. *The Letters of Oscar Wilde*, ed. Rupert Hart-Davis, London, 1962, p. 36 n. 3.
64. Ibid., p. 35.
65. John Pentland Mahaffy, *Rambles and Studies in Greece*, 2nd edition, London, 1878, pp. 286–7.
66. *The Diaries of Evelyn Waugh*, ed. Michael Davie, London, 1976, p. 277.
67. Allen Ginsberg, *Journals Early Fifties Early Sixties*, ed. Gordon Ball, New York, 1977, p. 235.
68. Nikos Kazantzakis, *Travels in Greece (Journey to the Morea)*, trans. F.A. Reed, Oxford, 1966, pp. 65, 67–8.
69. William Mure, *Journal of a Tour in Greece and the Ionian Islands*, Edinburgh, 1842, Vol. II, p. 270.
70. Mahaffy, *Rambles and Studies*, pp. 343–4.
71. Kazantzakis, *Travels in Greece*, p. 76.
72. Richard Ridley Farrar, *A Tour in Greece 1880*, Edinburgh, 1882, p. 164.
73. *Kolokotronês. The Klepht and the Warrior. Sixty Years of Peril and Daring. An Autobiography*, trans. Mrs Edmonds, London, 1892, p. ix.
74. Ibid., pp. 255, 270.
75. Ibid., pp. xxii, xix.
76. Ibid., pp. 255–6.

THE IONIAN ISLANDS, MISSOLONGHI, EPIROS

1. Quoted by Ferdinand Whittingham, *Four Years in the Ionian Islands*, ed. Viscount Kirkwall, London, 1864, Vol. I, p. 6.
2. D.T. Ansted, *The Ionian Islands in the Year 1863*, London, 1863, pp. 70–1.
3. Andreas Kalvos, 'Zante', Ωδαι, ed. Filippo Maria Pontani, Athens, 1970, p. 32.
4. William Biddulph, *The Travels of Certaine Englishmen*, London, 1609, p. 5, quoted by Terence Spencer, *Fair Greece, Sad Relic: Literary Philhellenism from Shakespeare to Byron*, London, 1954, p. 28.
5. Quoted by Romilly Jenkins, *Dionysius Solomos*, Cambridge, 1940, p. 54.
6. Rudyard Kipling, *The Complete Verse*, London, 1990, p. 77.
7. Diana Cooper, *The Light of Common Day: Autobiography*, London, 1984 (1959), p. 185.
8. William Napier Bruce, *Life of General Sir Charles Napier*, London, 1885, p. 105.
9. '*For Freedom's Battle*': Byron's Letters and Journals, Vol. XI, ed. Leslie A. Marchand, London, 1981, pp. 33–4.
10. *Trelawny's Recollections of the Last Days of Shelley and Byron*, London, 1906, p. 136.
11. Lord Byron, '*For Freedom's Battle*', p. 18.
12. *Trelawny's Recollections*, pp. 136–7.
13. Heinrich Schliemann, *Ithaque, le Peloponnèse, Troie*, Paris, 1869, Chapter III.
14. Nicholas Fraser and others, *Aristotle Onassis*, London, 1980 (1977), p. 298.
15. *The Works of Liudprand of Cremona*, trans. F.A. Wright, London, 1930, pp. 235, 270, 274–5.
16. John Addington Symonds, *Sketches in Italy and Greece*, London, 1874, pp. 232–3.
17. Viscountess (Emily Anne) Strangford, *The Eastern Shores of the Adriatic in 1863*, London, 1864, p. 57.
18. Whittingham, *Four Years in the Ionian Islands*, Vol. I, pp. 226–7.
19. Homer, *The Odyssey*, VI. 204–5.
20. *Edward Lear: the Corfu Years*, ed. Philip Sherrard, Athens, 1988, p. 237.
21. Cooper, *Light of Common Day*, p. 183.
22. Sir William Napier, *Life and Opinions of General Sir Charles James Napier*, London, 1857, Vol. I, p. 427.

23. Ibid, Vol. I, p. 285.
24. Bruce, *Life of Napier*, p. 83.
25. Napier, *Life and Opinions of Napier*, Vol. I, p. 348.
26. Cooper, *Light of Common Day*, p. 183.
27. Gerald Durrell, *My Family and Other Animals*, Harmondsworth, 1959 (1956), p. 31.
28. Ibid., pp. 35–6.
29. *Lear: the Corfu Years*, ed. Sherrard, p. 107; *Letters of Edward Lear to Chichester Fortescue Lord Carlingford and Frances Countess Waldegrave*, ed. Lady Strachey, London, 1907, p. 68.
30. Evelyn Waugh, *Labels: a Mediterranean Journal*, London, 1974 (1930), p. 156.
31. *Trelawny's Recollections*, p. 148.
32. Kostis Palamas, 'Missolonghi', Απαντα, Vol. III, p. 14.
33. Lord Byron, 'For Freedom's Battle', p. 107.
34. Lord Byron, 'On This Day I Complete My Thirty-Sixth Year' (1824) in *Poetical Works*, ed. Frederick Page and John Jump, London, 1970, p. 112.
35. Lord Byron, 'For Freedom's Battle', p. 29 n. 1.
36. *The Collected Works of Louis MacNeice*, ed. E.R. Dodds, London, 1966, p. 292.
37. Quoted by William Mure, *Journal of a Tour in Greece and the Ionian Islands*, Edinburgh, 1842, Vol. I, pp. 167–8. For Byron on Meyer see 'For Freedom's Battle', pp. 132, 139.
38. Lord Byron, *Childe Harold's Pilgrimage*, II. xlvi in *Poetical Works*, p. 201.
39. Nicholas Gage, *Eleni*, London, 1989 (1983), pp. 31, 32.
40. Edward Lear, *Journals of a Landscape Painter in Greece and Albania*, London, 1988 (1851), pp. 173–4.
41. Thomas Smart Hughes, *Travels in Sicily, Greece and Albania*, London, 1820, Part One, p. 431.
42. Lear, *Journals of a Landscape Painter*, pp. 173, 185,
43. Sir Steven Runciman, *Byzantine Style and Civilization*, Harmondsworth, 1975, pp. 168–9.
44. Sir Osbert Lancaster, *Sailing to Byzantium: an Architectural Companion*, London, 1972 (1969), pp. 115–16.
45. 'In My Hot Youth': Byron's Letters and Journals*, Vol. I, ed. Leslie A. Marchand, London, 1973, p. 229.
46. Lord Byron, *Childe Harold's Pilgrimage*, II. xlv in *Poetical Works*, p. 201.
47. Hughes, *Travels*, Part One, p. 416.

48. Lear, *Journals of a Landscape Painter*, p. 181.
49. Hughes, *Travels*, Part One, p. 421.
50. William Martin Leake, *Travels in Northern Greece*, London, 1835, Vol. IV, p. 198.
51. *The Chronicle of Ioannina*, quoted by Donald M. Nicol, *The Despotate of Epiros 1267-1479*, Cambridge, 1984, p. 145.
52. Ibid., pp. 143-9, 153-4.
53. Lord Byron, *Childe Harold's Pilgrimage*, II. lxii in *Poetical Works*, p. 203.
54. Lord Byron, 'In My Hot Youth', pp. 227-8.
55. *Travels in Southern Europe and the Levant, 1810-1817: the Journal of C.R. Cockerell R.A.*, ed. Samuel Pepys Cockerell, London, 1903, p. 243; John Cam Hobhouse, *A Journey Through Albania and Other Provinces of Turkey in Europe and Asia*, London, 1813, Vol. I, p. 110.
56. Hughes, *Travels*, Part One, p. 474.
57. Hobhouse, *A Journey Through Albania*, Vol. I, pp. 52, 117-18.
58. Cockerell, *Travels*, p. 236.
59. Lord Byron, 'In My Hot Youth', p. 226.
60. Hughes, *Travels*, Part One, p. 461.
61. Bruce, *Life of Napier*, p. 84.
62. *Home Letters Written by the Late Earl of Beaconsfield in 1830 and 1831*, ed. Ralph Disraeli, London, 1885, p. 91.
63. Lear, *Journals of a Landscape Painter*, p. 200.

THESSALY, MACEDONIA, MOUNT ATHOS

1. Kevin Andrews, *Ikaros Rising: a Journey into Greece*, London, 1959, p. 225.
2. William Eton, *A Survey of the Turkish Empire*, London, 1798, p. 345.
3. *Hippocrates*, ed. W.H.S. Jones, London, 1923, pp. 165-7.
4. Xenophon, *Anabasis* VII. iv, ed. C.L. Brownson, London, 1961, p. 308.
5. *The Complete Letters and Works of Lady Mary Wortley Montagu*, ed. Robert Halsband, Oxford, 1965, Vol. 1, p. 361.
6. Arnold Toynbee, *The Greeks and their Heritages*, Oxford, 1981, p. 76.
7. 'Sailing to Byzantium', in *The Collected Poems of W.B. Yeats*, London, 1950, pp. 217-18.
8. Edward Lear, *Journals of a Landscape Painter in Greece and Albania*, London, 1988 (1851), p. 205.

9. 'On the Vale of Tempe,' *Memoirs Relating to European and Asiatic Turkey*, ed. Robert Walpole, London, 1817, p. 518.

10. Lear, *Journals*, pp. 208–10, 220.

11. C.R. Cockerell, letter of 9 February 1814, quoted in Lear, *Journals*, p. 206.

12. Lear, *Journals*, p. 206.

13. Robert Curzon, *Visits to Monasteries in the Levant*, London, 1983 (1849), p. 288.

14. Patrick Leigh Fermor, *Roumeli: Travels in Northern Greece*, London, 1983 (1966), pp. 86, 89.

15. Karl Baedeker, *Greece: Handbook for Travellers*, 2nd edition, London, 1894, p. 229.

16. Curzon, *Visits to Monasteries*, pp. 291–2.

17. Donald M. Nicol, *Meteora: the Rock Monasteries of Thessaly*, London, 1975 (1963), pp. 15–16.

18. Ibid., p. 105.

19. Ibid., p. 99.

20. Leigh Fermor, *Roumeli*, p. 85

21. Nicol, *Meteora*, pp. 179–80.

22. Curzon, *Visits to Monasteries*, p. 293

23. Leigh Fermor, *Roumeli*, p. 79.

24. 'Ode on a Grecian Urn', in *The Poems of John Keats*, ed. Miriam Allott, London, 1970, p. 534.

25. 'On the Vale of Tempe', *Memoirs Relating to European and Asiatic Turkey*, ed. Robert Walpole, London, 1817, p. 520.

26. Richard Monckton Milnes, *Memorials of a Tour in Some Parts of Greece*, London, 1834, p. 77.

27. Eric Newby, *On the Shores of the Mediterranean*, London, 1984, pp. 172–3.

28. Ibid., p. 178.

29. Henry Fanshawe Tozer, *Researches in the Highlands of Turkey*, London, 1869, Vol. II, p. 18.

30. Ibid., Vol. II, p. 12.

31. *Travels in Southern Europe and the Levant, 1810–1817: the Journal of C.R. Cockerell R.A.*, ed. Samuel Pepys Cockerell, London, 1903, pp. 169–70.

32. Peter Levi, *The Hill of Kronos: a Personal Portrait of Greece*, London, 1991 (1981), p. 202.

33. Demosthenes, *Olynthiakos B*, in *The First Philippic and the Olynthiacs*, ed. J.E. Sandys, London, 1897, p. 46.

34. Robin Lane Fox, *Alexander the Great*, London, 1973, p. 19

35. *Handbook for Travellers in Greece*, London, 1884, p. 709.

36. Henry Fanshawe Tozer, *Lectures on the Geography of Greece*, London, 1873, pp. 202–3.

37. Osbert Lancaster, *Sailing to Byzantium*, p. 46.

38. William Martin Leake, *Travels in Northern Greece*, London, 1835, Vol. III, pp. 238–9.

39. John Julius Norwich, *Byzantium: the Apogee*, London, 1991, p. 110.

40. Eustathios, *De Thessalonice urbe a Normannis capta narratio* in *Opuscula*, ed. T.L.F. Taffel, Frankfurt, 1832, pp. 296–8.

41. Edward Gibbon, *The History of the Decline and Fall of the Roman Empire*, ed. J.B. Bury, London, 1909 (1776–88), pp. 181–2, 185.

42. Henry Fanshawe Tozer, *Researches in the Highlands of Turkey*, 1869, Vol. I, p. 148.

43. *Handbook for Travellers in Greece*, Vol. II, p. 714.

44. Lancaster, *Sailing to Byzantium*, p. 54.

45. R.F. Hoddinott, *Early Byzantine Churches in Macedonia and Southern Serbia*, London, 1963, p. 149.

46. Eustathios, *Opuscula*, p. 296.

47. *Handbook for Travellers in Greece*, Vol. II, pp. 714–15.

48. Cyril Mango, *The Art of the Byzantine Empire 312–1453: Sources and Documents*, Englewood Cliffs, N.J., 1972, pp. 155–6.

49. Ibid., pp. 155–6.

50. Efthymios Tsigaridas, *Latomou Monastery (the Church of Hosios David)*, trans. Deborah Whitehouse, Thessaloniki, 1988, p. 38.

51. Hoddinott, *Early Byzantine Churches*, p. 176.

52. Ibid., p. 112,

53. See Edmund Keeley, *The Salonika Bay Murder: Cold War Politics and the Polk Affair*, Princeton, 1989.

54. Lear, *Journals*, p. 23.

55. *The Itinerary of Benjamin of Tudela*, ed. and trans. Marcus Nathan Adler, London, 1907, p. 11.

56. *Ben Gurion Looks Back in Talks with Moshe Pearlman*, London, 1965, p. 44.

57. H.G. Dwight, *National Geographic Magazine*, September, 1916, p. 224.

58. Israel Cohen, *The Jewish Chronicle Supplement*, August 27, 1926, pp. ii–iii.

59. Quoted by Robert Byron, *The Station. Athos: Treasures and Men*, London, 1984 (1928), p. 250.

60. Edward Lear, letter to Chichester Fortescue, 9 October 1856, in *Letters of Edward Lear to Chichester Fortescue Lord Carlingford and Frances Countess Waldegrave*, ed. Lady Strachey, London, 1907, pp. 41–2.
61. Ralph Harper, *Journey from Paradise: Mount Athos and the Interior Life*, Beauport, Quebec, 1987, pp. 84, 103.
62. Robert Byron, *The Station*, p. 251.
63. Robert Curzon, *Visits to Monasteries*, pp. 401–2.
64. Dr Hunt, 'Mount Athos: an Account of the Monastic Institutions and the Libraries of the Holy Mountain,' *Memoirs Relating to European and Asiatic Turkey*, ed. Robert Walpole, London, 1817, p. 520.
65. Curzon, *Visits to Monasteries*, p. 357.
66. Robert Byron, *The Station*, p. 128.
67. Curzon, *Visits to Monasteries*, pp. 357–9.
68. F. W. Hasluck, 'The First English Traveller's Account of Athos', *The Annual of the British School at Athens*, no. xvii, 1910–11, pp. 106, 124–5.
69. Curzon, *Visits to Monasteries*, p. 375.
70. Robert Byron, *The Station*. pp. 131–2.
71. Ibid., p. 238.

THE AEGEAN ISLANDS

1. Bernard Shaw, *Collected Letters 1898–1910*, ed. Dan H. Laurence, London, 1972, p. 109.
2. David Marr, *Patrick White: a Life*, London, 1991, p. 507.
3. *Don Juan*, II. 145, 171 in George Gordon, Lord Byron, *Poetical Works*, ed. Frederick Page and John Jump, London, 1970, pp. 677, 680.
4. Ibid., II. 185, p. 682.
5. Robert Byron, *The Byzantine Achievement: an Historical Perspective A.D. 330–1453*, London, 1987 (1929), p. 7.
6. Joseph Pitton de Tournefort, *A Voyage into the Levant*, trans. John Ozell, London, 1718, Vol. I, pp. 177–8, 179.
7. J. Theodore Bent, *The Cyclades: or Life Among the Insular Greeks*, London, 1885, p. 242.
8. Ibid., p. 243.
9. Ibid., pp. 247–8.
10. Lawrence Durrell, *The Greek Islands*, London, 1978, pp. 244–6.
11. Tournefort, *A Voyage*, Vol. I, p. 245.

12. 'Syra: a Transmitted Reminiscence', in *Collected Poems of Herman Melville*, Chicago, 1947, p. 251.
13. *The Writings of Herman Melville, Volume 15. Journals*, ed. Howard C. Horsford and Lynn Horth, Evanston and Chicago, 1989, pp. 53, 71.
14. Ibid., p. 71.
15. Willy Russell, *Shirley Valentine and One for the Road*, London, 1988, p. 18.
16. Jean Baelen, *Mykonos: chronique d'une île de l'Égée*, Paris, 1964, p. 35.
17. Durrell, *The Greek Islands*, p. 228.
18. Ibid., p. 230.
19. Russell, *Shirley Valentine*, p. 26.
20. Ibid., pp. 27–8.
21. Ibid., p. 36.
22. Bent, *The Cyclades*, p. 230.
23. Sir Thomas Roe, letter to George Villiers, Duke of Buckingham, 24 January 1625, quoted by Terence Spencer, *Fair Greece Sad Relic: Literary Philhellenism from Shakespeare to Byron*, London, 1954, pp. 76–7.
24. Sir Kenelm Digby, *Journal of a Voyage into the Mediterranean, 1628*, ed. John Bruce, London, 1868, p. 57.
25. Sir George Wheler, *A Journey into Greece*, London, 1682, p. 56.
26. C.A. Trypanis, 'Delos', *Pompeian Dog*, London, 1964, p. 21.
27. Durrell, *The Greek Islands*, p. 236.
28. Marr, *Patrick White*, pp. 335–6.
29. *The Travels of Monsieur de Thévenot into the Levant*, trans. A. Lovell, London, 1687, p. 104.
30. William Miller, *Essays on the Latin Orient*, London, 1921, p. 176.
31. Bent, *The Cyclades*, p. 372.
32. *Vita S. Theoctistae Lesbae*, in *Acta Sanctorum*, Novembris Tomus IV, Brussels, 1925, p. 226.
33. Bent, *The Cyclades*, p. 379.
34. Ernle Bradford, *The Sultan's Admiral: the Life of Barbarossa*, London, 1969.
35. Lord Byron, *Don Juan*, IV. 72 in *Poetical Works*, p. 707.
36. Tournefort, *Voyage into the Levant*, pp. 150–1.
37. Fynes Moryson, *An Itinerary*, London, 1617, p. 257.
38. Bent, *The Cyclades*, pp. 104–5, 118–19.
39. Quoted by G.I. Alexakis, *Santorini Today and Yesterday*, Athens, 1987, p. 20.

40. Bent, *The Cyclades*, p. 110.
41. Alexakis, *Santorini*, pp. 21–3.
42. *Illustrated London News*, 1866, p. 257.
43. Bent, *The Cyclades*, p. 116.
44. William Lithgow, *The Totall Discourse of the Rare Adventures and Painefull Peregrinations*, Glasgow, 1906, pp. 91–2.
45. Bernard Randolph, *The Present State of the Islands in the Archipelago*, 1687, p. 49.
46. Lithgow, *Rare Adventures*, p. 93.
47. Randolph, *Present State of the Islands*, p. 46.
48. Anonymous letter quoted by Thomas Smart Hughes, *Address to the People of England Occasioned by the Late Inhuman Massacres in the Isle of Scio*, London, 1822, pp. 40–1.
49. *Le Spectateur Oriental*, no. 49, 26 April 1822, reprinted in *The Massacres of Chios Described in Contemporary Diplomatic Reports*, ed. Philip P. Argenti, London, 1932, pp. 235–6.
50. Ibid., p. xxxi.
51. Hughes, *Address to the People of England*, pp. 32–3.
52. *The Perilous and Most Unhappy Voyages of John Struys*, trans. John Morrison, London, 1683, pp. 109–10.
53. Sir Compton Mackenzie, *Greece in My Life*, London, 1960, pp. 23–4.
54. George Seferis, *On the Greek Style: Selected Essays on Poetry and Hellenism*, trans. Rex Warner and Th. D. Frangopoulos, London, 1966, p. 3.
55. Peter Green, 'King Fix: Bill Golding in Greece', in *William Golding: the Man and his Books. A Tribute on his 75th Birthday*, ed. John Carey, London, 1986, pp. 51–2.
56. Ibid., p. 53.
57. *The Letters of Rupert Brooke*, ed. Sir Geoffrey Keynes, London, 1968, pp. 685–6.
58. Patrick Leigh Fermor, *Roumeli: Travels in Northern Greece*, London, 1983 (1966), pp. 174–5.

CRETE, THE DODECANESE AND RHODES

1. Claude-Étienne Savary, *Letters on Greece*, London, 1788, p. 236.
2. H.H. Munro, 'The Jesting of Arlington Stringham', *The Penguin Complete Saki*, London, 1982, p. 135.
3. *Proceedings of the Hellenic Travellers' Club*, 1930, p. 89.

4. Antony Beevor, *Crete: the Battle and the Resistance*, London, 1991, p. 63.
5. Ibid., p. 194.
6. Ibid., pp. 98, 97, quoting a conversation with Nicholas Hammond and C.M. Woodhouse, *Something Ventured*, London, 1982, p. 18.
7. Patrick Leigh Fermor, quoted by Dilys Powell, *The Villa Ariadne*, London, 1973, p. 117.
8. Nikos Kazantzakis, trans. Peter Bien in *Nikos Kazantzakis: Novelist*, Bristol, 1989, p. 100.
9. Edward Lear, *The Cretan Journal*, ed. Rowena Fowler, Athens, 1985, pp. 64–5.
10. Nikos Kazantzakis, *Freedom and Death*, London, 1966 (1956), p. 9.
11. P. Daru, *Histoire de la République de Venise*, Paris, 1819, Vol. IV, pp. 616–25.
12. Fynes Moryson, *An Itinerary*, Glasgow, 1907 (1617), Vol. 11, p. 83.
13. Bernard Randolph, *The Present State of the Islands in the Archipelago*, 1687, p. 83.
14. Democratia Hemmerdinger-Iliadou, 'La Crète sous la domination venitienne et lors de la conquête turque', *Studi Veneziani*, Vol. IX, p. 585.
15. Quoted in Ibid., pp. 606–7.
16. Richard Pococke, *A Description of the East and Some Other Countries*, Vol. II, 1745, Part I, pp. 257–8.
17. Francesco Morosini, 'Relatione di Candia' [1629], in Stergios Spanakis, Μνημεια της Κρητηχης ιστοριας, Vol. II, Herakleion, 1950, pp. 38–40.
18. Nikos Kazantzakis, *Report to Greco*, trans. P.A. Bien, Oxford, 1965, p. 89.
19. Lear, *Cretan Journal*, p. 66.
20. Mary Renault, *The King Must Die*, London, 1970 (1958), p. 162.
21. David Sweetman, *Mary Renault: a Biography*, London, 1993, p. 170.
22. Rodney Castleden, *The Knossos Labyrinth*, London, 1990.
23. Sir Arthur Evans, *The Palace of Minos*, London, 1921–36, Vol. III, p. 301.
24. Powell, *Villa Ariadne*, p. 9.
25. Evelyn Waugh, *Labels: a Mediterranean Journal*, London, 1974 (1930), p. 137.

26. Kazantzakis, *Report to Greco*, p. 149.
27. Henry Miller, *The Colossus of Maroussi*, London, 1991 (1941), p. 122.
28. Waugh, *Labels*, p. 136.
29. Kazantzakis, *Report to Greco*, p. 151.
30. Powell, *Villa Ariadne*, p. 8.
31. Ibid., p. 11; Ann Brown, *Arthur Evans and the Palace of Minos*, Oxford, 1983, pp. 22, 29.
32. Beevor, *Crete: the Battle and the Resistance*, p. 178.
33. Ibid., p. 311.
34. W. Stanley Moss, *Ill Met By Moonlight*, London, 1968 (1950), pp. 70, 56.
35. Patrick Leigh Fermor, introduction to George Psychoundakis, *The Cretan Runner: his Story of the German Occupation*, London, 1955, p. 18.
36. Joseph Pitton de Tournefort, *A Voyage into the Levant*, trans. John Ozell, London, 1718, Vol. 1, pp. 41–2.
37. Ibid., pp. 46–7.
38. Miller, *Colossus of Maroussi*, pp. 165, 167.
39. *The Perilous and Most Unhappy Voyages of John Struys*, trans. John Morrison, London, 1683, p. 101.
40. Olfert Dapper, *Description exacte des isles de l'Archipel*, Amsterdam, 1703, p. 445.
41. Psychoundakis, *Cretan Runner*, p. 160.
42. Michael Llewellyn Smith, *The Great Island: a Study of Crete*, London, 1965, p. 152.
43. Nikos Kazantzakis, *Zorba the Greek*, trans. Carl Wildman, London, 1961, p. 294.
44. Pandelis Prevelakis, *The Tale of a Town*, trans. Kenneth Johnstone, London and Athens, 1976, pp. 15, 32.
45. Lear, *Cretan Journal*, p. 60.
46. Tournefort, *Voyage*, Vol. I, p. 40.
47. Lear, *Cretan Journal*, pp. 89–90.
48. Henry Fanshawe Tozer, *The Islands of the Aegean*, Oxford, 1890, p. 54.
49. Ibid., p. 26.
50. William Lithgow, *The Totall Discourse of the Rare Adventures and Painefull Peregrinations*, Glasgow, 1906, p. 73.
51. Rosemary Bancroft-Marcus, 'The Pastoral Mode', in *Literature and Society in Renaissance Crete*, ed. David Holton, Cambridge, 1991, p. 81.

52. Lear, *Cretan Journal*, pp. 103–4, 35.
53. Randolph, *Present State of the Islands*, p. 29.
54. Claude-Étienne Savary, *Letters on Greece*, pp. 109–10, 124.
55. Tozer, *Islands of the Aegean*, p. 178; Arthur Penrhyn Stanley, *Sermons ... in the East*, London, 1863, p. 225.
56. Tozer, *Islands of the Aegean*, p. 195.
57. Ibid., p. 182.
58. C. Diehl, 'Le Trésor et la bibliothèque de Patmos au commencement du 13e siècle', *Byzantinischer Zeitschrift* Vol. 1, 1892, p. 488.
59. A.R. Burn, *The Living Past of Greece: a Time-Traveller's Tour of Historic and Prehistoric Places*, London, 1980, p. 256.
60. Tozer, *Islands of the Aegean*, p. 187.
61. Randolph, *Present State of the Islands*, pp. 25–6.
62. Sir Compton Mackenzie, *Aegean Memories*, London, 1940, pp. 185–6.
63. Sir Compton Mackenzie, *Greece in My Life*, London, 1960, p. 152.
64. Lawrence Durrell, *Reflections on a Marine Venus: a Companion to the Landscape of Rhodes*, London, 1960 (1953), pp. 76–7.
65. *Caoursin's Account of the Siege of Rhodes in 1480*, trans. John Kay (1482), ed. H.W. Fincham, London, 1926, pp. 27–32.
66. William Makepeace Thackeray, *Notes of a Journey from Cornhill to Grand Cairo*, ed. Sarah Searight, Heathfield, 1991, p. 85.
67. *A Handbook for Travellers in Greece*, London, 1854, p. 347.
68. François-René de Chateaubriand, *Itinéraire de Paris à Jérusalem*, ed. Émile Malakis, London, 1946 (1811), Vol. II, p. 12.
69. *Handbook for Travellers in Greece*, p. 347.
70. Thackeray, *Notes of a Journal*, p. 82.
71. Durrell, *Reflections on a Marine Venus*, p. 127.
72. Savary, *Letters on Greece*, pp. 100–1.
73. Alphonse de Lamartine, *Voyage en Orient*, ed. Lotfy Fam, Paris, (1960), p. 290.
74. Durrell, *Reflections on a Marine Venus*, p. 152.

ACKNOWLEDGEMENTS

Acknowledgement is due to the following for kindly giving permission to reproduce copyright material:

Kevin Andrews, *The Flight of Ikaros: a Journey into Greece*, Weidenfeld and Nicolson, 1959, extract reproduced by permission of Weidenfeld and Nicolson; Antony Beevor, *Crete: the Battle and the Resistance*, John Murray, 1991, extracts reproduced by permission of John Murray (Publishers) Ltd; Peter Bien, *Nikos Kazantzakis: Novelist*, Bristol Classical Press, 1989, extract reproduced by permission of Bristol Classical Press; *The Letters of Rupert Brooke*, ed. Sir Geoffrey Keynes, Faber, 1968, extracts reproduced by permission of Faber and Faber Ltd; Robert Byron, *Letters Home*, ed. Lucy Butler, John Murray, 1991, extract reproduced by permission of John Murray (Publishers) Ltd; *Callas as They Saw Her*, ed. David A. Lowe, Robson Books, 1987, extract reproduced by permission of Robson Books; Diana Cooper, *The Light of Common Day: Autobiography*, Rupert Hart-Davis, 1984 (1959), extracts reproduced by permission of the Viscount Norwich; Roald Dahl, *Going Solo*, Jonathan Cape, 1986, extract reproduced by permission of Jonathan Cape Ltd and Penguin Books Ltd; Leo Deuel, *Memoirs of Heinrich Schliemann: a Documentary Portrait*, Hutchinson, 1978, extract reproduced by permission of HarperCollins Publishers Ltd; Gerald Durrell, *My Family and Other Animals*, Rupert Hart-Davis, an imprint of HarperCollins Publishers Ltd, 1956, extracts reproduced by permission of HarperCollins Publishers Ltd; Lawrence Durrell, *The Greek Islands*, Faber, 1978, extracts reproduced by permission of Faber and Faber Ltd, *Reflections on a Marine Venus: a Companion to the Landscape of Rhodes*, Faber, 1960 (1953), extracts reproduced by permission of Faber and Faber Ltd; Odysseus Elytis, 'Drinking the sun of Corinth . . .', in *Odysseus Elytis: Selected Poems*, ed. Edmund Keeley and Philip Sherrard, Anvil, 1981, extract reproduced by permission of Anvil Press Poetry; Eugenia Fakinou, *Astradeni*, trans. H.E. Criton, Kedros, 1991, extract reproduced by permission of Kedros Publishers; Patrick Leigh Fermor, *Mani: Travels in the Southern Peloponnese*, Penguin, 1984, extracts reproduced by permission of John Murray (Publishers) Ltd, *Roumeli: Travels in Northern Greece*, Penguin, 1983, extracts reproduced by permission of John Murray (Publishers) Ltd; E.M. Forster, *A Room With a View*, Penguin, 1955, extract reproduced by permission of the Provost and Scholars of King's College, Cambridge; John Fowles, *The Magus: a Revised Version*, copyright John Fowles, Jonathan Cape, 1977, extract reproduced by permission of Jonathan Cape; Robin Lane Fox, *Alexander the Great*, Allen Lane, 1973, © Robin Lane Fox, extract reproduced by permission of Penguin Books Ltd; Nicholas Gage, *Eleni*, Fontana, an imprint of HarperCollins Publishers Ltd, 1989, extract reproduced by permission of HarperCollins Publishers Ltd; George Giannaris, *Mikis Theodorakis: Music and Social Change*, Allen and Unwin, 1973, extract reproduced by permission of George Allen and Unwin; Allen Ginsberg, *Early Fifties, Early Sixties*, © Allen Ginsberg 1977, extract reproduced by permission of Grove/Atlantic Inc; *The Letters of George Gissing to Eduard Bertz 1887–1903*, ed. Arthur C. Young, Constable, 1961, extracts reproduced by permission of Constable Publishers; Allen Ginsberg, *Journals Early Fifties Early Sixties*, ed. Gordon Ball, Grove Press, 1977, extract reproduced by permission of Grove Press, a division of the Wheatland Corporation; Peter Green, 'King Fix: Bill Golding in Greece', in *William Golding: the Man and his Books. A Tribute on his 75th Birthday*, ed. John Carey, Faber, 1986, extracts reproduced by permission of Faber and Faber Ltd;

Peter Greenhalgh and Edward Eliopoulos, *Deep into Mani: Journey to the Southern Tip of Greece*, Faber, 1985, extracts reproduced by permission of Faber and Faber Ltd; *Ben Gurion Looks Back in Talks with Moshe Pearlman*, Weidenfeld and Nicolson, 1965, extract reproduced by permission of Weidenfeld and Nicolson; *Peter Hall's Diaries: the Story of a Dramatic Battle*, ed. John Goodwin, Hamish Hamilton, 1983, extract reproduced by permission of Hamish Hamilton Ltd; R.F. Hoddinott, *Early Byzantine Churches in Macedonia and Southern Serbia*, Macmillan, 1963, extracts reproduced by permission of Macmillan London; Hugo von Hofmannsthal, *Selected Prose*, trans. Mary Hottinger and Tania and James Stern, Routledge and Kegan Paul, 1952, extract reproduced by permission of Routledge Chapman & Hall; Romilly Jenkins, *Dionysius Solomos*, Cambridge, 1940, extract reproduced by permission of Cambridge University Press; Brian de Jongh, *The Companion Guide to Mainland Greece*, revised by John Gandon, HarperCollins, 1989, extracts reproduced by permission of HarperCollins Publishers Ltd; Nikos Kazantzakis, *Zorba the Greek*, trans. Carl Wildman, Faber, 1961, extracts reproduced by permission of Faber and Faber Ltd, *Report to Greco*, trans. P.A. Bien, Bruno Cassirer, 1965, extracts reproduced by permission of Faber and Faber Ltd, *Travels in Greece (Journey to the Morea)*, trans. F.A. Reed, Bruno Cassirer, 1966, extracts reproduced by permission of Bruno Cassirer (Publishers) Ltd; Photis Kontoglou, trans. Philip Sherrard, *The Pursuit of Greece*, Denise Harvey, 1987 (1964), extract reproduced by permission of Denise Harvey (Publisher) & Company; Osbert Lancaster, *Classical Landscape with Figures*, London, 1975 (1947), extracts reproduced by permission of John Murray (Publishers) Ltd, *Sailing to Byzantium: an Architectural Companion*, John Murray, 1972, extracts reproduced by permission of John Murray (Publishers) Ltd; Edward Lear, *Selected Letters*, ed. Vivien Noakes, Oxford University Press, 1990, extract reproduced by permission of Watson, Little Ltd, *The Cretan Journal*, ed. Rowena Fowler, Denise Harvey, 1985, extracts reproduced by permission of Denise Harvey (Publisher) & Company; Peter Levi, *The Hill of Kronos: a Personal Portrait of Greece*, Harvill, 1991 (1981), extracts reproduced by permission of John Johnson Ltd; *The Works of Liudprand Cremona*, trans. F.A. Wright, George Routledge, 1930, extract reproduced by permission of Routledge and Kegan Paul; Rose Macaulay, *Pleasure of Ruins*, Thames and Hudson, 1953 © Rose Macaulay, extracts reproduced by permission of Thames and Hudson Ltd; Sir Compton Mackenzie, *Aegean Memories*, Chatto and Windus, 1940, extracts reproduced by permission of the Society of Authors; Harold Macmillan, *War Diaries: Politics and War in the Mediterranean January 1943–May 1945*, Macmillan, 1984, extract reproduced by permission of Macmillan London; *The Collected Works of Louis MacNeice*, ed. E.R. Dodds, London, 1966, extract reproduced by permission of Faber and Faber Ltd; Rosemary Bancroft-Marcus, 'The Pastoral Mode', in *Literature and Society in Renaissance Crete*, ed. David Holton, Cambridge, 1991, extract reproduced by permission of Cambridge University Press; David Marr, *Patrick White: a Life*, Jonathan Cape, 1991, extracts reproduced by permission of Jonathan Cape; *The Writings of Herman Melville, Volume 15. Journals*, ed. Howard C. Horsford and Lynn Horth, Northwestern University Press, 1989, extract reproduced by permission of Northwestern University Press and Newberry Library; Henry Miller, *The Colossus of Maroussi*, William Heinemann, 1991 (1942), extracts reproduced by permission of William Heinemann; Jan Morris, *The Venetian Empire: a Sea Voyage*, London, 1990, extracts reproduced by permission of Rainbird; H.V. Morton, *In the Steps of St. Paul*, Rich and Cowan, 1936, extracts reproduced by permission of Rich and Cowan; Eric Newby, *On the Shores of the Mediterranean*, Harvill, an imprint of HarperCollins Publishers Ltd, 1984, extracts reproduced by permission of HarperCollins Publishers Ltd; Donald M. Nicol, *Meteora: the Rock Monasteries of Thessaly*, Variorum, 1975, extracts reproduced by permission of Variorum; John Julius Norwich, *Byzantium: the Apogee*, Viking, 1991, © John Julius Norwich, extract reproduced by permission of Penguin Books Ltd, *Venice: the Greatness and the Fall*, Allen Lane, 1981, © John Julius Norwich, extract reproduced by permission of Penguin Books Ltd; Dilys Powell, *The Villa Ariadne*, Hodder and Stoughton, 1973, extracts reprinted by permission of the Peters Fraser & Dunlop Group; Pandelis Prevelakis, *The Tale of a Town*, trans. Kenneth Johnstone, Doric Publications, 1976, extracts reproduced by permission of Doric Publications; George

Psychoundakis, *The Cretan Runner: his Story of the German Occupation*, John Murray, 1955, extracts reproduced by permission of John Murray (Publishers) Ltd; Mary Renault, *The King Must Die*, Longman, 1970 (1958), extract reproduced by permission of the Longman Group and Curtis Brown Group Ltd; Willy Russell, *Shirley Valentine and One for the Road*, Methuen, 1988, © Willy Russell, extract reproduced by permission of Methuen London; George Seferis, *On the Greek Style: Selected Essays on Poetry and Hellenism*, trans. Rex Warner and Th. D. Frangopoulos, the Bodley Head, 1966, extract reproduced by permission of the Estate of George Seferis, the Estate of Rex Warner, and the Bodley Head; George Seferis, *A Poet's Journal: Days of 1945–1951*, trans. Athan Anagnostopoulos, the Belknap Press of Harvard University Press, 1974, extract reproduced by permission of Harvard University Press; Demetrios Sicilianos, *Old and New Athens*, trans. Robert Liddell, Putnam, 1960, extracts reproduced by permission of Curtis Brown Group Ltd; Michael Llewellyn Smith, *The Great Island: a Study of Crete*, Allen Lane, the Penguin Press, 1965, © Michael Llewellyn Smith, extract reproduced by permission of Penguin Books Ltd; Ethel Smyth, *A Three-Legged Tour in Greece*, Heinemann, 1927, extract reproduced by permission of Heinemann Ltd; Stephen Spender, *Journals 1939–1983*, ed. John Goldsmith, Faber, 1985, extracts reproduced by permission of Faber and Faber Ltd; Judith Swaddling, *The Ancient Olympic Games*, British Museum Publications, 1980, extract reproduced by permission of British Museum Press; Oliver Taplin, *Greek Fire*, Jonathan Cape, 1989, extracts reproduced by permission of Jonathan Cape Ltd; Arnold Toynbee, *The Greeks and their Heritages*, Oxford University Press, 1981, extract reproduced by permission of Oxford University Press; C.A. Trypanis, 'Delos', *Pompeian Dog*, London, 1964, extracts reproduced by permission of Faber and Faber Ltd; *The Diaries of Evelyn Waugh*, ed. Michael Davie, Weidenfeld and Nicolson, 1976, extracts reproduced by permission of Weidenfeld and Nicolson; Evelyn Waugh, *Labels: a Mediterranean Journal*, Gerald Duckworth, 1974 (1930), extracts reproduced by permission of the Peters Fraser & Dunlop Group Ltd; *The Letters of Oscar Wilde*, ed. Rupert Hart-Davis, Hart-Davis, 1962, extracts reproduced by permission of Oxford University Press and Merlin Holland; Edmund Wilson, *Europe Without Baedeker*, Martin Secker & Warburg, 1986 (1948), extracts reproduced by permission of Martin Secker & Warburg Ltd; Virginia Woolf, *A Passionate Apprentice: the Early Journals 1897–1909*, ed. Mitchell A. Leaska, the Hogarth Press, 1990, extracts reproduced by permission of the Estate of Virginia Woolf and the Hogarth Press.

While every effort has been made to secure permission, we may have failed in a few cases to trace the copyright holder. We apologize for any apparent negligence.

INDEX